Off the Beaten Tracks in Japan

Off the Beaten Tracks in Japan

A Journey by Train from Hokkaido to Kyushu

John Dougill

Stone Bridge Press • Berkeley, California

Published by
Stone Bridge Press
P.O. Box 8208, Berkeley, CA 94707
sbp@stonebridge.com • www.stonebridge.com

Cover and title-page: Original photograph by Akihiko Sayo on unsplash.com and paper texture by João Vítor Duarte on unsplash.com; edited and enhanced for this edition.

Maps are modified from their originals on d-maps.com:
d-maps.com/m/asia/japan/hokkaido/hokkaido34.svg
d-maps.com/m/asia/japan/honshu/honshu20.svg
d-maps.com/m/asia/japan/japon/kyushu78.svg
d-maps.com/m/asia/japan/japon/japon34.svg.

Book design and layout by John Sockolov.

All interior photos by John Dougill.

Printed in the United States of America.

p-ISBN 978-1-61172-082-2
e-ISBN 978-1-61172-963-4

Contents

List of Photos

Periods of Japanese History

Ancient

Jomon	14,000–300 BC
Yayoi	300 BC–AD 250

Classical

Kofun	250–538
Asuka	538–710
Nara	710–784
Heian	794–1185

Feudal

Kamakura	1185–1333
Muromachi	1336–1572
Sengoku	1467–1615
Tokugawa/Edo	1603–1868

Modern

Meiji	1868–1912
Taisho	1912–1926
Showa	1926–1989
Heisei	1989–2019
Reiwa	2019–present

Travel Route and Major Cities

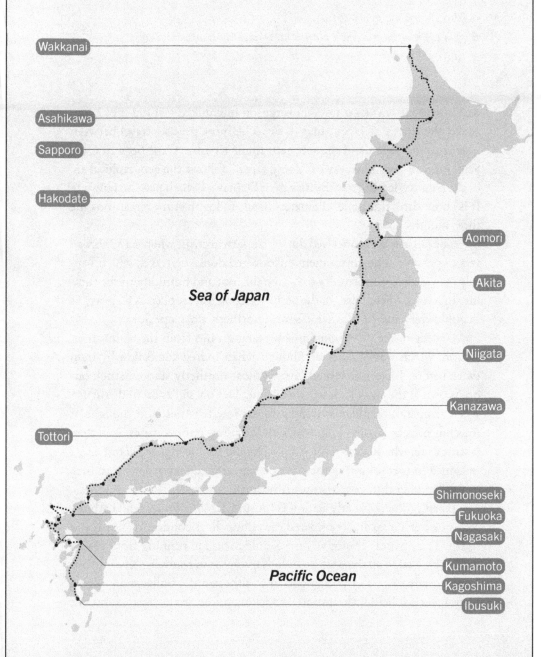

Wakkanai

Asahikawa

Sapporo

Hakodate

Aomori

Akita

Sea of Japan

Niigata

Kanazawa

Tottori

Shimonoseki

Fukuoka

Nagasaki

Kumamoto

Pacific Ocean

Kagoshima

Ibusuki

Preface

A good traveler has no fixed plans and is not intent on arriving.
    – Laozi

ALAN BOOTH WALKED IT. Will Ferguson hitchhiked it. I did it by train. Travel the length of Japan, that is, or to be more precise, travel between northernmost Japan and the southern tip of Kyushu. Cape Soya to Cape Sata, more or less. This way of "doing Japan" follows the geographical arc of the country, leaving out the islands of Okinawa (which have no railway). It is about three thousand kilometers in all, and with stopovers it took me three months.

The journey was conceived during the Covid crisis, when travel abroad was impossible. The government encouraged domestic travel, which happily provided an opportunity to escape the heat and humidity of the summer in Kyoto, where I live. In the desire for coolness, I looked as far north as I could, which meant Hokkaido's most northerly tip, Cape Soya.

Getting to the cape would involve taking a bus from the closest train station, which was Wakkanai. Though I had toured Hokkaido by train twice before, I had not visited Japan's most northerly station, stuck out on its own at the end of a long railway line. I set my sights on mid-August, when temperatures there would be in the low twenties, and thought of traveling back to Kyoto in tandem with the falling temperatures. And then it struck me: why stop at Kyoto? Like Donald Richie in *The Inland Sea*, I imagined forever following the sun as it retreated southward, so as to bask in the lingering glow of late-summer warmth.

Japan's most southerly station is Ibusuki, famous for its sand bathing, so I took out a map and considered the railway lines connecting north and south. The obvious choice was the Shinkansen line running from Hakodate in Hokkaido all the way down to Kagoshima in southern Kyushu, but I had already done all the segments and, although the bullet train offered convenience, it held little appeal. By sticking to the Sea of Japan, however, the route opened up exciting possibilities. I would avoid the big cities on the Pacific coast and bypass the touristic Golden Route of Tokyo, Kyoto, Osaka, and Hiroshima. Instead I could explore towns on Japan's less glamorous side, including several attractive castle towns that had been the seats of feudal lords in Edo times (1603–1868). Still today they remain regional centers of art, crafts, and cultural activities. Conveniently for a train traveler they are spaced an hour or two apart, like stepping stones the length of Japan.

The absence of bullet trains along the Sea of Japan coast suited my intentions, as I was looking for a more leisurely pace. Local trains would do nicely for short stretches, and express trains for the longer distances. My plan was to explore the rich diversity of the country by seeking what was unique to each of the places I would visit. As elsewhere, modernization has had a leveling effect on Japan's cities, but scratch the surface and there is great regional pride in the distinctive features. To a large extent the spirit of place remains manifest in such aspects as the famous products, literary associations, religious customs, ancient traditions, and above all the local food.

Travel books tend to be by younger people, footloose and fancy-free. Alan Booth was thirty-one when he did his heavily blistered walk, and Will Ferguson was around the same age when he stuck out a thumb to hitchhike north. Donald Richie was still in his thirties when he started the trips that were woven together in *The Inland Sea*. I was twice their age, but I hoped that would work to my advantage. "Write about Japan after three weeks or thirty years," is the sage advice given to newcomers. I had missed the boat for the first option; I was determined to catch the train for the second.

There are two types of traveler. One likes to prepare meticulously, the other to travel on a whim, relishing the unexpected. Put me down in the latter group. Sure you sometimes miss out, sure you sometimes run into trouble, but that is more than compensated for by the joy of discovery and the thrill of surprise. Besides, with train travel in Japan you very rarely go wrong. The general impression is of cleanliness, punctuality, and considerate passengers. If hell is other people, it is much less so in Japan. Trains are by and large a delight. Passengers talk in low voices so as not to cause a nuisance, and talking on mobile phones is not allowed. Leaving litter is rare. And should you feel lost on arrival, just ask a random stranger and you will likely experience the kindness of ordinary Japanese.

It is no exaggeration, then, to regard travel by train as one of the great joys of Japan, which is why it felt such a privilege to have the opportunity to journey the length of the country. I invite readers to join me. Along the way there will be some surprises, several unexpected encounters, and not a few adventures. This is no conventional travel guide—other books and Tripadvisor do that well enough. My journey draws rather on over thirty years of cultural immersion to give a personal account of the fascination that Japan holds for foreigners. Every country is different, they say, but Japan is more different than anywhere else, and the book unpacks one individual's response to the conundrums this often presents. As such it is as much a journey in time as place, ranging over the three decades I have spent in Japan. Along the way you will get to meet my friend Hirota-san and my partner Lili too. And along with the personal journey is the physical journey, through some of the country's lesser-known gems that lie off the beaten track. Aomori, Akita, Sado Island, Dewa Sanzan, Matsue, Hagi, Iki Island, Hirado, Shimabara, Kagoshima—these may be unfamiliar names to many, but each holds a special appeal. So do please get on board, and let our great train journey begin.

———

IN THIS BOOK NAMES of Japanese living after the Meiji Restoration (1868) are presented in the Western style—that is, given name followed by family name. Those who lived prior to the Meiji period are rendered in the traditional fashion of family name followed by given name.

Periods of Japanese history are given dates at their first mention only. An overview can be found on page 8.

Poetry and prose originally in Japanese have been translated by the author unless otherwise noted.

Acknowledgments

DURING MY JOURNEY THROUGH Japan, I was struck on numerous occasions by the courteous kindness of Japanese strangers when I asked for directions. I was also lucky enough to benefit from the company of friends and volunteer guides in various places. I'm very grateful to all of them, for the journey would have been far less rewarding without their support. They include above all Yuriko Suzuki and Yuji Ota, who joined me at different points and shared their cultural perspectives. In Sado, Takayuki Tsukakoshi was particularly generous in taking time out to drive me around the island. He proved an excellent guide. In Toyama, two longterm friends, Hiroko Terada and Mikiko Oshigami, shared their intriguing life stories. In Kanazawa the artist John Wells was kind enough to drive me around, and a friend from my earliest days in Japan, Chigako Omori, told me of the changes in the city as we tucked in to some delicious seafood. In Hagi, Izumi Makino went far beyond the normal duties of a volunteer guide by inviting me to meet her husband and inspect the kiln he had built. In Tsuwano I was guided by the enthusiastic Akemi Yuda, who made my brief visit a thorough joy, and in Imari I was able to interview veteran potter Sofu Mizokami and meet his family. In Hirado volunteer guide Yoshio Koteda gave me the benefit of his local expertise, as did Mr. Tai in Kumamoto when we toured the earthquake-damaged castle. Mention should be made too of the unfailingly pleasant and helpful staff at information offices located in the stations I visited.

A word of thanks also to Mark Stanley for drafting a map of my route along the "back side" of Japan. I would like to express here my appreciation of Stone Bridge's Peter Goodman for taking on the project and producing the wonderful cover design and to John Sockolov too for guiding the manuscript towards publication. Finally, a huge thank you to novelist Julie Highmore for her unfailing support throughout and for the valuable suggestions.

Hokkaido

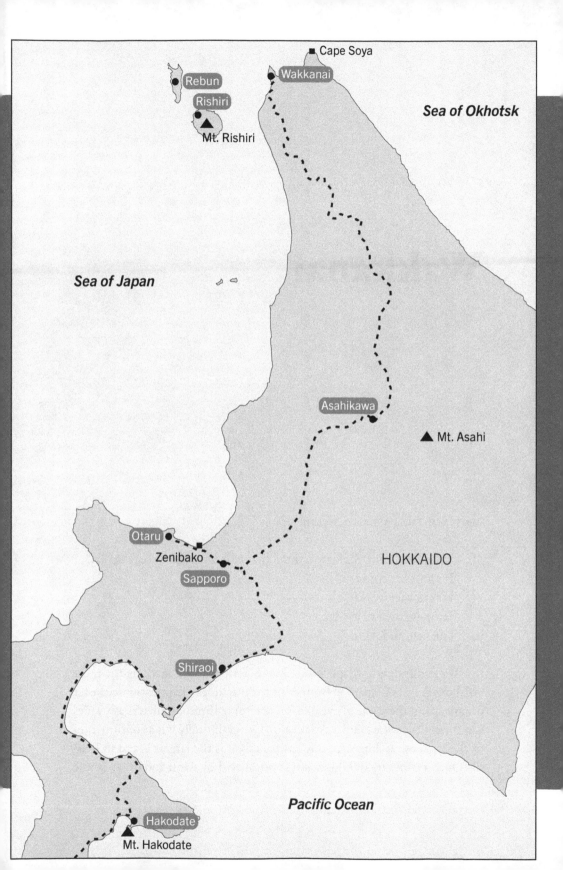

Wakkanai

"YOU SEE THAT ISLAND over there?"

"Yes."

"That's Sakhalin. Strange to think that you can actually see Russia."

"It's another country."

"It's another world."

"Japanese used to live there."

"Japanese and Ainu."

"Yes."

We're standing at Cape Soya, next to a monument marking the most northerly point of Japan. In front of us the placid sea disappears into the far distance, and there, clearly visible, a mere forty-three kilometers away, lies Karafuto, otherwise known as Sakhalin. Geographically it is a continuation of the Japanese archipelago, but territorially it is the largest island in Russia. Once a tributary of China, it was populated by Ainu and other ethnic groups until in modern times it became a source of conflict between Japan and Russia. Before World War II Japanese controlled the southern half, but in the closing stages of warfare Russia moved to occupy it. In the Treaty of San Francisco (1951) Japan ceded the territory.

My companion, Hirota-san, is a Buddhist priest in the True Pure Land sect (Jodo Shinshu). He was expected to take over the family temple but had managed to extend his graduate studies to such good effect that at thirty-nine he was that most unusual figure, a Japanese "eternal student." His interests had veered from Sanskrit to American Literature, and I was never quite sure how many masters courses he had started. When he heard of my plans to head for Wakkanai, he asked to be a Boswell to my Johnson. It was an amusing notion, but I wanted the freedom to roam at will. Besides, I am one of nature's loners. In the end we agreed he would come for the first leg only. So there we were, staring out at Sakhalin.

The chief attraction at Cape Soya—the whole point of it—is a monument marking Japan's most northerly point, in front of which visitors pose for photos. Nearby is the statue of a samurai holding a yardstick. Mamiya Rinzo (1775–1844), a famous cartographer, had led an expedition to Sakhalin, which confirmed for the first time that it was an island. Accompanying him were six Ainu, yet there was no mention of them—a bit like celebrating Hillary but omitting Tenzing in the conquest of Everest.

In 1976 an Englishman called Alan Booth stayed here overnight in a *minshuku* (guesthouse), and as he was leaving the next morning the owner offered him a bus schedule. He replied that he was going to walk. "How far?" queried his host. "The length of Japan," came the unexpected answer. It took four months, and the result was the celebrated *Roads to Sata*.

Booth's walk took place not long after a song about Cape Soya had become a national hit. It was an *enka*, a style dubbed "Japan's country music" because of similar themes of loneliness, lost love, and longing. The music tugs at the heartstrings of older Japanese and is popular in hostess bars. Here at the cape, a memorial rock had a button , when pressed, replayed the song, and as the plaintive tones filled the air, I even felt nostalgic myself.

> The drifting ice is melting
> Spring wind is blowing

The Rugosa rose in bloom
And seagulls crying
Along the distant shore
Happily the smoke trails
Of ships from overseas—
Ah, that's Cape Soya!

It is a curious fact of life in Japan that Russia lies so close, yet is so remote in the national consciousness. In my thirty years in the country I have overheard countless conversations about America and Europe, yet I cannot recall a single one about Russia, though it takes roughly the same time to fly from Tokyo to Vladivostok as to Okinawa.

"What's your image of Russia?" I asked Hirota-san.

"They are like thieves, I think."

"Thieves? That's not very fair, is it?"

"But they entered World War II just at the finish and they stole our islands. Japanese don't think that is right. And they treated prisoners badly. You know, many died in Siberia after the war."

"So you have a bad feeling towards them. Is that usual, do you think?"

"Yes."

When Will Ferguson visited Hakodate on his hitchhiking tour across Japan, he was told that Russian sailors steal bicycles and remove car tires. The legacy of the Soviet Union still taints Russia's image, and when Monty Python's Michael Palin flew from Siberia to Japan in his travel series *Around the World in 80 Days*, he described the experience as moving from a country where nothing works to one where everything does. He was spot on. Customers may be kings in Japan, but in Siberia they are simply a nuisance. I remember my first impression of U-ra-ji-o-sto-ku (Vladivostok), when a hotel receptionist kept me waiting a full forty minutes while she chatted to a friend.

There were no such worries at Cape Soya, where stalls were doing a brisk business selling seafood souvenirs like scallops, clams, crabs, and octopus. There was Soya black beef too. The sole restaurant offered sea urchin rice and soft seaweed soba. Tasty. The atmosphere was delightfully local, for the tourist industry had somehow passed it by—no chain stores, no resort hotels, no crass commercialism.

Behind the ramshackle buildings was a grassy knoll with a dozen miscellaneous monuments, the tallest of which commemorates the shooting down of a Korean Air plane in 1983 after it strayed into Sakhalin's airspace (ironically, it was numbered 007). Sculpted in the shape of a crane (symbol of Hokkaido), the monument was a reminder of just how cold the Cold War got. All 269 people on board perished.

Another monument was dedicated to a different kind of warfare—the sinking of the US submarine *Wahoo* in World War II. It had destroyed several Japanese ships, and the enlightened inscription, which shows compassion for both sides, is a model surely for how such monuments should be.

> Eighty Americans sleep in the Soya Strait twelve miles northeast of here. Many Japanese sleep in the Sea of Japan from *Wahoo* attacks. This monument was erected by the members of the Japan Attack Group and relatives of Americans lying in the *Wahoo*. Old enemies met as brothers to ensure that our countries will have lasting peace and we will never again destroy the friendship we enjoy today.

Hirota-san had rented a car for the short journey from Wakkanai to the cape (about thirty kilometers). Giant wind turbines stood on rolling green hills, and a signboard cautioned that our coastal road was only three meters above sea level. Winters are harsh in these northern parts, though the houses looked far from robust and, like most Japanese buildings, seemed designed for summer. Only the chimneys hinted at the winter cold. The snow here is dry and not as heavy as the moist variety found further south, where houses have steep roofs with thick tiles to cope with the weight.

Ahead of us lay a wide bay, the curving coastline of which led the eye to Japan's most northerly town, but on rounding a bend we were confronted by a most improbable sight—Mt. Fuji. Graceful slopes rose to fashion a familiar shape, and the perfect symmetry took the breath away. It wasn't *the* Mt. Fuji of course; it was the Rishiri Fuji, which stands on an island beyond Wakkanai.

Throughout Japan there are regional versions of Japan's iconic mountain, and there is another in Hokkaido called Mt. Yotei. I knew too that at the end of the tracks in Kyushu would be yet another, the Satsuma Fuji. My journey would thus begin and finish beneath the protective presence of local Fujis. It surely augured well.

WAKKANAI IS A HYBRID town, part industrial port, part summer resort. In among the modest buildings two high-rise hotels soar skywards out of all proportion to their surrounds. What were the city authorities thinking— or rather, what were they taking? They had sold the soul of the town for the lure of tourist money. Yet despite that there is something very appealing about the place. It has an end-of-the-line feel, and like a real-life *Truman Show* the station entrance is roped off for large portions of the day, as if to signal there is no escape.

While I was sipping a drink in a coffee shop, a family of deer wandered past, nonchalantly munching the front lawn. It is that kind of a place. Virtually all the shops and restaurants shut at five—it is that kind of a place, too. My room overlooked the port, and though there were several docks there were only two ships, one of which was a car ferry. Was the town always this quiet, I wondered, or was it the Covid effect?

For dinner Hirota-san and I tracked down the only open restaurant and ordered *bukkake-don*, which turned out to be a bountiful bed of rice topped by salmon roe, tuna, salmon, scallop, *wakame* seaweed, and succulent shrimp. Best of all was the sea urchin (*uni*), described by Matt Golding in *Rice Noodle Fish* as "arguably the sexiest food on the planet." Perhaps that was why I drew Hirota-san's attention to the waitress, aware that he was looking for a girlfriend. "She seems charming," I ventured. "I don't think so," he replied.

"What's wrong with her?"

"She poured very little sake into my cup. It wasn't polite."

"Really, let me pour you some more. Perhaps it will change your mind!"

"Also she reminded me of my old girlfriend. She is from Wakkanai."

"Your old girlfriend? Is she still here?"

"Maybe not. But once I came here to visit in winter."

"What was it like?"

"I had to buy a special tool for my shoes."

"What kind of tool?"

"A rubber covering the shoe, it has spikes. I needed to cover my face with muffler."

"It sounds like Siberia. Did you do any snow walking?"

"No, there was a problem."

"What was that?"

"She was not friendly."

Hirota-san had not mentioned his previous visit, but perhaps the memory was too painful. He had not had much luck with women; "I've never been on a car date," he told me wistfully. As heir to his father's temple his chances were limited, because few females these days arc willing to take on the onerous duties of being a priest's wife.

The next day we visited Wakkanai's main attraction, a small park with a view of Sakhalin, and, yes, more monuments. It took all of fifteen minutes from the station to walk across town, past the main Shinto shrine and up a small hillside, at the top of which were views over the Okhotsk Sea. The monuments exuded a mournful atmosphere, the most prominent commemorating "nine maiden telephone operators" who committed suicide in southern Sakhalin rather than live on under the Soviet invaders of 1945.

Another monument showed the grotesque figure of a woman with head thrown back, looking upwards. Her mouth was open in a Munch-like scream, and her arms were outstretched. The statue honored the 420,000 people summarily expelled from Sakhalin in 1949. Overnight they had lost their homes, and their homeland.

In among the tales of human tragedy the statue of a dog stood out. In 1956, some forty huskies that had been trained in Wakkanai were dispatched to the Antarctic. When it came time to return, atrocious weather conditions meant fifteen of the dogs had to be abandoned. A year later, against all expectations, it was discovered that two had miraculously survived. The story won worldwide attention and formed the basis for a well-received movie, *Antarctica* (1983), starring Ken Takakura—and, of course, two huskies.

THERE IS SOMETHING ALLURING about small islands. Self-containment makes them manageable, the sea air makes them invigorating. In a big city like Osaka, you can easily feel insignificant, but on an island, you soon become a known entity. Beach or rocky shore, the never-ending swell of waves lulls the soul into a sense of ease. Small wonder that ancient Chinese sited their paradise on an island (Penglai in English, Horai in Japanese).

To the northwest of Wakkanai lie two attractive islands, Rebun and Rishiri. They make a natural pair, one playing yin to the other's yang.

Rishiri is round and tall, Rebun long and low. It is as if they are sentinels guarding against unwelcome elements, like the lion dogs found at the entrance to shrines. Ferries shuttle back and forth, but the weather can be unreliable, even in mid-August. Time was on my side, however, and I was able to head for Rishiri with clear skies and a warm day. Hirota-san claimed to have work to do, though I suspected "work" involved a female.

There were few other passengers aboard the capacious ferry, which I was told was usually crowded in August. Once out at sea, horizons broadened, and the vast expanse invited the soul to fly free. Kenji Miyazawa, the popular children's writer, made a trip to Sakhalin in 1923, and a verse he wrote was composed on the deck of the ferry, looking back to the land left behind and forwards to his destination.

> Dark mottled green
> is Cape Soya
> and to the north
> slumbering in deep blue
> Sakhalin's eastern tip

Rishiri lies fifty kilometers off the Hokkaido coast, which oddly makes it more distant than Sakhalin, and the latter part of the journey was dominated by the 1,721-meter Mt. Rishiri. On arrival a large tourist coach awaited us, but barely a dozen got in. That did not stop the guide from throwing herself into a nonstop commentary about all things Rishiri. No snakes, no bears, no coronavirus, but please wear masks, wash hands, and keep social distance, a refrain repeated throughout the day. In between came a stream of statistics, schedules, sightseeing spots, and safety tips. Such is the way with Japanese tours.

Special attention on these excursions is lavished on local specialties, and the bus drew up at souvenir shops where passengers flocked to the neatly packed gifts. The fascination with souvenirs is said to date back to the pilgrimages of Edo times, when bringing back unusual items was a way of sharing the travel experience with those unable to go. Writing in the 1890s, Lafcadio Hearn noted that "such small gifts and memories make up much of the unique pleasure of Japan. In almost any town or village you can buy for a souvenir some pretty or curious thing made only in that one place."

Driving round Rishiri is simple: you drive round the volcano. "The last eruption was eight hundred years ago," said our guide, "so there is a good chance that we'll be safe." The mountain has sixteen different faces, she continued, but it is unusual to see all of them in a single day because the peak gets covered with cloud. Along the way were stops at scenic spots, the first being a small lake with footboards over its marshy margins. It was a smaller version of the more famous walkway at Shiretoko, a World Heritage site in Hokkaido's northeast. Both have spectacular views, but Shiretoko offers the extra thrill of possibly encountering a bear. Here the only danger was a rival busload of tourists.

At one point the bus passed a simple rock monument close to the sea, of great interest to me personally but not so much to the others. It marked the spot where the splendidly named Ranald MacDonald arrived on a one-man mission in 1848. His was an extraordinary story. Son of a Scottish father and Chinook mother, he was raised in western Canada where he developed an obsession with the forbidden land on the far side of the Pacific. Japan was still in self-imposed isolation, and imprisonment or death awaited intruders. Nonetheless, bored of his job as a bank clerk, Mac-Donald signed on to a whaling ship and persuaded the captain to abandon him off Hokkaido. The crew must have thought him insane.

When he washed up on Rishiri, MacDonald pretended to have capsized and was taken captive, then dispatched to Nagasaki where those in charge of foreign affairs were based. For some time American and British ships had been skirting Japanese waters, and the captive offered a chance to learn their language, so fourteen samurai who had previously learnt Dutch were appointed to study with him. MacDonald thus became Japan's first-ever English teacher.

The lessons came to an abrupt end after ten months, when MacDonald joined a group of shipwreck survivors released to an American warship. In later years he tried his hand at business but died a poor man, his last word being "sayonara." History suggests he did a great job as teacher, for one of his students, Moriyama Einosuke, became a leading interpreter in the historic negotiations of 1854 with Commodore Perry.

Back in the bus the commentary continued at full speed. Mackerel were once so plentiful that in the poverty following World War II people flocked to fish at Rishiri. Fishermen put up Shinto shrines in gratitude, which explains the large number. Scallops too were found in abundance. "Now, if you would please turn to the left, you can see the kelp hanging up to dry, while on the right is another famous face of Mt. Rishiri. Please look left again and you can see the Hokkaido mainland." Heads were swiveling from side to side as at a tennis match.

Our midday meal was soba noodles with shredded kelp. Delicious. Even as we ate, a small white cloud attached itself to the Rishiri Fuji, obscuring face number fifteen. "What a pity," said the guide, "we were so close to seeing all sixteen." Afterwards we stopped at a cliff face where lava had run into the sea during the last eruption, and while the others shopped, I sat for a while looking down at the rocks, mesmerized by the motion of waves. My musings were interrupted by the buzz of a smart phone. How absurd, I thought, here in unfettered nature, yet tied by a gadget to everyday life. So I hurled it over the rocks and into the sea.

Well, I confess that though I wanted to, I didn't. And when I saw the message, I was glad I hadn't, because my partner, Lili, had written a haiku that spoke to the delicacy of the Japanese soul. Translated, it went:

Why does your head droop?
What do you pray for,
Japanese rose?

The flower of which she wrote, in seasonal bloom at the time, is called *nekojarashi* and hangs down like a bluebell. Though she had never studied haiku, Lili had absorbed the essence, whereby personal feelings are expressed through allusion to nature. Much of the population is steeped in the tradition, and one of the most popular primetime television programs, called *Purei Batto* (Play Battle), features a haiku competition. Moved by her message, I tried to respond in kind, and that's one reason why Japanophiles love Japan. It brings out our better selves.

OUR GUIDE FOR THE trip round Rebun looked so young I thought she must be a schoolgirl. She showed not the least dismay about our small number, but embarked on a nonstop commentary that was so loud and fast it was a wonder she could breathe. The tour was scheduled to last two and a half hours; surely, I thought, she cannot keep up that pace. But she did.

In much of the world one might assume she was after a tip, but in Japan the *ganbaru* (do your best) ethic ensures the work is done well. Collectivism means too that there is awareness of representing something larger than self, which is why uniforms and name cards are so important. As well as acting on behalf of her company, our guide was representing the island, and the explanations aimed specifically at me as a foreigner showed that for outsiders she was also speaking for Japan.

Rebun's population of three thousand is aging and in decline, a situation faced by most of Japan's 430 inhabited islands. A low birth rate is compounded by limited job opportunities, which means crisis is looming for many island communities. Our guide presented a rosier picture, however.

"When we were at school, we learnt about special flowers on the island. They are volcanic plants that we cannot find anywhere else. Since there were only a few students, we could go by minibus on fieldwork. It was fun. Just imagine: Rebun has over three hundred different flowers. That's why we call it 'Flower Island.' And that's why I want others to know about the beauty of our island."

At the picturesque Cape Sukai, a fellow traveler approached me with a question: "Can you speak Japanese?" When I replied in Japanese that I could, he continued in pidgin English.

"Where you from?"

"England," I said.

"This Sukai Misaki. You know the meaning?"

"Is it Ainu?"

"No. Maybe English."

"Well, *misaki* is cape in English."

"Yes, no." Then he pointed upwards. "You see? It is sky. Sukai Misaki."

When Alan Booth walked the length of Japan in 1977, he had scores of such conversations. They make up the pattern of life for gaijin (foreigners in Japan), not so much in cities anymore but certainly in the provinces. One learns to enjoy or endure them, and while my fellow passengers were raiding the souvenir shop, I sought relief in "the most northerly public toilet in Japan."

One of the shop assistants, a student from Tokyo, was having a cigarette break, and we compared notes about "empty tourism." As in Kyoto, the capital's tourist sites had been emptied of visitors. Looking around I said, "It must be paradise to work surrounded by all this natural beauty?"

"Not really," he replied, "the Wi-Fi signal is weak."

On the way to the ferry port our guide entertained us by singing an *enka* about Rebun. She was good, very good, and the performance was a joy. When she finished, there was a smattering of applause. "You sound as if you're not impressed," she responded, "so I better not sing another one." But of course she did, and we loved it.

On Track ||||||||||||||||||||||||||||||||||||||||||||||||||

Wakkanai is the end point of the Soya Line from Asahikawa. The line first started in 1898 but only reached Wakkanai in 1922. The terminus is marked by buffers and a sign stating that it is the country's most northerly station. There is a single platform with a daily average of just eighty-three passengers, indicative of the crisis JR Hokkaido faces in terms of usage. In front of the station is a small section of uncovered track, which remains from a former line to the ferry connection for Karafuto (Sakhalin). The extension was closed following World War II.

Asahikawa, the next significant town, is 259 kilometers distant. The Sarobetsu limited express takes a little over three and a half hours for the journey, running through a vast expanse of empty land, including the Sarobetsu Plain. Operating trains across the sparsely populated region has proved a costly business, which is one of the reasons why JR Hokkaido is running at a loss.

Asahikawa

FROM WAKKANAI, ASAHIKAWA IS the next significant outpost of civilization. The long train journey is indicative of the scale of Hokkaido, for in much of Japan a journey of nearly four hours might take you past three major towns and a couple of volcanoes. Before departing, Hirota-san and I had a "sayonara splurge" on a Wakkanai Bowl, which turned out to be much the same as we had the previous evening: a bed of rice covered with seafood. Nonetheless it was delicious and nutritious, a fitting way to say goodbye to an area we had both enjoyed.

As we pulled away from Japan's northernmost station, urbanization gave way to mixed woods of maple, conifer, and silver birch, the latter glistening in the sunshine. After Honshu's monoculture of allergy-inducing cedar, the diversity was a delight. The undergrowth was thick with broadleaf bamboo, while the rolling green hills and tree-lined embankments were reminiscent of England. There were hillside meadows too like those of the Swiss lowlands.

The sight of cows made my heart jump, and I realized how Japanese I had become. As the saying goes, you know you've been in Japan too long when you bow while on the telephone; when you object to other gaijin; when you wait for the door to open automatically; when you expect the toilet to greet you; and, sadly, when you get excited by cows.

As the terrain became flatter, horizons withdrew, and the open expanse seemed to stretch forever. Stations were few and far between. Clouds of white and grey dappled a boundless blue sky, liberating after the hilly confines of Kyoto. Here and there among the patchwork fields were farm buildings, varied in type and color. Hedgerows were conspicuously absent.

For a while Hirota-san and I played a form of I Spy, seeing who could first identify the crops we were passing. The island boasts a lengthy list: millet, sweet corn, melons, asparagus, pumpkin, leak, cucumber, tomato, green pepper, fruit trees, and three types of potato (three types of rice too).

Everywhere you looked there was luxuriant growth, quite different in nature from Honshu's rice fields and mountainsides. The greenery led me to think of Isabella Bird, who made a trip to southern Hokkaido in 1878. Told in her youth to travel for her health, she made the advice a lifelong mission, journeying to exotic parts of the globe and writing perceptive travel books. She was the first Western woman to travel to Hokkaido, where she made a study of the Ainu for Christian missionaries. Roads were rough (accommodation even rougher) and she was thrown from her horse on several occasions, bringing her face to face with the thick vegetation. The result is a passage that shows her remarkable ability to record details:

> The undergrowth is simply hideous, consisting mainly of coarse reedy grass, monstrous docks, the large leafed Polygonum cuspidate, several umbelliferous plants, and a "ragweed" which, like most of its gawky fellows, grows from five to six feet high.

In our carriage were twenty-three other passengers. I counted them to be sure, for it was so quiet I had hardly noticed their presence. Apart from one or two couples, they were male, young, and on their own. Some were staring at the vast open expanse, but most had their eyes closed or ears sealed with headphones. We were socially distanced, as we surely would have been even without Covid. None were causing the slightest disturbance, and as the train rumbled on it was possible to slip into a meditative state. Not for the first time I felt grateful to be in Japan.

Diagonally across from me a young man sported a T-shirt saying "My life, my gas." It took me back to my first days in Japan and a student who had "Dickhead" written on the back of his jacket. Despite specializing in English, he had never bothered to read the word. And why should he? The writing was decorative. Roman letters look chic, advanced, sophisticated. Only a Dickhead would worry about the meaning!

Decorative English is one of the enjoyable traits of contemporary Japan. "Let's bilingual," exhorted one of my writing pads, to which a pencil case responded, "I feel basically you should sport yourself." A T-shirt declared, "I love everybody, and you're next," which sounded like a promise but might have been a threat. Occasionally the whimsy aspires to poetry: "When I jumped far beyond your imagination, I found myself a gust of wind," said a shopping bag I came across in Kanazawa.

The more you look out for English, the more of it there is. Pubs have suggestive names like Let's or Pink Banana, while scooters are called, inappropriately, Jog or Squash. "Grass wine" is a popular item on menus, and in vending machines you can get a drink called Pocari Sweat, a type of milk powder called Creap, and a condom named Rony Wrinkle. Speaking of which, a jeweler in Tokyo once put up a sign inviting passersby to "Come in and get your thing engraved." Let's bilingual, indeed!

"ROUGH, LITTLE-KNOWN AND THINLY populated" was Isabella Bird's summary judgment of Hokkaido. These days it is not rough nor little-known, but it remains thinly populated. She compared the scenery to her native Scotland with its mountains, lakes, and open space. At the time Japan was dubbed "the Britain of the Far East," and in those terms Hokkaido clearly fit Bird's bill, so to speak.

Given the northern feel, it comes as a surprise to learn that Hokkaido is on a similar latitude to southern France and northern Spain. Within Japan, it is very much an oddity too. For one thing, it is not just an island but a prefecture and a region all in itself. As an island it is the second in size after Honshu, but it is easily the biggest of the eight regions. Japan has forty-seven prefectures, and here again Hokkaido is the largest. In fact, it contains an impressive twenty-two percent of Japan's total landmass but has just four percent of the people. If you hear Japanese complain of cramped conditions, tell them to relocate to Hokkaido.

The region is unusual in terms of climate too. Few typhoons and no rainy season make it decidedly different from other parts of Japan. You won't find any haiku here about glistening moss. Winters on the other hand can be severe, and it has claim to be one of the snowiest places on earth. Cold air from Siberia propelled across the relatively warm Sea of Japan generates clouds that unload snow in truckloads over the mountains, creating ski slopes that in recent years have been popular with Australians and East Asians.

Along with the distinctive geography, Hokkaido has a distinctive history. For millennia it was under the sway of the Ainu, but following the Meiji Restoration of 1868 it was integrated into the new nation state. (Still today eighty percent of place names are Ainu.) The development is often compared with the taming of the Wild West, as impoverished farmers from Honshu were urged to build a new life in the wide-open spaces. "Go North" was the message. I hoped to learn more when I visited the Ainu Museum at Shiraoi.

Thirty years ago, there had been a popular television serial called *Kita no kuni kara* (From the North Country), which captured the pioneering spirit in the story of an individual called Goro. A divorcee through no fault of his own, he leaves Tokyo for Hokkaido to make a new life for his children by single-handedly building a house. The climate is harsh and life is hard, but the family struggle through difficulties with heart-warming perseverance. The honest and hard-working Goro became a much-loved character who embodied ideal Japanese traits—hardworking, stoic, modest, and above all sincere even if shy and a little naive.

AS THE TRAIN NEARED the end of its four-hour journey, unfettered nature gave way to agribusiness and "wagon wheels" of harvested wheat. But there was none of the disfiguring development that characterizes other parts of the country. No concrete hillsides, no ugly industry. Just stands of trees and arable land. In the distance clouds hovered over mountain peaks, some of which wore a silvery sheen as if in a trial run for the blanket of snow to come.

Asahikawa is Hokkaido's second biggest city, with a population of 350,000, but one hears little about it. You might even be forgiven for thinking it is just what the name says—Morning Sun River. Hirota-san had a relative to visit, so we agreed to meet up later in Sapporo, but before parting he introduced me to a verse by Kenji Miyazawa, who visited the town in 1923 on his way to Sakhalin. He had arrived on a sunny day in October and took a cab ride, noting the fine buildings and distinctive trees (larch grow in colder regions, and poplars are a useful wind break).

As we turn now into Rokujo
ah, larches, larches,
and blue trembling poplars;
in this part the planners have done well,
a row of administrative buildings
lined up with the Junior High

A surprise awaited me on arrival, for stepping out of the station I found an idyllic scene of flower beds and grassy slopes leading down to a tree-lined river. Schoolchildren were scattered here and there, some on benches and some huddled around smart phones. Near me, with not the slightest hint of self-consciousness, two schoolgirls were practicing dance moves. The sun had not yet begun its descent behind the western hills, though crows in profusion were already flocking to their evening assembly. But for an elevated roadway, it might as well have been open countryside.

Unwittingly I had stepped out the back of the station. Outside the main exit, on the other hand, was the usual townscape of taxi stand, convenience store, and station hotels. The contrast was striking: Exit one side, and high-rise concrete blocks jostle for attention. Exit the other, and there was a pastoral setting. I was so taken with this that early the next morning I headed back again, and in the early light, bereft of schoolchildren, it looked even better. Skirting the riverside, I rounded a bend and came upon a lone angler holding a pose so motionless I thought it must be a statue. Eventually he moved, and I watched as he attached bait and cast off.

"What kind of fish can you catch here?"

"Pike and *funa*," he grunted.

"Do you usually catch much?"

"No."

"How long have you been here?"

"Since earlier.'"

A train went past. "It's amazing that you can fish so close to the main station."

"*So desu ne.*"

"Amazing that there's only you here too."

"*So desu.*"

It was as close as Japanese get to telling you to mind your own business. When Alan Booth walked across Hokkaido, he was plagued by children yelling "gaijin" at him. Now the tables were reversed, I thought wryly, and the gaijin was annoying the locals. Booth was an irascible type, and he had a low tolerance for fools, but I am forever grateful to him, for it was largely thanks to his encouragement that I got into writing about Japan. He had come to Japan to study noh and was something of a Renaissance man, active in multiple fields. His work as movie critic for the *Asahi Evening News* came to a jaw-dropping conclusion when he declared that he could no longer stand being subjected in the dark to films of mind-numbing mediocrity.

When he reached Asahikawa, Booth was told the winters were so cold that Coca-Cola bottles exploded. The town holds Japan's record for low temperatures, with a toe-curdling minus forty-one Celsius, and in recent years it has taken to holding an annual ice sculpting festival. That sounded great for winter, I told the woman at the information office, but how about events in August?

"I'm looking for something special that only Asahikawa has."

"Where are you from?" she responded.

"England," I said.

"Then you will certainly like the English flower gardens."

I assured her I wouldn't.

"How about the zoo?" she suggested, handing me a brochure.

"I'm afraid I'm not in favor of zoos."

"But you'll like the penguins." she insisted. "They are very cute. And they are only found in Asahikawa."

"Oh," I said in jest, "so they are native to Asahikawa. That is special indeed."

"No," she replied, "they are from the Antarctic."

Not for the first time my attempt at humor had fallen flat. One lesson every Englishman soon learns in Japan is that irony is trumped by sincerity. And just to make sure I had understood her point, the information officer added, "The penguins are very cute. Everybody likes them."

"Cute" is deeply ingrained in the Japanese psyche. Koala bears, mannequins, cats, dolls, Lolita girls. Police stations line up toy animals in their windows, and virtually every town or sports team has some kind of cute mascot. Even Kyoto Station has one. No one finds it strange because cuteness is its own justification. It speaks to a willingness to embrace innocence and the childlike. By contrast, being adult is a virtue in the West and children are often told to "Grow up."

A student of mine once described as cute the fattest of fat sumo wrestlers called Konishiki, a giant hulk of rolling blubber. The funny thing was I knew just what she meant. Cuteness can grow on you—or even in you. Tokyo's Unko Museum (Turd Museum) marks the ultimate example of Japan's ability for cutification, for, to a background of soft music, you can walk among representations of human excrement. There's even a takeaway toy modeled on whipped cream.

Meanwhile back at the information office, I was still looking for something special about Asahikawa. Guidebooks pitch it as the gateway to the Daisetsu Mountains, which is Hokkaido's number one tourist destination. "Do you have something on mountains, perhaps?" I asked, and sure enough a glossy brochure was produced—"Coexisting with the *Kamuy*: The Kamikawa Ainu." (*Kamuy* is the Ainu name for spirits; Kamikawa, a sacred river.)

The brochure spoke of "magnificent waterfalls," "mysteriously shaped rocks," and "enigmatic lakes." There were religious sites too, such as a riverside rock from which shaved sticks called *inau* were offered to the river god for safe passage through the rapids. Inside was a map of Ainu villages and an area labeled "Playground of the gods." One caption spoke of "gorges filled with snow which has not melted in ten thousand years." I needed a moment or two to take in the time scale. Seeing that snow, touching it, savoring it—now that would be special!

HOKKAIDO WAS ONCE TWO separate islands, which merged into each other as the tectonic plates beneath them collided. The movement forced up the Daisetsu Range, which the Ainu named, descriptively, "Vast Roof Covering Middle Hokkaido." The tallest of the mountains, the highest in Hokkaido, is Mt. Asahi (2,291 meters), and the visitors center at its base has a list of adventurous activities, which, along with hiking and river rafting, include snowshoeing, air boarding, dog sledding, and even "treeing."

The route to the top is six kilometers, and it takes eight to nine hours to complete the walk there and back. The volcano is still active, and there is no shortage of hot springs available afterwards, to soak weary limbs. Skiing is particularly popular, because, according to the visitors center, the mountain has "the best powder snow in the world."

Near the visitors center a ropeway runs up to 1,600 meters, transporting passengers literally and figuratively to a different realm. In ancient times mountains with a special sense of presence were considered sacred, and Mt. Asahi was sacred to the Ainu. The ride is spectacular—the rarefied atmosphere, the soaring heights, the magnificence of nature. With its waterfalls, pristine lakes, and alpine flowers, you can see why the Ainu would have thought it a paradise on earth.

At the top, a one-hour walk leads to a volcanic landscape with crater lakes. It is the first place every year to display autumn colors in Japan, and the crowning glory is the sight of bright red maple leaves against thick white snow. How divine is that! In winter there are pillars of light and sparkling ice crystals known as "diamond dust," while in spring streams burst into life with the melting of the snow, surging down to the valley below. As in India, the fresh mountain water was seen as a living entity, gifted from the gods on high. Among the animal life here are brown bears and—new to me—a furry relative of the rabbit called pika, which burrows underground. Cute!

Within this paradise were swarms of dragonflies, darting back and forth in delight at the sunshine. It reminded me of Emperor Jomei, who as early as the seventh century had written of "My Yamato, Island of Dragonflies." It was only when I got back to the Wi-Fi comfort of my hotel that I discovered there are a staggering five thousand varieties worldwide, of which two hundred exist in Japan alone. Dragon is a powerful moniker for such a fragile creature, yet it captures the appeal of the brightly colored insects, for in their flight and love of water they evoke the vision of transitioning between realms. Perhaps the Pure Land priest Issa had something similar in mind when he wrote:

dragonfly—
distant mountains reflected
in its eyes

Another writer with an affinity for insects was Lafcadio Hearn, whose interest resulted in a remarkable twenty essays on the subject. His eyesight was abysmal, but his one-eyed myopia led him to focus on close-ups through a magnifying glass. He particularly appreciated the value given to insect song in Japanese culture, for "the music of insects and all that it signifies in the great poem of nature tells very plainly of goodness of heart, aesthetic sensibility, a perfectly healthy state of mind."

Refreshed and reinvigorated by my sortie into the mountains, I was ready for the next stage in my journey. The "bright lights, big city" awaited me in Japan's fifth-largest metropolis, and Hirota-san had texted me to say that he was already there. Sapporo was his favorite town, he had told me, because of the food; his brother had been a student at the university, so he used to be a frequent visitor. Eating, I suspected, would be top of our menu.

On Track ||||||||||||||||||||||||||||||||||||||||||||||||||||||

The station for Hokkaido's second city was first opened in 1898, and the present building makes use of the region's abundance of timber. As well as the Soya Line to Wakkanai, there are the Hakodate Line, running south to Sapporo, and the Sekihoku Line, running east to Abashiri, famous for its prison. In addition, a branch line runs to Furano, a popular skiing resort that is also famous for its lavender fields in July.

From Asahikawa to Wakkanai the limited express Sarobetsu runs alongside the Teshio River and across a park in the Sarobetsu Plains. Rishiri Island and its volcano are visible from Bakkai Station. To access the Daisetsuzan Ropeway the nearest station is Kamikawa on the Sekihoku Line, then thirty-five minutes by bus. Kamikawa and its neighbor Shirataki form the longest distance between JR stations in the whole of Japan (37.3 kilometers).

Sapporo

AMID THE THRONG OF humanity at Sapporo Station stands a striking sculpture. Busy commuters hurry past, but the lone figure stands defiantly still. Carved out of yellowish wood, it depicts an Ainu hunter in headdress with a long arrow gripped firmly between his teeth. In his hands he holds out a bow in welcome, yet no one pays him any heed. Dignified and rooted, he speaks to another age.

Sapporo in the Ainu language means Vast Dry River (i.e., Plain), a reference to the open land on which it is located. With the influx of migrants from the Honshu mainland, kanji characters were allocated to the name based on the sound and without regard to meaning. In this way, the descriptive Ainu name was written as something akin to Tablet Hood—a tablet on which is written a sad history.

In 1869 the Ainu of Ishikari Plain were pushed aside for construction of a capital fit for a thriving new region. The layout was conceived in grid-like straight lines, and once you step out of the station it becomes apparent, and modernity hits you in the form of a building with thirty-seven stories. A hundred and fifty years ago there were only a handful of village houses; now Sapporo has a population of nearly two million. Yet despite its size there are wide avenues and open areas, startling for those used to the cramped conditions of Honshu. All that unused space!

Sapporo's reputation as a food destination draws on Hokkaido's fertile land and bountiful waters. The island is surrounded by three different seas, fed by differing currents, meaning that the seafood is abundant and varied. In addition, Hokkaido's dairy products are a quality brand, and the first lick of a Hokkaido ice cream is never forgotten. Fresh, smooth, and deliciously creamy.

But the food most associated with Sapporo is meat. Lots of it. The most popular dish is Jingisukan, named after the Mongol tyrant Genghis Khan. For reasons best known to Sapporans, copious amounts of lamb and mutton are grilled in his name and swilled down with Sapporo beer. Such is its reputation that overworked office workers in Tokyo take weekend flights to indulge in all-you-can-eat-and-drink sessions, followed by a visit to the lively entertainment area.

Ramen fans, too, flock to Sapporo, said to have the country's best miso-style ramen. The noodles are made of wheat, and along with miso, the broth contains chicken stock, vegetables, and ground pork, resulting, if done properly, in a thick soup and rich *umami* flavor. Toppings might include sliced pork, dried seaweed, fish cake, green onions, or corn. Virtually every area in Japan boasts its own variation, and as Hirota-san considered himself a connoisseur, I asked about the difference between miso and *shio* (salt) ramen.

"*Shio* is simpler," he said. "If you want thick taste you should try miso ramen."

"I see."

"If the weather is cold, try miso."

"I see, okay."

"If you are sensitive to smell, *shio* is safer."

"Okay, I think I've got it."

There was a pause. "If you want sweet corn, you should ask for *shio*."

"Why?"

"With *shio* ramen you can taste ingredients. With miso ramen the taste is miso."

Ramen appreciation is something of a cult, and fanatics get up early to queue at shops that have built up a reputation. Hirota-san found us a restaurant that offered a seafood broth, and I was handed an English-language guide about how to slurp properly. (Anyone who has seen Juzo Itami's *Tampopo* will know about good slurping.) "Lean towards your bowl and support it with one hand," began the instructions:

> Start by admiring the sight and smell. Then begin on the noodles, being sure to slurp as you ingest the flavors sucked up from the broth. Not only is it the ideal way to enjoy a bowl of ramen, it can be insulting to the chef if you eat too quietly.

WHEN I FIRST CAME to Japan, university students spent the first year and a half in a liberal arts department, and many of the English-language textbooks featured essays contrasting Japan with the West. There would sometimes be reference to a puzzling phrase attributed to an American called William Clark. "Boys, be ambitious," he unremarkably said. None of my colleagues could explain why those words should be so famous, and in a classic case of circular logic I was told that the phrase was famous because it was well known.

Flipping through a brochure about Sapporo, I came upon a picture of William Clark's bust. It is mounted on a pillar in the grounds of Hokkaido University where he taught, and as the campus is situated not far from the rail station, I decided to head there the following morning. My curiosity was piqued; here perhaps was a chance to solve the mystery of Clark's words. Hirota-san was happy to join me, and so we set off to do some serious sleuthing.

The university campus is one of the city's sights, with trees galore and a clover lawn divided by a flowing brook. On the far side, kindergarten kids were running around in high spirits. There were few others—students had been told to stay home because of Covid. It seemed we were lucky, for a pamphlet spoke of "throngs of tourists" admiring its poplar avenue and "scores of tourists" arriving in autumn for the yellowing ginkgo trees.

Clark's bust showed a dignified and bearded figure, next to which was a board giving information about his life. A professor at Amherst College, he had been invited to Sapporo in 1876 to help set up an agricultural college and left after just eight months, job done. As he was departing he turned round to the students who had come to see him off and uttered three words: "Boys, be ambitious." It was his sayonara.

This was all very fine, but it hardly explained why such a humdrum phrase should be remembered over a hundred years later. At this point one of the teaching staff happened to walk past, so I seized the opportunity to question him.

"Well, first of all you have to understand it was a special time for Japan," he responded.

"In what way?"

"You see, in Meiji times it was important to catch up with the West. That was when Clark Sensei came, and he brought us new knowledge. Over there for instance is a model barn built to his instructions, because Japanese were not used to giving animals shelter in winter."

"I see. I understand he was a good teacher. But what's so special about the phrase 'Boys be ambitious.' After all, plenty of other teachers must have said good phrases."

"Yes, but Mr. Clark was special. He could understand Japanese feelings. He gave us encouragement. And he taught with respect. We Japanese appreciate that. Even after he went back to the US, he continued to help Japan. His students became important in shaping agricultural policies, so we never forget what he contributed. And we will never forget his final words."

"But are the words so meaningful?"

"For we Japanese, yes. It reminds us what he taught."

"So 'Boys, be ambitious' is a way of honoring his memory."

"Yes. that's right."

Now it all made sense. It was an example of the deep sense of gratitude felt to foreigners who contribute to Japan (whereas those who are critical are quickly accused of "Japan-bashing"). In the terms of George Bush, the Japanese way is either you are with us or against us. It helps explain the high profile of a writer such as Lafcadio Hearn, little known in the wider world. Like Clark, he is viewed not exactly as "one of us," but "one with us."

The campus was so pleasant that Hirota-san and I lingered for a while.

The pond has Ainu origins, and until the 1920s salmon came upstream as far as this. Urban development caused the river to dry up in the 1950s, when the boom years were beginning, but in recent years clear water has begun flowing once again. It reflects a greater concern with the quality of life, now that catching up with the West is no longer a priority.

On display in the university museum are sample entrance exams, one of which was an English-language exam for science students in 1932. (At the time there were four compulsory subjects: Japanese, Chinese, math, and English.) The passage for translation ran as follows: "It sometimes happens, during a lively conversation at a dinner party or in a group of people on a train, that there is one silent person who knows more about the subject than anybody else." Ah, the Japanese love of silence; it even raises its head in a test of English.

Not far from the university a souvenir shop offered Hokkaido specialties, including corn on the cob, oysters, potatoes, and juices—maple, prune, blueberry, and, intriguingly, silver birch. Eager to taste a tree, I chose the latter but disappointingly it was much like water. It reminded me of the delicate aromas found in incense, when the fragrance of tiny bits of wood worth thousands of dollars is so subtle you wonder if there is anything there at all.

One of the physical features that marks Sapporo as different is Odori Park (*odori* means main or wide street), with its fountains, flowerbeds, and monuments. It separates the northern administrative district from the southern residential area and extends twelve blocks, as if a town planner had sat down with a ruler and drawn a mile-long green line through the urban landscape. Laid out in 1871, it was conceived as a firebreak, for if there is one thing that Japanese history teaches, it is that fire is as great a threat to wooden buildings as earthquakes. Ironically, it means that Japan's newest city is closest in design to the ancient capital of Kyoto, which was also built with a grid system and huge central firebreak.

As is the way with parks in Japan, someone had bothered to count the 4,700 trees and categorize them into ninety-two different species. A large percentage, nearly a quarter in all, are lilac. Why? Because it is Hokkaido's official tree. (Each prefecture has a representative bird, flower, and tree.) Along with the arboreal abundance the park boasts a number of Soviet-style monuments to agricultural workers. The Dairy Farmers Association for example is represented by an idyllic young boy and calf looking forwards in visionary unison to a future of supplying the nation's milk. There are literary monuments too, among which is a statue of a boyish Takuboku Ishikawa, who wrote the following short verse in 1907.

> In the silence
> of an autumn evening
> in the town's wide street
> there wafts the aroma
> of grilled corn

Ishikawa was part of a modernizing movement that sought to break free of tradition, and his poem captures the spirit of place by referencing sweetcorn, a famous Hokkaido product. Though it captures a moment from another age, the silent emptiness felt strangely fitting for a time of Covid. There is a tragic aspect too to the life of the poet, for though he burned bright he died all too young (just twenty-six).

WHEN I TOLD HIROTA-SAN I was going to visit Hokkaido Shrine, he showed little interest. Shinto is often said to be key to an understanding of Japanese culture, yet it is not recognized by Hirota-san's sect of Buddhism (Jodo Shinshu, True Pure Land sect). The founder, Shinran Shonin, regarded Japanese spirits, called kami, as a distraction from the only thing that mattered—salvation through Amida's saving grace.

Shinto's major shrines often boast ancient origins, but those in Hokkaido only date from Meiji times (though a couple in the extreme south claim a seventeenth-century foundation). For millennia Hokkaido was the domain of Ainu spirits, called *kamuy*, and the decision in 1868 to construct a large Shinto shrine, authorized by the teenage Emperor Meiji, was an assertion of authority. The main kami, written in a brochure as Okuni-Tama-no-Kami, is translated by the shrine as Divine Spirit of the Land of Hokkaido, indicative of the new order.

The imperial character of the shrine is evident in its stately approach, lined by massive cryptomeria. Unusually, there are wooden cloisters, as if to mimic the grandeur of medieval cathedrals. At the water basin, intended for ritual cleansing, the ladles had been removed to prevent Covid contagion.

The irony was striking—a religion that promotes purity had been disrupted by impurity.

At the worship hall were the usual trappings of Shinto, and I wondered if somewhere there might be recognition of the Ainu past. Instead I came upon a subshrine, established in 1938 to mark the seventieth anniversary of the "founding of Hokkaido." It enshrines thirty-seven pioneers for overcoming difficulties in the development of the island. There was not a single mention of the Ainu or of the *kamuy*, who for so long had co-existed with them.

These days Shinto is being recast by some as a nature religion concerned with environmental matters, though officially it remains centered on the emperor as representative of a divine lineage. The spread of Shinto abroad has prompted greater examination of its claims to universality, based on the animist belief in kami-imbued natural phenomena, such as rocks and trees. Supporters of this view like to point to the sacred groves with which shrines are surrounded as evidence of their green credentials. Hokkaido Shrine is no exception, being set in a large area of mixed woodland. A noticeboard claims it is proof of Shinto's bond with nature, though with no hint of irony it stands alongside a sign banning pets.

The woods are home to red fox and squirrel, as well as a variety of birds. Though it was early autumn, the shrine was offering herbal tea with pickled cherry blossom, and the subtle taste was much in keeping with Japanese traits: understated, refined, and delicate. Inevitably, someone had counted the cherry trees (1,400 in all), and it is worth noting that because of the difference in temperature they flower almost two months later than in Kansai, the region surrounding Kyoto and Osaka. Travel tip: visit Honshu in May for the fine weather, then enjoy a bonus of cherry blossoms in Hokkaido.

I WAS IN HOT water. Literally. Immersed up to the neck, I lay facing a window with a hand towel dumped messily on my head. Before me was a large square windowpane filled with every shade of green, comprising the lush vegetation of an adjacent slope. Here inside was a hot-water paradise, which lent itself to physical ease. "Spartan sybarites," Arthur Koestler called the Japanese. They work hard, but they sure know how to enjoy life too.

Hokkaido has some notable hot springs (*onsen*), one of which is

Jozankei. Technically it is in Sapporo, but it takes a one-hour bus ride to get there. With its massively oversized hotels, it typifies Japan's modern resorts. Imagine a small river valley in which sits a ten-story cruise ship, and you have an idea of the mismatch in proportions.

I was beginning to slowly cook and turn lobster red, so I knew it was cold-tub time. Lili might be waiting, and I had the sole key to our room. Happy to have found an excuse, I rinsed myself off, slipped on a *yukata* (summer kimono), and hurried upstairs having skipped the cold bath. It was a good half an hour before my pickled partner arrived.

Lili and I have been together for over twenty years, though we do not cohabit. "Live separately, stay happy," said Katherine Hepburn when asked about her long-term relationship with Spencer Tracy. He was married and found it impossible to divorce. Lili also.

Katei nai rikon (in-house divorce) refers to married couples who no longer have an emotional involvement but continue to share the family home. In this way the form of marriage is maintained, though not the substance. The fact that there is a special phrase in Japanese suggests that the situation is relatively widespread. It used to be common in the West too, typified by couples staying together for the sake of the children.

In the past, the basic social unit was the *ie* (family household), and to some extent it still is. Based on patriarchal lines, it involves the wife being registered as a member of her husband's household. Ancestor worship, which is said to be Japan's true religion, depends on continuity of the *ie*, and the wife is expected to honor her husband's ancestors and care for his parents. Divorce would mean being excluded from the household. Things are changing, but still today traditional values persist, exemplified by married women not being allowed to use their maiden name for official purposes.

In Lili's case she had married at a young age and brought up three sons virtually single-handed while her husband was at work. Or said he was. As a company chairman he kept long hours, had overseas trips, and sometimes did not return for the evening. It turned out he had another woman—and another child. She was distraught, broke down, had a miscarriage. The trauma destroyed her trust in love, but rather than divorce she opted for *katei nai rikon*. Her parents would have been horrified by a split, besides which she was on good terms with her father-in-law, whose house she shared, and she did not want to disrupt the lives of her sons.

Around the change of millennium, a gaijin unexpectedly appeared in her life. They met at a picnic at the foot of Mt. Hiei. He had also suffered a trauma involving lost love, but one of a completely different kind. Boarding School Syndrome (BSS) was first theorized in the late 1990s but did not become widely known until a decade later. The basic premise is simple: children sent away to boarding school at a young age cut off their feelings in order to cope with the sudden loss of parental affection. The result is distrust of intimacy and an inability to commit to a loving relationship. In my own case the problem was exacerbated by the abandonment at age seven taking place within four months of the birth of my only sibling. I was not just ejected from the family nest, but usurped.

So where does that leave Lili and I, she with in-house divorce and me with boarding school blues? Strangely enough, it means we are perfectly matched. She is happy to have a love interest, while maintaining a role as mother and grandmother. For myself, I am grateful for the gift of security with the freedom she provides.

In *Autumn Light* Pico Iyer writes of his Japanese partner with admiration for her grace under pressure and the spark of joy she imparts. Lili embodies similar traits, with the polite charm of someone raised in Kyoto. She is steeped in Japanese culture; she knows the rules for the tea ceremony, for wearing kimono, for appreciating the seasonal round. Religion for her is a custom, not a belief. She is talented but modest, very modest, and seems to lack all sense of ego. If I ask what she wants to do, she replies with a question—What do you want to do? Where do you want to go?

Now together in our room, we sit on cushions on the tatami floor, radiating warmth from the hot spring and sipping green tea. There is a knock on the door and a kneeling female figure slides open the door to announce dinner has arrived. As usual the quality is superb and the volume overwhelming. The great thing about eating while dressed in *yukata* is the feeling of being untied, unbuttoned, unconstrained. And the great thing about sitting at a low table is that you can lie down whenever you like.

The next morning we found a pleasant pathway along the small Toyohira River, around which, according to a noticeboard, a total of fifty-six different hot springs emerge. Amazingly, eight tons of hot water are discharged every single minute, with a top temperature of around eighty Celsius. Ranged around the stream are some typical Japanese curios: a shrine for *kappa* (a type of water monster), a communal foot bath, and a cave with thirty-three statues of Kannon (deity of mercy).

There is also a large statue of spa-founder Jozan Miikuni, a wandering Zen monk who in 1866 was guided here by the Ainu. He saw an opportunity for a healing business, and settled down to be a spa keeper. The springs are noted for their efficacy: sodium chloride for neuralgia, sodium bicarbonate for digestive diseases, sulphur for just about anything. The one-time ascetic had found a way to channel his spiritual merit to benefit others, for in Japan cleanliness is not just next to godliness; it actually is godliness.

On Track |||||||||||||||||||||||||||||||||||||||||||||||||||

In keeping with a city of two million people, Sapporo Station is a big and busy complex, with a west and east concourse. It was first opened in 1880, and its present form dates from 2003, with an underground mall and several stories of shops. Unusually there is a special Food and Tourism Information Office, as well as the usual tourist information. The thirty-eight story JR Tower Center has four different shopping zones, and an underground walkway leads all the way in climate-controlled conditions to Susukino, the nightlife area, useful for a city that has six-month winters. The extension to the Shinkansen line from Hakodate is due for completion by 2030, when there are plans for a new high-rise development.

Otaru

THE SEASIDE TOWN OF Otaru is just half an hour from Sapporo. It is said to be exotic—exotic for Japan that is, which means it has historical Western-style buildings. The train runs along the coast as it nears the town, with views of picturesque outcroppings on which sit clusters of cormorants and seagulls, sometimes socially distanced but sometimes in mixed groups of black and white. The sea is gentle here, and makeshift houses are squeezed improbably into the narrow space between tracks and beach. "Beware tsunami," said a curt sign, with no explanation as to how.

Otaru burst into view as we rounded a bend, set in a bay with buildings ascending the nearby hills. It is a city of slopes, some of them steep, though the name, which derives from Ainu, means "river running through a sandy beach." Fifteen taxis waiting patiently at the station told of a busy little town, and color brochures told of its tourist appeal. "Shinkansen is coming to Otaru in 2030," screamed a large poster. Yes, within a decade the small town of 120,000 is going to be Japan's northern terminal, just a five-hour train trip from Tokyo. Money, tourists, and investment are sure to follow.

For the present the town's attention seems focused elsewhere, and bilingual signs announce that it is twinned with Nakhodka, a similarly sized Russian port on the Sea of Japan. Although Japan is often depicted as an isolated country, the long arc of its archipelago means it has maritime connections with a variety of neighbors: Okinawa with Taiwan, Kobe with Shanghai, Nagasaki with Hong Kong, Tsushima with South Korea, Niigata formerly with North Korea. And here in Hokkaido, Russia is a real presence.

The neighborly interest dates back to the late eighteenth century, when Adam Laxman arrived, asking for trade rights in exchange for the return of castaways. Despite his best efforts he only secured permission for a single ship, and even then nothing came of it. Next up was Nikolai Rezanov in 1809, appointed Russian ambassador to Japan with a mission to develop trade. This time his ship managed to get as far as Nagasaki, but the shogunate used a tactic the Japanese had refined to perfection: they made him wait for an answer that never came. Frustrated, he returned home empty-handed.

Shortly afterwards in 1811 Captain Golovnin was captured while surveying the Kuril Islands and detained in Hokkaido. The book he wrote about his two years of captivity became an international bestseller. It was just one incident in a fabled life, for in his youth, when Russia was allied to Britain, Golovnin saw action under Horatio Nelson. After Russia flipped sides to the French, he was detained on board his ship for a year until he made an audacious escape. His later life was hardly dull either, for he circumnavigated the world on two separate occasions.

Following the opening of Japan in 1854, Russians were quick to see trading opportunities, and as early as 1861 a Russian Orthodox church was established at Hakodate. Around this time Vladivostok was settled by European Russians and became the country's Pacific naval base. With the opening of the Trans-Siberian Railway in 1891, a connection was made with far-off Europe, such that instead of hazardous months at sea, a fifteen-day train ride would take you as far as Warsaw.

Then in 1904 an emergent Japan took on Russia in war. Astonishingly they declared victory the next year, and the world looked up in surprise. It was the first time one of the Great Powers was defeated by a "lesser" country. Japan was moving fast, and Otaru would play an important part.

HIROTA-SAN AND I WERE headed for the town's main tourist site—a canal completed in 1923, lined by warehouses. Brochures present it as "Romantic Otaru," with nighttime shots enhanced by subdued lighting, carefully editing out nearby multistory buildings. Rickshaws with runners in traditional clothing further the image, and the whole atmosphere resembles a historical film set amid the contemporary world.

If imitation is a form of flattery, Japan does a great job of flaunting its love of the West. Christian weddings with Caucasian "priests" are a prime example. French bakeries, Italian restaurants, German beer halls, Irish pubs, and English tearooms are dotted throughout the land. Some mimic the originals with such care that they import features such as brick, fireplace, and window frame. Love hotels and pachinko parlors act out fantasy versions of Las Vegas or royal palaces, while popular theme parks such as Huis Ten Bosch recreate whole villages.

The canal promenade had few promenaders, though it was easy to tell from the souvenir shops that there would normally be large crowds. Otaru prides itself on being "a city of glass" and a nearby museum promised much, but instead of arty works there were stained glass windows imported from European churches. The most interesting item was unintended: a queue of young women waiting to take selfies alongside the Virgin Mary.

In the surrounding streets there were a number of historical buildings all about one hundred years old. In 1865 Otaru had been a small fishing village of one thousand people. Forty years later it was a booming port city. It owed its prosperity to the concentration of banks built to fund development at a time when the town was the gateway to more remote parts of Hokkaido. At one time there were twenty-six sizeable banks, and one street had so many it was dubbed "the Wall Street of Northern Japan."

As well as banks, the area is full of old warehouses and historical shops. Helpful information boards explain the architectural significance and make the area a veritable outdoor museum. The design details are impressive. Pride of place goes to the National Bank of Japan, which was considered a wonder of its time, with ceilings so high that people made special journeys just to see them.

The Western buildings have a wonderful solidity, for the granite stone and Greek pillars were built to last. There is something reassuring about them, as if to say your money is safe—and appreciated! In the case of the

Chamber of Commerce, stone was imported from Ishikawa Prefecture and marble from Shikoku. Many of the buildings combine a Western structure with Japanese touches, such that West here truly does meet East.

The development of Otaru was boosted by a railway line built in 1880 with the help of American engineers. The opening up of Hokkaido led to a huge volume of coal and agricultural products being shipped out to Honshu, and for roughly a century the line was kept busy. Now a short stretch of the disused track serves as "a romantic walkway," with flower boxes where couples pose for photos. It prompted Hirota-san and me to think of captions, such as "On Track for Romance" or in country-music style, "Missed the Train, but I Found You."

The whole charm of Otaru is captured in Sakaimachidori, a wonderful street with funky art and craft shops. Here you can browse displays of goods from artisan workshops, and there are cafes with the pleasant clinking of glass wind chimes. A shop named Kamuy, dedicated to Ainu goods, says for its sales pitch, "Fire, mountains, valleys, the ocean, animals, plants, even tools and clothing the Ainu make and use, all are *kamuy*." It was a reminder that we live in an enchanted world.

A few minutes' walk away lies Sushi Street, with reputedly the town's best seafood. Seasonal delicacies include sea urchin and octopus in spring, salmon in summer, and herring in autumn. So abundant were the latter that the town once boasted herring millionaires. Just how opulent was their lifestyle can be seen at the Old Aoyama Villa with its gorgeous painted *fusuma* sliding doors and decorated ceiling panels.

In the past the sea was said to be so full of fish that they leapt into fishermen's arms. Ninety percent of the catch was not even used as food—it was made into high-quality fertilizer for such crops as cotton and indigo. Sadly, the cornucopia was ruined by overfishing, and now with the warming of the sea, fish stocks are in dangerous decline.

Hirota-san chose a restaurant for us, and we were ushered to the counter in front of which two impassive chefs were performing a form of ritualized theater. Swaying gently side to side in white uniforms, they took a handful of moist rice with one hand, squeezed it into shape, and with the other added a dash of wasabi. This was topped with a slice of fish, wrapped with a strip of nori, and finally placed very deliberately in an eye-pleasing arrangement on the decorated dish that was set before us. Meanwhile, hands were dipped in water and wiped clean on a white cloth, then the whole process started again. This was synchronized sushi at its best.

The stylized, polished, perfectly timed theatrics reminded me of taiko drum performers, so well-rehearsed that each movement is in absolute unison with others. Along with the precision was a concern with aesthetics. The dish for the sushi was decorated with the image of a *sasa* leaf, which echoed the real one placed among the food, and an acorn on the sashimi plate added a seasonal touch. Most pleasing of all was a thin orange line painted on the little soy dish, which resembled the final flourish of a calligraphic masterstroke.

Imagine this for a meal—sushi portions of salmon, shrimp, tuna, squid, flying fish eggs, and Japanese flounder, served along with miso soup and six *kappa* rolls (small sushi rolls of tuna and cucumber). All of it perfectly presented and followed by sorbet and coffee for just fifteen dollars. Where else could you get such value for money?

We had ordered the smallest set lunch on the menu, and once again I was moved to wonder at the capacity of Japanese stomachs. I eat less than just about every Japanese person I know, yet it is my stomach that protrudes, quite unfairly. When challenged about their capacity for cake, Japanese women often say that they have two stomachs, one of which is reserved for dessert, but Hirota-san had a different take.

"We Japanese have two faces."

"You mean two stomachs?"

"No, two faces. One for outside world. And one private, in secret."

"So?"

"So I think we can use our second mouth too."

During our meal three young women in *yukata* at the counter had been enjoying the attention of the young chefs, receiving their remarks with delight. They sat with perfect poise, straight backs rising above handbags tucked neatly behind their bottoms, and they ate with a graceful elegance. It resembled a scene from a woodblock print: the young bucks with their headbands, an adoring audience, and kabuki posters on the walls. And what exactly was I doing in this quintessentially Japanese tableau?

If I had any doubts, the middle-aged waitress made my role clear enough. Everything I said to her in Japanese, she responded to with exaggerated English for the amusement of others—"Want more?" "What drink, please?" "You understand?" It was rude of course, but over the years one learns to accept it as the flip side of being an honored guest, a privileged outsider. Donald Richie wrote eloquently of this, noting that foreigners look in at the culture but are never fully integrated. It suits a certain kind of character, and for a writer it is a goldmine.

IN MY EARLY DAYS in Japan, Otaru was a hot topic because of a legal case about discrimination. It centered around a bathhouse with a Japanese-only policy, which had been introduced in 1993 due to the lack of "bath etiquette" by Russians. Washing their hair in the communal bath, for example. Drunken rowdiness had not endeared them to the regulars, and in the most extreme case a sailor had gone on a rampage and caused an eye-popping eight hundred thousand yen worth of damage (no mean feat in a bathhouse).

The city government claimed to be powerless to stop the Japanese-only policy, since there was no law against discrimination in Japan. It was a red rag to an international group campaigning for gaijin rights, and when they tried to enter the bathhouse, Japanese wives and children were allowed in but foreign-looking husbands were not. Japaneseness was thus reduced to the slippery slope of appearance.

When one of the Americans naturalized, he was able to show proof of his Japanese nationality. Surely now there could be no debarment. Ah, said the bathhouse manager, you don't look Japanese and that will make our regulars uncomfortable. Litigation followed, and both bathhouse and city government were sued for damages. The bathhouse made the unexpected defense that banning Russians would have been discriminatory, so they chose to ban all foreigners. (From their perspective it made sense, as foreigners could not be expected to know Japanese customs.)

The city authorities were sued for not enforcing the 1995 International Convention on Elimination of All Forms of Racial Discrimination, which Japan had signed. The case went all the way to the Supreme Court, with the final verdict denying any wrong by the city. However the Sapporo District Court did rule that banning foreigners was an illegal act and awarded the plaintiffs a token compensation.

Still today there is no anti-discrimination law in Japan, a situation which is most apparent when it comes to house rentals. Applicants may be told, in the nicest possible way, that the owner has specified no foreigners. Cultural differences are cited as the reason. Refraining from noise, not causing a nuisance, cleaning up before leaving, putting out the rubbish in the right place on the right day—these are traits the Japanese hold dear. Foreigners may ignore or not even be aware of them.

Underlying all this is the shared thinking of a largely monocultural nation. For those of us who live here, it is rarely a problem though it surfaces from time to time. During the Covid crisis, while advanced countries in the West were proceeding with vaccination, Japan was at least three months behind. Why? Because special tests had to be carried out to see how Japanese bodies reacted, even though the vaccinations had already been tested on a range of volunteers.

At one point in the crisis Japanese abroad were allowed to return to Japan, but non-Japanese with permanent residency were not. It made no sense. Even after the restriction was lifted, different standards were applied. My friends might serve as example, for on arrival at Kansai Airport the French husband was taken aside to be tested, while his Japanese spouse was waved straight through.

The issue brings up the whole matter of Japaneseness. There are basically two forms of nationality, one territorial (*jus soli*) and one based on blood (*jus sanguinis*). The former privileges place of birth, the latter parentage. In this sense Japan is at the opposite end from the French model, which accepts immigrants but is resistant to outside culture. By contrast, Japan readily embraces foreign culture, but is resistant to immigrants. Take asylum seekers, for instance: in 2018 Japan accepted a total of 42, whereas France took in 20,710.

A letter to *The Japan Times* by a bemused American illustrates the ironies. A newcomer to Tokyo, he saw a bar called Manhattan displaying a large Stars and Stripes. Being from New York, he wanted to enter but was told that there was a no-foreigners policy. "Maybe you can't understand our customs," they told him. He quite genuinely couldn't. Multiculturalism had run up against monoculturalism and was nonplussed.

Given the global nature of modern life, it is remarkable that Japan manages to retain such insularity. Nonetheless change is happening, for international marriages are on the increase and labor shortages necessitate acceptance of overseas workers. The change is most apparent in sports, with the national rugby team of 2019 including every possible gradation of Japaneseness, from full-blooded to only one grandparent, and even naturalized Japanese.

Change is evident elsewhere too: Miss Japan 2015 was mixed race, born to a Japanese mother and an African American father. Tennis star Naomi Osaka, chosen to light the torch at the Olympics opening ceremony in 2021, has a Haitian father and was raised in the US from the age of three. She was just one of thirty mixed-race Olympians representing Japan, including judo gold medalist Aaron Wolf (American father), basketball player Rui Hachimura (Beninese father), Monica Ooye (Nigerian father), and Evelyn Mawuli (Ghanaian parents).

The result is that, almost by stealth, a new Japan is taking shape. Tokyo is home to over half a million foreigners, and in Shinjuku one person in eight was born overseas. Statistically, around two percent of babies have at least one foreign parent, and though the "one race, one nationality" discourse remains influential, a younger generation will soon be speaking with a different kind of voice.

HIROTA-SAN AND I DECIDED on different options for the afternoon. He was headed for the Otaru Literary Museum, while I was headed for fresh sea air. Just twenty minutes away by train, Zenibako has a delightfully sandy beach with nothing much but a love hotel at one end. It was full of students from Sapporo, and as I walked barefoot among the youngsters, I realized with a shock that I was the oldest there by a good forty years. The only person to show the slightest interest in me was a surfer girl with bleached hair who called out in Japanese: "Gaijin-san (Mr. Foreigner), don't your feet hurt walking on those stones?" Somehow it felt wonderfully refreshing.

Back in Otaru, I got a report from Hirota-san about two authors associated with the town. One was the young poet Takuboku Ishikawa, whose *tanka* we had come across in Sapporo's Odori Park. He was just twenty-six when he died of TB (one year older than John Keats), and his short life was full of problems, partly the fault of a fiery spirit. His visit to Otaru in 1907 serves as example.

Ishikawa's brother was the Otaru stationmaster, and he helped find him a job with the local paper. However, Ishikawa soon fell out with an editor and had to leave. Nonetheless Otaru honors him by displaying one of his poems where it is set, in the station car park. With a humorous touch it captures the severity of the Hokkaido winter.

Carrying our child
on her back
in the snow-blown car park
it seems the brows of my wife
are what's seeing me off

The Otaru-born Takiji Kobayashi, who also died young, is remembered for his proletarian novel *Crab Cannery Ship*, a big hit in 1929. Some seventy years later it enjoyed a second life as a film, when the harsh conditions of life at sea resonated with Japan's modern "freeters" (contract workers with no job security and dismal prospects).

Both Ishikawa and Kobayashi opposed Japanese colonialism. Ishikawa spoke out against the takeover of Korea, and Kobayashi was tortured to death in 1933 by the dreaded Tokko (Special Police Force). He was just twenty-nine and had all the bravery (or foolhardiness) of youth, for having been cleared of belonging to the Communist Party he went ahead and joined it. As in Europe, the 1930s were a perilous time when people had to make invidious choices. I often wonder if I would have the courage of Ishikawa and Kobayashi to stand up and speak out when the time comes. I sincerely hope it never comes, though.

On Track ||||||||||||||||||||||||||||||||||||||||||||||||||

From Sapporo the rapid train takes thirty minutes to Otaru, along the Hakodate Line. After Zenibako the train runs close to the sea, and for those with time, it is worth taking a local train to better appreciate the shoreline.

Otaru was the birthplace of railways in Hokkaido. The island's oldest railway opened in 1880, originally as a freight line for coal and marine products. It was closed just over a hundred years later in 1985. Now railway buffs head down the slope from the present station in quest of the former tracks, which are maintained in part as a tourist attraction. Not far away is the Otaru General Museum, housing a collection of historical trains. Features include snow-clearing equipment special to Hokkaido, a dining carriage serving food, interactive exhibits, and a short ride aboard a steam engine, popular with children.

Shiraoi

HIROTA-SAN AND I WERE headed for Shiraoi, our destination the newly opened Ainu National Museum, just an hour's train ride from Sapporo. It had proved controversial. On the one hand it was promoted as a showcase for Ainu culture and the focus of a drive for revival. On the other hand, it was criticized as nepotistic and a case of the government asserting control of the narrative for their own ends. The majority of those running the museum are non-Ainu.

Isabella Bird visited Shiraoi on her trip to Hokkaido in 1878. At the time the indigenous folk lived in separate settlements from mainstream Japanese (known as Wajin), and she found her Ainu hosts to be unfailingly courteous and mild-mannered, with a lifestyle that was underwritten by a strong religious code. Her purpose was to see if they were good missionary material, but it seemed they had no need of Christianity for they were "more truthful, hospitable, honest, reverent and kind to the old than the lower class of Western cities."

From the station the museum is a few minutes' walk away, and the picturesque setting beside a woods-encircled lake certainly promised well. In the spacious exhibition hall was an attractive display of patterned robes, which were painstakingly made in a process that began with the making of thread from inner bark fiber. The robes were embroidered, sometimes appliquéd, and the swirling patterns indicated the region from which they came. Like kimono, the robes became treasured heirlooms.

Around the room were panels explaining aspects of the culture. One section gave an overview of the history, suggesting the Ainu were a branch of the Jomon linked to ethnic groups in Sakhalin and northeast Siberia. For millennia Ezo (Hokkaido) was their home base, but the Meiji Restoration brought forced integration. Their land was appropriated, the language banned, religious practice suppressed, and customs such as tattooing forbidden. Meanwhile, compulsory education taught children Japanese language and culture. It is a familiar story of the way native people were treated by conquerors around the world.

Just as in the US, newly arrived settlers brought disease with them to which the Ainu had no immunity. It led to a drastic decrease in numbers, and as communities were broken up by forced relocation, many sought escape by intermarriage or passing off as mainstream Japanese. Ignored by Tokyo, the Ainu were discriminated against and not even officially recognized.

Only in 2008, after international pressure, did the government acknowledge "an indigenous people with a distinct language, religion, and culture." By this time a once vibrant culture had been reduced to scattered villages, and though numbers are disputed, it is thought that fewer than thirty thousand self-identify as Ainu. Many work in tourist shops where they put on ethnic clothing and carve wooden goods or make fabrics with traditional markings. Isabella Bird would be horrified. Writing one hundred and fifty years ago, she claimed that the Ainu way of life was so well rooted that there was little danger of them dying out.

The use in the exhibition of one tiny word is particularly striking—"we." Intercultural encounters are a common topic on television, and one often hears the phrase *"ware ware Nihonjin"* (we Japanese), indicative of collectivist thinking. So pervasive is the mantra that it comes as a shock to find a totally different perspective here. "We Ainu have stood up against discrimination leveled at us by Wajin," states one of the panels, "and have supported one another to help pull ourselves out of poverty."

There are two ways of looking at this. You could see the exhibition as a welcome instance of victims allowed their voice in the land of their victors. More cynically, you could see it as an empty gesture, akin to a condemned man allowed his say before execution—or in this case, extinction. In 2014, a Hokkaido politician tweeted that "Ainu people of course no longer exist. At best, they are Japanese of Ainu ancestry who claim government subsidies."

The existence of the Ainu is a thorn in the side of nationalists, who like to assert a single monocultural identity. In 2005 Aso Taro, later to be foreign minister, described Japan as having "one nation, one civilization, one language, one culture, and one race." In fact, apart from the Ainu there are over half a million Korean residents as well as a disputed number of Ryukyuans in Okinawa, not to mention those of mixed parentage. Though rarely acknowledged, *ware ware Nihonjin* should include them too.

ON THE MUSEUM GROUNDS is a performance area where music, dance, and storytelling are staged. Like other aspects of the culture, such activities were an expression of Ainu spirituality, designed to enhance the relationship with the *kamuy*. The musical instruments featured a type of mouth harp called *mukkuri*, and a guitar-like instrument called *tonkori*. These accompanied dances, one of which was an inclusive circle dance of such simplicity that old and young alike could take part—the audience too.

One feature I had expected was a section on sake, or the Ainu version of it, for Isabella Bird was struck by the vital role it played in the culture. "[It is] the one thing they care about," she wrote. Rituals were initiated with libations involving the sprinkling of alcohol (as in Siberian shamanism), and imbibing was seen as a means of communing with the *kamuy*. "Break on through to the other side," sang Jim Morrison, and for Ainu, sake was the means. Something of the intoxication of an Ainu gathering is captured in verse by Itakutono, who under his Japanese name of Takeichi Moritake wrote poetry about the sad decline of Ainu culture.

The Ainu Dance

From a big bowl full of homemade sake
The Ainu drink. Dance, dance!
Clapping to the fascinating rhythm
All through the autumn night,
Hoya—hoya!
Jangling earrings, sparkling necklace,
Glistening sword enliven the dance,
The gods are happy too. Dance, dance!
All through the autumn night,
Hoya—hoya!

Language is the very lifeblood of a culture, so the stark heading of one of the exhibition panels spoke volumes—"Linguisticide." Ainu has the same structure as Japanese (subject-object-verb) but is otherwise grammatically different and belongs to a separate language group. Some linguists even assign it to a group of its own with regional variations in Sakhalin and the Kuril Islands. The language has no script, but there was an opportunity to hear it spoken on the day I went when a traditional tale was recited. In abridged form, it went something like this:

Long ago there was a hunter of bears and deer who felt the urge to
go to the mountains, so he took his boat and paddled upstream, but
it took longer than he expected, and foolishly he had taken no food.
By the time he reached the mountain he was exhausted and hungry.
It was growing dark and unpleasantly cold. He wondered if he would
survive the night, but crows took pity on him, brought him meat, and
covered him over like a blanket. Next morning when he awoke, they
were gone. Not a single one was to be seen.

At this point the storyteller got up and left, though no one in the small audience seemed sure if it was the end or just a dramatic pause. Was it about connections, about being an integrated part of nature? Or did it imply that the crows were divine agents of a protective mountain god? Whatever the subtext, it was easy to imagine it as the kind of mythic entertainment that once gripped the imagination of young children seated round a fire, in an age when the world truly was magical.

AT THE LAKESIDE WERE a few houses built in traditional manner, by which an A-shaped wooden frame is covered with thatched reed and woven bamboo fiber. We were invited into one of the buildings, to find a single large room with high ceiling and open hearth. Here we were told about the bears with which Ainu are closely associated.

The bear cult is the most well-known part of Ainu culture, but it is also the most misunderstood. The idea that Ainu worship bears is so widespread that even Alan Booth repeated it, but it is not bears as such that they worship but the Great Bear Spirit. There's a big difference, as big as that between worshipping humans and worshipping a Great Human Spirit named God.

For the Ainu, bears were the strongest and bravest of animals, with which they felt a kinship through sharing similar hunting patterns. Killing bears was a perilous and bloody business, and to ensure success the Ainu made offerings to the Great Bear Spirit. The biggest festival of their year, called Iyomante (or Iomante), consisted of the ritual sacrifice of a bear cub that had been raised by an Ainu "foster family" in a small cage. As with bullfighting, it involved drawing blood by firing arrows into the animal.

The blood sacrifice is intended to release the spirit of the bear, which would attain immortality through joining with the Great Bear Spirit. It was carried out with respect and gratitude, the intention being to ensure a further supply of bears to hunt in the coming year. Life must die so that life may live. Or as Joseph Campbell, the great mythologist, puts it, "You die to the flesh to be born in the spirit." (The practice of Iyomante has stopped now, but a YouTube video shows the whole ceremony performed in 1931, complete with dancing, drinking, and feasting.)

In her account of the Ainu, Isabella Bird repeatedly stresses their gentle and courteous character, yet the blood sacrifice is hard to watch for a modern audience. Western visitors to an earlier museum at Shiraoi were appalled by the conditions there, for adult bears were confined in cramped concrete pens with no freedom, no vegetation, and no company. The suffering was self-evident, and only when the museum closed were the bears handed over to a charitable organization, which flew them to a sanctuary in the north of England. It must have seemed like bear heaven.

So how does one explain the cruelty? The antiquity of the practice may be a factor, for it dates back to a time when kill, capture, or maim was a matter of survival. For Joseph Campbell, the ritual constitutes a form of atonement; through their pact with the Bear Spirit, the Ainu transform the killing of a sentient being into an act of benevolence. The bloodletting of a transcendent individual is reminiscent of Jesus on the cross. Similarly by drinking the blood and eating the flesh, the Ainu partake in an act of communion. In a sense Isabella Bird was right; they had no need of Christianity, for they had their own equivalent.

AFTER THE MUSEUM VISIT Hirota-san and I happened on a soba shop, run by a middle-aged Ainu woman. There were a few patterned fabrics around the room and a carving of an owl. "It is a lucky charm," she explained. "Owls are *kamuy* which protect the village."

There were no other customers, and she told us of her childhood in Biratoricho, a town with a sizeable Ainu community. She remembered being teased at school, and she could even remember attending the Iyomante ceremony as a child. "It was very cruel," she noted.

Her response to the museum was unexpected. "Too late. . . ." she said dismissively. "It's not for Ainu, it's for Japanese. To make themselves feel better."

"But surely it's good to show the culture and explain what happened?" I objected.

"What for? From Meiji times we were destroyed. And now there is no meaning."

"But isn't it good to show the Ainu viewpoint?"

"It is just a showpiece. It's for Japanese so they feel better about things. Even the people working there are mostly Japanese. We don't need a museum. They should give us back our land. And our right to fish and hunt."

The previous day I had seen an article in the *Hokkaido Shinbun* about the demand of an Ainu group to be allowed to catch salmon in rivers, which is currently illegal. As the first lawsuit to claim back indigenous rights, it was a landmark case, yet it was tucked away on an inside page.

"So you don't feel there's any kind of revival?" I continued.

"Revival of what? There is nothing to revive. I'm Ainu but what do I have? I don't speak Ainu, no one speaks any more. I can remember my grandfather had a long beard and my mother painted her face. They practiced old customs, but in secret. They didn't want anyone to know. But my parents were not so interested. They thought it better not to know. They wanted to protect me. There was a lot of discrimination in those days. There still is. Maybe you can't understand."

Actually, I could, for there were parallels in my own family. Two of my grandparents were Jews in central Europe who did not survive the Holocaust, and my mother sought to protect her children by hiding her Jewishness. It was only after her death, when I was working in Japan, that I learnt the truth about her background.

"Did you learn Ainu history at school?" I continued.

"No. There was just one mention in our textbook. But it did not explain anything. So I read books on my own. About the Matsumae clan in Edo times and how they used us like slaves. Then in Meiji times everything was banned. Our language, our religion, our lifestyle. Now it's all gone."

"But there are still Ainu villages, aren't there? Up near Mt. Asahi."

"They are dying. Everything changes. Maybe it's sad, but everything changes. We're all humans, why make a difference. Japanese are mixed: Korean blood, Chinese blood, Polynesian, Ainu. We're all mixed."

"Me too," I said.

"You see," she said, "we are all mixed. We should live in peace. Discrimination is stupid. Nationalism is stupid."

Afterwards Hirota-san and I took the train back to Sapporo. He had been quiet during the conversation and I wondered why. "I have an ability to digest bad food," he said enigmatically. What did he think of the Ainu? "They are good at getting subsidies, I think." It might have been a Japanese politician speaking.

Conversation turned to his family business of running a temple. I remembered that he had missed a class one week, which was unusual, and when he turned up the next time his head was shaven. His absence and haircut were necessary to qualify as a priest, he explained. I was intrigued. How long had it taken him to qualify? Ten days, he answered.

"Ten days?" I said in surprise.

"Yes, it was a special course," he answered.

"What kind of course?"

"A ten-day course."

"A ten-day course in what?"

"Jodo Shinshu. To be a priest."

"You can become a priest in just ten days?!" It was hard to believe.

"Yes. No."

"What do you mean?"

"Because my father is a priest. So when I was young I could learn with him."

"So what is the failure rate?"

"Maybe nobody."

"Nobody! It can't be very hard if no one fails."

"No. It is very hard. We have training in our home temple."

"But in what way is it hard if everyone passes?"

"We must sit *seiza* for a long time."

"How long?"

"Maybe one hour."

I told Hirota-san about a conversation that I had once had with a Shinto priest, who said that during training the group had had to sit *seiza* until one of them damaged his knee and was forced to drop out.

"Yes, it's the same," Hirota said.

"You mean people with knee problems can't qualify?"

"Yes."

"But that's discrimination, isn't it?"

"Yes."

At this point I was eager to pursue a more pressing topic. Mindful of the bears at Shiraoi, I wanted to know more about the Jodo Shinshu attitude to animals. Buddhism teaches compassion to all sentient beings, yet Jodo Shinshu priests happily eat meat. How come, I asked?

"Some eat for medicine," said Hirota-san.

"But you eat meat, and it's not for medicine."

"We can eat meat, but we cannot kill."

"Did the Buddha say that?"

"Yes, in his teaching there are three things. The person who offers the food should be clean. The person who receives should be clean. And the food also should be clean."

There was a short pause.

"Actually the Buddha died from food poisoning," Hirota-san continued.

"Really? That's ironic."

"Yes. Maybe it was rotten meat. Or maybe poison mushroom."

"So how about compassion to sentient beings? Does Jodo Shinshu do anything about that?" I pressed.

"Yes. In Hiroshima where my temple is, Jodo Shinshu butchers don't offer meat once a month on Shinran's memorial day." (Shinran is the sect founder.)

"But one day a month isn't a great deal of compassion, is it?"

"Also people there don't make silk because of killing a lot of worms in boiling water. Also there was a low rate of killing babies. Because in those days there was famine and people killed babies to save food."

"I see," I said, bringing the conversation to a close. It had been a long day, and infanticide in a time of famine was not something I wanted to get into. But I did have one last question.

"Does Jodo Shinshu make a difference between seafood and meat?"

"Maybe. My teacher said mammals scream before dying, but fish don't."

I mulled that over for a while. I was well aware of animal terror, as was Lafcadio Hearn, whose description of the hell-like conditions in an American slaughterhouse is heart-wrenching. But I had no need of such second-hand accounts, for my father, who was a veterinary surgeon, took me as a young boy to farms, where I was overwhelmed by the cacophony of squeals as he went about the business of castrating pigs. It seared itself into my consciousness, and as our train passed deeper into the darkness of the Hokkaido night, I found myself contemplating a startling image— an open-mouthed fish out of water uttering as loud as it could a silent scream.

On Track ||||||||||||||||||||||||||||||||||||||||||||||

Shiraoi stands on the Muroran Line, which opened in 1892 when it linked various coal mines to Muroran Port. As such it played an important part in the opening up of Hokkaido for natural resources. For much of the route, the line skirts the shoreline along the Iburi coast, with the

28.7-kilometers section between Shiraoi and Numanohata forming the
longest straight stretch of railway in Japan.

The station sees few passengers, owing to the small population
of seventeen thousand. In a sign of the times JR Hokkaido's president
announced in 2016 plans to rationalize around fifty percent of the network. This included a proposal to lease out the section of the Muroran
Line that runs to Shiraoi, so its future depends on agreement with local
governments.

Hakodate

THE ROOM I HAD booked in Hakodate was a converted *kura*. These Edo-period storehouses are squat one-story buildings with whitewashed walls, tiled roofs, and tiny windows. In the past they acted as a private vault in which to keep valuables such as kimono, artwork, and antiques. They not only safeguarded against theft, but, more importantly, against fire, the ogre that ravaged Japan's wooden towns.

When Isabella Bird arrived in 1878, it was after a disastrous crossing from Honshu in an old paddleboat that was buffeted by a gale. She was drenched and exhausted, but nonetheless found the port town to her liking. The setting round a bay felt to her "northern" (she was from Scotland), and from the harbor she made her way uphill to the church mission where she looked down on houses "splashed with mud, large boulders holding down the roofs on which were laid sods of grass as a fire precaution against flying sparks."

Just over a hundred years later Will Ferguson, having hitchhiked from southern Honshu, saw a town that had passed its heyday. "Today," he wrote, "Hakodate has fallen half asleep. A threadbare, somewhat seedy city, it is one of the few areas in Hokkaido where the American influence doesn't dominate." He did however find the fish market "exuberant."

From the train station I took a taxi, expecting to be delivered to my accommodation. I had the address in Japanese, but addresses are fickle friends in a country where streets often have no names. After a couple of wrong turns, the driver dropped me in front of a warehouse and drove off. Contrary to what I had been told, the front door was padlocked. This was odd, as the instructions had been clear enough. I even had a photo. How could things go so wrong?

Thinking there may be another entrance, I squeezed along a narrow gap running down the side of the building and came out at the far end into an empty scrap of land where a man seated on a rickety old chair was smoking a cigarette. "*Bikkurishita*" (What a surprise!), he exclaimed. It was an expression I was used to, for in the days when I had a red beard there was a *bikkurishita* every time I turned a corner.

Early visitors to Japan were known as *nanbanjin* (southern barbarians, so named because they arrived from the Portuguese colony of Macao to the south). Later, when a different kind of European arrived, *komojin* was used for the fair-haired people from Holland and England. Redheads like myself stood out even from a distance, and what is more we had similar coloring to Japanese demons.

"What are you doing here?" the man demanded.

"Sorry, I was looking for the way into this warehouse."

"Eh?"

"I wanted to get inside this warehouse."

"The door is at the front."

"I know, but it's not open."

'That's because nobody can enter."

"But I'm supposed to stay there tonight."

"Eh?'

"I booked it through Airbnb."

"Eh?" He looked at me, baffled. "There's nothing in there. It's empty."

"Eh?" It was my turn to be baffled. "But I talked to the owner yesterday."

"Eh?" He was already outscoring me in "ehs," but then he served an ace. "I'm the owner," he said.

At this point I indulged in the ritual necessary to get out of trouble, with profuse apologies and repeated bowing. After all I had trespassed on his land and for all he knew I could have been casing his warehouse.

It turned out there was another *kura* close by which took in guests. Sure enough the front entrance was open; inside were two apartment doors. Mine opened onto a newly furnished room with modern fittings. There was everything a traveler could need, and I was just unpacking when a knock came at the door. "Hi," said the owner, a young Japanese with the casual manner of someone who has spent time in the States. He had already heard of my mishap.

"Don't worry about it," he reassured me. "That man is just trouble-maker. You know, we Japanese are very conservative, don't like change. So some don't like foreigners. Haha. That man is the same residents' group as me, you see, but his way of thinking and my way completely differ-ent. I think Japan must change, open up and be more like outside, you understand?"

When I assured him I did, he went on.

"But that man doesn't think like that. He thinks Japan way is best way. So he thinks foreigner can't understand Japan way. And here many think like that. Maybe I'm first person here to open guesthouse like this. You know, many foreigners like Japanese style. So why not stay in a *kura*? I think your country doesn't have like this, right? So you are happy to stay here. But that man thinks maybe many problems. Foreign people can't under-stand language. And trash. It is small problem, but it is big problem. You understand? And there is another problem. Noisy. Foreign visitors talk too loud, maybe drinking, they feel happy, go back, it's very noisy. Neighbors don't like that. Music, party, not good. Here in the evening very quiet. Can you understand?"

"Yes," I answered, "I can."

Complaints about foreigners are common, and understandable too. After all, "When in Rome" isn't just about Italy. Long-term residents in Japan get annoyed with newcomers who break the rules, for we have learnt to adjust our behavior—not to eat while walking, not to talk in a loud voice, and not to cause annoyance to others. When in Japan, do as the Japanese!

My friendly landlord took me to a local restaurant, where he explained that *shio* ramen is Hakodate's "famous food." When I said I did not eat meat, he showed me a menu with fifty different combinations of seafood. When it came to ordering I chose at random, distracted by his telling me of his time in New York. The result was I got more than I bargained for—crab, giant shrimp, red caviar, herring roe, scallops, and egg roll, all on a bed of rice. Afterwards it was all I could do to waddle to a bus stop, from where my host assured me I would be taken to the town's most celebrated sight.

"One of the three best night views in Japan" is Hakodate's proud boast (Nagasaki and Kobe are the others). As usual, no one had the slightest idea how or when the best three were decided, but ranking along these lines has been going on since the Edo period. Then again, the city's tourism department might well have made it up. All power to them if they did. By restricting the best to a limited number, you create a sense of order and make visiting them manageable. Besides, ticking off numbers is very satisfying, as any trainspotter will tell you.

From Mt. Hakodate, the view of the city at night resembles an almost perfect hourglass, with a narrow waist widening towards top and bottom. I had seen it once before, but it had been unpleasantly crowded. Now, I thought to myself, there would be an opportunity to view it in peace. I was wrong. As dusk began to darken, coachloads of schoolchildren arrived and the hillside was covered in frenetic activity, very little of which had to do with the night scene. Mobile phones flashed, selfies were snapped, delighted shrieks filled the air. So much for "empty tourism." I took the first bus back.

NEXT MORNING I HEADED for Hakodate's morning market. The Covid effect was much in evidence in the empty stalls, yet row upon row of fresh fish was laid out in neat display, as if through force of habit. Some of the workers were up to their elbows in guts and gills, while others were out hustling passersby. Set on its own in the middle of the market, like a prime showpiece, was a gigantic crab singled out for its size, and feebly moving its legs against a narrow glass tank. A wave of crustacean compassion washed over me.

It was lunchtime, so I let myself be hustled into a surprisingly spacious dining room in which sat a single Japanese couple. What was it like pre-Covid, I asked the waitress. "A full house," she answered. How many would that be? "Eighty," she said. "They come in large groups." I presumed that was in summer, "No, they come all year round. Mainly tour groups for pensioners."

Despite the disastrous downturn she seemed cheerful enough, and I wondered if they were being kept afloat by government subsidy. There was generous funding available for small businesses, and rumor even had it that some places were enjoying more income than pre-Covid.

The market is known for squid, so I ordered a set meal and waited. Tanks of the creatures lined one of the walls, and there were notices warning against sprayed ink. Restaurant staff in *happi* coat and headband stood around with nothing much to do, and I was scribbling down a few notes when out of the corner of an eye I noticed something moving next to me. Turning to look, I found myself staring straight into the face of a living creature with eerily undulating tentacles. I thought it must be moving postmortem, like a headless chicken, but the continued wriggling indicated it was very much alive. "*Sumimasen*," I yelled out, "Please take this away." "But you ordered it," responded the puzzled waitress.

Realizing I was adamant, she took the plate off to the kitchen, returning minutes later with neatly cut strips of fresh squid. I looked at the plate, then at her. "Is that the same one you brought before?" I asked, and hearing it was, I hesitated. Somehow in our eye-to-eye encounter I felt that we had bonded. Was I really going to eat it? For a moment I wavered on the point of refusing, but then I thought of the Ainu, who would see it as a divine gift from the Great Squid Spirit, and I thought of Buddha, who said not to refuse what had been served by another. But most of all, I thought of the kitchen staff staring at me. There was no way I was going to confirm their prejudice about weak-willed gaijin unable to stomach Japanese food. And so, dear reader, I ate it.

Afterwards I had some questions for the waitress.

"Is it usual to serve the squid while it's still alive?"

"Yes," she said, "Japanese customers like it."

"They like it! Why?"

"Maybe they want to know it's fresh. And if they watch it dying, they know it is fresh."

"You mean they like to watch the squid die?"

"Yes. Maybe it will change color," she said matter-of-factly.

"Then what happens?"

"Then it's sliced and served."

At this point I plead guilty to hypocrisy. I happily chew dried squid with a glass of sake, but I am squeamish about seeing one dying. Humans are emotional by nature, and little of what we do makes rational sense, though we like to think it does. We pamper certain animals, and torture others. The French eat horsemeat, the Koreans dog meat, the Japanese serve live squid. We defend practices that suit us and oppose those that are alien. It is all cultural, for sure. But still . . . watching your food die on your plate?

The history of the treatment of animals in Japan throws up some interesting quirks. In 675 Emperor Tenmu issued a ban on meat eating, particularly domestic animals, though seafood was allowed because reincarnation was thought to be restricted to land animals. Venison and wild boar had previously been popular, but as time passed the ban was applied to all four-legged animals—except rabbits, which were counted as birds. Many Japanese think this is because of their large ears, which flap like wings, but in fact it is due to a linguistic oddity. In Japanese the verb *tobu*, which means jump and fly, is applied to both rabbits and birds.

The haiku master Kobayashi Issa (1763–1824) was a Pure Land priest with a great compassion for animals, including insects. Such was his depth of feeling that he would hold out his arm for hungry mosquitoes. In the haiku below he shows pity for a stranded insect, identifying perhaps with its poetical chirping in what Buddhists call a "floating world."

Still chirping
the insect is carried away—
floating branch

When it comes to animal rights, not even Issa can compare with the "dog shogun," Tokugawa Tsunayoshi. In a remarkable series of laws between 1687 and 1709, he issued *Orders on Compassion for Living Things*, which stipulated that those who abused animals should be punished. The strictures were progressive, even by today's standards. A weight limit was set for the loads pulled by working horses, and the caging of singing insects was banned. Punishments were severe: in one case a public officer was exiled to a remote island for having thrown a stone at a dove.

Tsunayoshi was born in the Year of the Dog, hence his preference for the animal. If any dog was injured, the owner was held responsible and punished. It led to the mass abandonment of pets, and kennels had to be built to cope with the strays. The number of dogs in care is estimated to have ranged between one hundred thousand and two hundred thousand, all of which had to be fed. It was big business, and for each dog the kennels received the equivalent of a man's salary. Such was the cost that it depleted government coffers, surely the only example in human history of dogs virtually bankrupting an economy.

BEADS OF SWEAT WERE running down my shirt. It was the tail end of August, and there was an unseasonable heatwave as I walked around downtown Hakodate with its port and historical Western buildings. On the waterfront an unassuming monument marked the spot where the first agricultural pioneers from Honshu had arrived in 1873. A small step for a human, but a giant leap for Hokkaido. As I contemplated the scene, a movie began to form in my mind featuring Ken Takakura in the lead role as an impoverished farmer jumping onto the quay, taking a deep lungful of air, and looking around in great expectation.

But that sunny morning it was not Japanese pioneers with whom I was concerned, but foreign pioneers. First to arrive had been Commodore Perry in 1854, following Hakodate's designation as an open port for American ships. After more than two hundred years of isolation, his arrival caused great excitement, and the gold buttons on his jacket proved a particular source of fascination. But the prospect of foreign sailors arriving in the town was at first so alarming that women and children were evacuated for their safety.

It was not long, however, before the citizenry settled to the foreign visitors and embraced their fashions. Import shops did a brisk business in novelties, such as photographs, cigarettes, and coffee, as well as Western alcohol and medicine. European food caught on too, and the elite took to eating meat. In the meeting of East and West new styles of building appeared, and innovative architects created hybrids with a Japanese first floor and a Western second floor.

Such was Hakodate's importance that at one time it housed fourteen different consulates, grandest of which was that of the British. (The former consulate, now a museum, is one of the city's chief sights.) This was an age in which Japan was dubbed "the Britain of the Far East" because of the similarities between the two island countries. Relations were close and culminated in what for historians was a breakthrough moment: the 1902 Anglo-Japanese Alliance. It was formed to counter Russian expansionism and gave tacit approval to Japan's decision to go to war with its neighbor in 1904.

JAPAN HAS FOUR SIZEABLE *gaijin bochi* (foreign graveyards), located at the treaty ports of Hakodate, Kobe, Nagasaki, and Yokohama. Even in death a distinction was drawn between native and outsider. In Hakodate the first foreign burials took place with the arrival of the first ever foreign ship, for when Commodore Perry arrived here in 1854, he brought with him a Mr. Wolfe, age fifty, and a Mr. Remick, age nineteen, both recently deceased.

A special cemetery was set up, sited on a slope with a fine view of the Pacific. Hydrangea bush and twisted pines beautify the site, and in the summer warmth of late August this final resting place is everything a foreigner might wish for—apart from being on the other side of the world.

There are some forty graves in all, comprising American, British, French, and German. A nearby cemetery is specifically for Chinese, and there is one for Russians too. Interestingly, there is no mention of nationality in the early gravestones, just a date and occasionally an occupation. The most poignant has the simplest inscription: "Baby, May 21st, 1874."

By midday the temperature had reached thirty-three Celsius, and since there was no one around, I lay on the grass in the shade of a bush, looking out to sea and contemplating death in a distant land. At this point a Japanese couple walked past, and though they must have seen me they showed not the slightest indication of anything unusual. This ability not to see things is a fine art in Japan and a cultural trait foreigners sometimes speak of with envy.

Opposite the gaijin cemetery is a Buddhist temple with a graveyard for parishioners, and to one side there is a third graveyard, reserved for Japanese Christians. It seemed symbolic of the halfway house they occupy. In Edo times Christianity was banned as a tool of colonialism, and only after 1873 was it tolerated, though it was not long before it fell under suspicion again for the refusal of believers to accept the divinity of the emperor. Still today Christians stand out from the Japanese norm: they keep different festival days, cleave to monotheism, and don't observe ancestral rites (explicitly forbidden in the Bible).

The sun was setting as I left, and it felt fitting that the cemetery should mark my last evening in Hokkaido. The next day I faced the long ride to Aomori, which would take me back to Honshu, and I had mixed feelings. Many years previously, when I wanted to visit Okinawa, Japanese friends had told me it was like a different country, and it was true that away from the capital there was a Polynesian feel. Hokkaido too has the feel of a foreign country, and the humidity and restricted horizons of Kyoto that I was used to had been replaced by fast-flowing streams and endless greenery. The resulting ease of mind owed itself not just to the openness of the landscape but to the friendliness of the people, descendants of pioneering adventurers who had arrived to build a new life. All in all, it felt indeed as if I had been to a foreign country—without even going abroad.

On Track ||||||||||||||||||||||||||||||||||||||||||||||||||

Hakodate Station opened in 1902 and was renovated in 2003. It is the terminus for a number of lines in southern Hokkaido, the main one being the Hakodate Main Line running to Asahikawa. The Super Hokuto limited express from Sapporo takes three and a half hours and runs roughly every hour. When the Hokkaido Shinkansen opened in 2016, regular trains to Aomori and Tokyo were discontinued, including overnight sleeping carriages. Now the high-speed Hayabusa to Tokyo takes a little over four hours.

The station for the Shinkansen, oddly, is located fifteen kilometers north of Hakodate Station in a different town, hence its cumbersome name: Shin-Hakodate-Hokuto Station. (The location was chosen for financial reasons to do with subsidies and the cost of tracks.) Regular trains arrive on the ground level, and Shinkansen trains on the upper level. The new station has large windows and support pillars modeled after poplar trees, while the inside uses locally sourced cedar. Relay trains connect to Hakodate Station in twenty minutes.

Tohoku

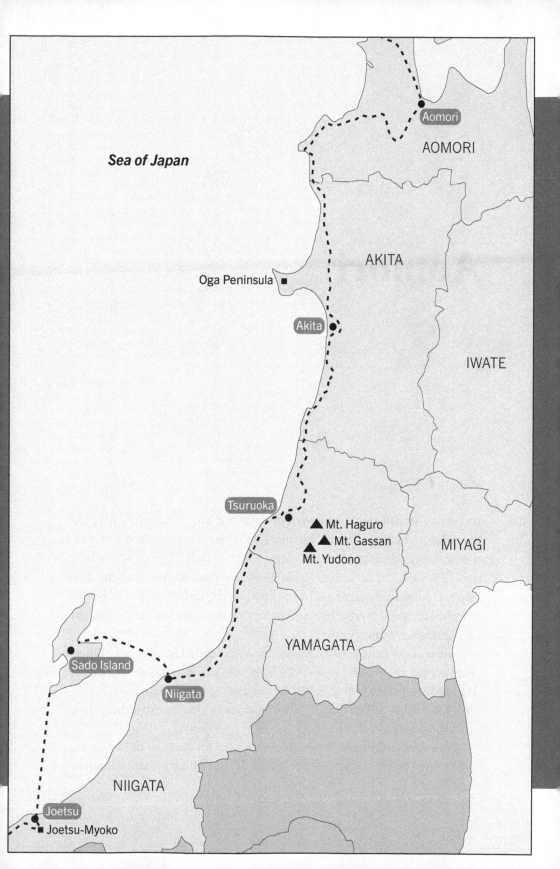

Sea of Japan

AOMORI

Aomori

AKITA

Oga Peninsula

Akita

IWATE

Tsuruoka

▲ Mt. Haguro
▲ Mt. Gassan
▲
Mt. Yudono

MIYAGI

YAMAGATA

Sado Island

Niigata

NIIGATA

Joetsu
Joetsu-Myoko

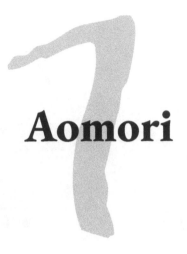

Aomori

BETWEEN HOKKAIDO AND HONSHU lies the Tsugaru Strait, where the Sea of Japan meets the Pacific. It is just a little over 19.5 kilometers at its narrowest, but in times past it was a formidable obstacle. When Isabella Bird crossed in 1878, she took an old paddleboat that got caught in a storm. The ship was completely unsuited to the high winds, and the journey lasted a wretched fourteen hours. To make matters worse, there was no equipment for nighttime navigation.

Around the same time, the naturalist Thomas Blakiston noted a difference between animals in Hokkaido, which were related to those in northern Asia, and animals in Honshu, which were related to southern Asia. Blakiston's Line, named after the Englishman, marks a clear zoological division. Hokkaido really is different.

Nowadays Isabella Bird would have no need for boats, as the Strait was undermined by the Seikan Tunnel in 1988. It runs for fifty-four kilometers, of which just under half is beneath the sea. At the time of its completion, it was the longest tunnel in the world, and at 240 meters below sea level it was also the deepest. That could be worrying if you think about it too much, but so smooth is the journey that the first time I traveled through it I slept and never even noticed.

This time my attention was caught by two young women eating a *bento*. They were so much in unison they could have won gold for Synchronized Eating. First they spread a handkerchief over their laps, then unwrapped the string and, removing the lid, looked appreciatively over the contents. It was done with such unconscious elegance that it brought to mind the words of Lafcadio Hearn that Japanese women are "the most wonderful aesthetic products of Japan."

When I arrived in Aomori, "Land of Hope and Glory" was playing over a public address system and rain was pelting down. A very British welcome, you could say. Ironically, Isabella Bird was far from pleased with the town, calling it "a miserable looking place, a town of grey houses, grey roofs, and grey stones on roofs, built on a beach of grey sand, round a grey bay." The thunderous rain that greeted me seemed determined to support her, but much has changed since then, and the thrusting high buildings, the busy port, and lively downtown gave a different impression.

Say Aomori to a Japanese and they may well respond with "apples." On his hitchhiking journey through Japan, Will Ferguson joked that as soon as he entered the prefecture, "everything changed as if by clockwork from rice fields to apples." The city promotes the connection too, and its huge fifteen-floor information center has an enormous letter A as its frontage. A as in Aomori; and A is for apple too.

On my first evening in the town I dodged the large rain drops and raided a *konbini* (convenience store) for dinner: sushi roll, vegetable sticks, grilled mackerel, and a packet of nuts called Rocabo. Only later when I read the label did I realize Rocabo was Japanese English for Low Carbo(hydrate). The appeal of living in Japan, as Donald Richie noted, is that each day brings a fresh surprise. Rocabo was today's.

HOT SPRINGS AND FINE food and colorful festivals—these are a few of my favorite things. Japan must have more festivals than any other country

I can think of, outside India. Typically a procession with portable shrines parades around the neighborhood. Since every Shinto shrine has an annual festival, and many Buddhist temples too, there are festivals going on somewhere pretty much every day, particularly in spring and autumn (important times for rice cultivation). Some have a wider fame, because of their prestige or spectacular nature. One such is Aomori's Nebuta Matsuri. In a town of 280,000, it attracts some two million visitors.

The festival's centerpiece is an evening parade of illuminated floats in scintillating colors, which depict larger-than-life heroes and monsters. The effect is spectacular. Up to twelve meters long, the floats are spun around at intersections, accompanied by pounding taiko, cymbals, and flutes. Following them are costumed dancers called *haneto*. Dressed in flower hats and *yukata*, they hop and bounce energetically, frenetically. This is one of those occasions when buttoned-up Japan lets go and gets wild.

Each year a different theme is chosen, whether mythological or historical or contemporary. In 2019, in honor of the new emperor, imperial accession was the theme, and the most elaborate float featured the rock cave into which the sun goddess, Amaterasu, retreated after falling out with her brother. The mythical matriarch is the supposed progenitor of the imperial line.

In 1926 Emperor Hirohito, who claimed direct descent from her, assumed the throne as a living god, but renounced his divinity at the end of World War II. That did not prevent his grandson, the current emperor, from spending the night communing with Amaterasu in the ascension rites of 2019. Quite an experience, one would imagine, for someone who did postgraduate studies at Oxford in Thames navigation.

The Nebuta Museum is ideal for a rainy day, since you can see the floats up close without being jostled by two million others. Made of *washi* (Japanese paper) on bamboo frames, they are shaped, painted, and lit internally by up to eight hundred electric bulbs. (Traditionally it was illuminated by candlelight; talk about a fire risk!) The floats can weigh up to four tons and are pulled by teams of thirty or more. Each year the best designs are selected for special attention, and some of the artists have become well known. It is said festival connoisseurs can identify them by the shape of the noses in their creations.

Not far from the museum was a restaurant advertising Aomori's most famous dish, *kaiyakimiso*. A scallop shell is heated over a flame, in which mushrooms and onion simmer in a broth of miso sauce topped with an egg. A little too salty for my taste, but it certainly felt wholesome, complemented with a sip or two of the local sake. Even despite the rain Aomori looked anything but grey.

YOU DO NOT HAVE to be a history buff to be fascinated by Japan's Jomon period (c. 14,000–300 BC). Over ten thousand years of peace, sustainable living, harmony with nature, small communities, a seasonal diet, stunning pottery, and goggle-eyed dolls. What is there not to like? Well, in contrast to contemporary Japan, underpopulation might have been a concern. Estimates vary, but one scholar put the number at around two hundred thousand for early Jomon, just about enough for a large rock festival. Or put another way, the total number of Jomon people would barely make up one of modern Japan's lesser towns. Think of all the empty space there would have been.

Hunter-gatherers are known for being nomads, but the Jomon settled in villages even as they continued to hunt and gather. They lived near the coast or along estuaries so as to complement produce from the land with that of the sea. One of the most famous of their settlements, not far from Aomori City, is known as Sanmai-Maruyama, a World Heritage site with museum and reconstructed village.

The site offers guided tours, and for the morning session there was just myself and parents with their sons, aged seven and five, from neighboring Iwate Prefecture. The guide was an elderly volunteer who was slightly deaf. "I'll have to tune my hearing aid to understand your English," he said, and when I answered in Japanese he turned to the family with, "What, what? I can't hear him." He was so pleased with his little joke that he repeated it every time I asked a question. Eventually I gave up and asked the children, who were far more helpful.

The village flourished for over 1,500 years, which is impressive if you think of the short lifespan of people in the past. Basho wrote once of an ancient monument, which had stood for a thousand years, "through which I could see into the hearts of the men of old." I had a similar feeling with the reconstructed village in front of us.

The site was near a stream, which led to the sea four kilometers away, the reason no doubt it was chosen. The reconstructions stood on excavated sites, meaning that the layout was the same as it would have been originally. "Take a good look," our guide said, motioning towards the terrain. "Next time you come it will be packed with tourists."

"Now let me ask you. What are Japanese most interested in?"

We racked our brains. . . . Smart phones? Brand names? *Talento* (television entertainers)?

"Football," suggested one of the boys.

"No, no. The correct answer is food," said our guide.

He had a point. Food is a constant topic, and from television programs to restaurant fare, you are never far from an emphatic "*oishii*" (delicious). Only France, it is said, can equal Japan's level of food culture, and even then Tokyo outdoes Paris in Michelin stars.

"Okay, I will explain to you," continued the guide. "You see those trees over there. That was where the forest used to be, where they could gather chestnuts and walnuts. Very convenient, don't you think? Now what else could they eat? Yes, they could eat salmon and trout from the river over there. And they could follow the river to the sea. Actually we have found fifty different kinds of seafood here. Can you tell me fifty types of seafood?"

We put our collective heads together, and came up with something close to thirty, most of them popular sushi items.

"Actually I couldn't do fifty either," confessed the guide, "but they found here the remains of clams, octopus, squid, shrimp, and so on. As for hunters, they used bows and arrows, traps, pits, and spears. What do you think they hunted? Yes, that's right, wild boar. Also flying squirrels and hares. They could eat many types of food, but their life was not easy. Not at all. Around the village they have found eight hundred child graves. You see, life was very fragile. You children should be careful, haha. Now this is interesting. The children were buried in sealed jars, and in the jar a hole was made. Why? What do you think? Okay, I will tell you. Maybe it was for their spirit to escape. Sometimes too there were flat round stones, but we don't know why."

That last bit of information set off a chain of thoughts. Stones are a symbol of the everlasting, the eternal, the dead, and thus the unseen world of pure spirit. Round shapes also have spiritual connotations, for ancient Chinese believed the soul to be a shining white disc. Plato too said the soul was a circle, and shamans wear round discs on their costumes for similar reasons. When Amaterasu sent her grandson to earth, she gave him a circular bronze mirror as a token of herself, which is why to this day round mirrors are found in Shinto shrines. Look in the mirror, it is said, and you see the divine within.

Meanwhile our guide had moved on and stood by a track leading out of the settlement. "Adults were buried in oval pits either side of this pathway," he said. "We don't know why." Since the lane led in the direction of the sea, I thought that perhaps the souls were being seen off to Tokoyo, a mythical paradise beyond the sea. I put the idea to the guide, who laughed nervously and turned to the others. "Interesting, isn't it?" he said (Japanese being non-specific, the "it" seemed directed at me).

By now we had arrived at a reconstructed pit house. The roof and walls were thickly thatched, held by a wooden frame made of chestnut, the hardest wood available. The result was a robust ten-meter-square building, able to ride out storms and bad weather. Here the seven-year-old came in useful; at 150 centimeters, he was roughly the height of a Jomon adult and able to demonstrate how it was possible to slip in through the low doorway. Inside was a sunken floor made of earth, in the middle of which was a hearth for cooking.

Following this we walked over to a young chestnut tree, planted forty years ago. So how old did we think were the trees used in making the house? Over a hundred, guessed the oldest child, and he was right. Chestnut trees that old can no longer be found in Japan, so the reconstruction had to use timber specially imported from Siberia.

The largest of the buildings was an assembly hall, able to house up to three hundred people, the size of which suggested a major settlement, perhaps even a regional capital. The making of the roof required advanced skills, unexpected in hunter-gatherers. A three-story platform, thought to be for shamanic rituals, enabled sight of the sea, which I seized on as support for my Tokoyo theory. Perhaps, I speculated, the rituals held there were to honor ancestors who came from overseas.

The platform was supported by pillars tilted inwards at a twenty-degree angle for sturdiness, and our guide gleefully posed the question of how this was managed. Our collective brows furrowed, but no one could come up with the right answer, though it was simple enough. The bottom of the two-meter hole that held the pillar was lined with a twenty-degree incline of stones. "Well," pointed out the father of the family, "Jomon people had longer to think about it than we did."

With the tour over, we were left to explore the museum on our own. The exhibits suggested the people here not only enjoyed a sophisticated culture but traded with a wide range of neighbors. Some of the pottery, with its trademark cord patterns, was simply stunning, alongside which were ornamental items such as hair combs and stone pendants, not to mention jewelry made of amber, jade, and obsidian. Put together with a peaceful and sustainable lifestyle, the Jomon people seemed altogether admirable. The curators certainly seemed to think so, for a board declared they were "models of wisdom and ingenuity."

Thousands of years separated us, but it was easy to relate to these ancient people. One of the tableaux featured Jomon Man fishing with a long branch, while Jomon Woman was shown teaching her children how to plant. Among their main sources of food were mushroom, bracken, flowering fern, and elderberry seed. Interestingly, elderflower ferments easily, so perhaps inebriation helped them cope with the long winter nights. They kept fox-like dogs too, which were used for hunting and buried with respect. Kudos to them for that.

More intriguing than the dogs, though, were the *dogu*. These figurines of goggle-eyed space cadets and big-bellied earth mothers are Japan's earliest examples of cuteness. About the size of a hand, they are at once fanciful and futuristic, weird images from the far side of the imagination. Some two thousand have been excavated here, the most at a single site, yet no one knows for certain what they represent. Perhaps lucky charms. Or spirit containers. Or personalized offerings.

A work room offers the opportunity to make your own *dogu*, so I had a go along with a group of junior high students. Kits were handed out with clay already prepared for molding, together with a toothpick for punching in holes, either to represent facial features or make patterns on the bodies. My creation was sadly uninspired (later its head fell off), but the students produced wide-eyed figures that could have starred in a manga. One of the weirder ones, I fancied, was modeled on me.

It had been a full morning, so I headed off to try some "Jomon-style rice," which turned out to be white, red, and brown grain mixed with chestnut and shaved scallop. Dessert was apple cider jelly, hardly Jomon but definitely Aomorian. There were two other local delicacies on my to-eat list: rice cracker soup and ginger *oden* (a kind of hotpot). I made them my target for dinner, and though there were plenty of outlets around the station, none seemed to fit the bill. Hamburger was no problem. Nor were noodles. There were Indian and Chinese restaurants, a Mister Donut too, and even some likely looking *izakaya* (pub restaurants), but whenever I asked for rice cracker soup or ginger *oden*, all I got was a pained look. Such is modern Japan. I should have gone for apple pie.

On Track ||||||||||||||||||||||||||||||||||||||||||||||||||

Aomori Station opened in 1891 as the northern terminus of the main line from Tokyo to the Tohoku region. People disembarked here for the ferry to Hokkaido, a scene captured in a famous *enka* song, "Tsugaru Kaikyo Fuyugeshiki," about a young woman who leaves behind a lover in Tokyo to return home.

The station was destroyed in World War II, since when it has been twice rebuilt, with the present building dating from 2021. The old site is being rebuilt with a multiuse ten-story building planned for completion in 2024.

The Shinkansen line runs to Shin-Aomori Station, a five-minute train ride away. It opened in 1986 and was rebuilt in 2010. It serves as the terminus for the unusual Ou Main Line, which runs from Fukushima and is divided into sections, one of which, uniquely, sees regular trains and Shinkansen trains share the same line. To enable this, the track makes use of three parallel rails to cope with both narrow and wide gauges.

Akita

JAPAN IS OFTEN CHARACTERIZED as a crowded country, but Akita defies the description. The prefecture is huge, as big as Tokyo, Chiba, and Saitama put together, yet it is home to fewer than a million inhabitants. Of all Japan's prefectures it has suffered the steepest depopulation, and every year it suffers a loss of some ten thousand people. At current rates, by 2060 there will be fewer than half a million in an area larger than Cyprus.

The prefecture is noted for its scenic beauty, and the train from Aomori skirts the coastline, offering tantalizing glimpses of sandy beaches on one side and mountains on the other. From my seaside seat I could see white foam sparkling in the sunshine as waves crashed against rocks, and in secluded bays closely packed houses jostled each other for space. Meanwhile, on the other side the rolling hills of Aomori gave way to the soaring peaks of the Shirakami Mountains.

Hardworking figures in protective hat and clothing were bent double in the fields, overshadowed by monstrous wind turbines in intrusive white. All of a sudden the perfect symmetry of Mt. Iwaki, a.k.a. the Tsugaru Fuji, came into view and made me gasp in astonishment. Here was the second mini-Fuji on my journey, iconic miniatures in a country that loves imitation.

I was on the lookout for Kisakata, which marks the point where my route intersected with that of Matsuo Basho (1644–1694) in his wanderings described in *The Narrow Road to the Deep North*. The poet had gone out of his way to get there, for it was a renowned scenic spot with literary connections. In his poem, Basho personifies the seascape as the legendary Chinese beauty, Seishi. Alas, it is not possible to see it now as Basho did, because a devastating earthquake in 1804 raised the area by a massive two meters, meaning that the bay with its picturesque islands was turned into hills in open countryside.

Kisakata—
Seishi in the rain
wet silk tree blossom

It was rainy when Basho arrived, and he stayed overnight in a fisherman's hut. The next day he took a boat to visit the island retreat of a Heian poet, Noin Hoshi, then went to view a submerged cherry tree that the wandering monk Saigyo had memorialized in a short verse. As a Buddhist, Saigyo was concerned with the illusionary nature of our "floating world," captured in the image of fishermen in boats. Cherry blossom is a well-known symbol of transience, and by inverting the usual perception of humans looking up at the trees, the verse suggests hidden depths and an underlying truth.

At Kisakata
a cherry tree
covered by waves—
above the blossom
fishermen rowing boats

After Kisakata the train veered inland, past rice crops, which glistened in the afternoon sun. Here and there were stands of cedar and apple trees, while in the distance stood the menacing presence of dark mountains. They loom large in folklore as places of trepidation, and still today they can be perilous as I well knew, for I had firsthand experience.

As part of the research for *Japan's World Heritage Sites* I had to explore the Shirakami Mountains, recognized by UNESCO as containing one of the world's largest virgin beech forests. They survived here because of the unwelcoming terrain, even as elsewhere such forests were depleted by logging and land development.

The mountains straddle the border between Aomori and Akita. Faced with the vastness of the area, Lili and I rented a car and chose a route that ran through the middle of the mountains. It was marked as a minor road, and though there was no asphalt the track was smooth enough. We were soon immersed in thickly wooded surrounds, with steep rises to either side and an occasional gorge or waterfall. It was all very delightful, and I was admiring the nature when the car swerved violently to the right and headed straight for an embankment. There was a sickening noise, then a sudden thud as the car ground to a halt at a thirty-degree angle. Lili had fallen asleep at the wheel.

A quick appraisal revealed neither of us were hurt, but that one of the front wheels was wedged in a deep open gutter that ran alongside the road. The engine still worked, but there was no way to move the car. We would have to ring for help. Then came a sickening realization; we had crashed in one of the few places in Japan where there was no phone signal, no passing traffic, and no sign of civilization. What's more, it was bear country.

The accident happened around four in the afternoon, and dusk was not far off. From what I could tell, we were something like a five-hour walk from the nearest village. But just as our thoughts were turning gloomy, we heard the sound of a vehicle and around the corner appeared a van. Saved!

The van contained three foresters on their way home from work, and we asked for a lift. They said that legally one of us should stay with the car, but we were reluctant to split up with darkness descending, so we agreed to both stay put while they informed the police. Though the car was tilted at a thirty-degree angle, it was stable enough and we got in and waited. An hour passed. Then another. Stars appeared, and a crescent moon. We speculated what might have happened. Had the men actually told the police?

We were just dozing off when light spread through the forest like a

UFO in a Spielberg film. Then from the hill behind us a vehicle appeared and drew up alongside. It was the police. At last!

Finding a foreigner in such parts piqued their interest, and they took their time examining my "gaijin card" and asking how I liked Japan. The discussion that followed was directed at Lili: What was a gaijin doing in their mountains? Why had we chosen such a minor track? And what did we intend to do with the car? Their shift was over, they explained, but they would take us to the town where we had booked a room. Things were finally moving in the right direction. Or so I thought.

The budget for Akita police must be very tight, for the car provided for our rescue was a tiny two-door affair. We were invited to get in the back with our luggage, but being claustrophobic I balked and insisted I would rather stay on my own in the car. At first they treated this as some kind of gaijin joke, but Lili managed to convince them it was deadly serious so one of them squeezed in the back with my suitcase on his knees.

There followed a scene straight out of the Keystone Cops, as our tiny car raced off into the pitch darkness at top speed along a narrow road with a sheer drop to one side. As we hurtled round hairpin bends, the policemen were both on their phones talking animatedly. "What is going on?" I whispered to Lili. "Not sure," she replied. I wondered if she was having as much trouble with the local accent as I was.

After some forty minutes of high-speed confusion, we came to a main road and roared into an empty carpark lined with shuttered shops. The policemen left in a hurry after telling us to wait for a truck. "This is Aomori," they explained, as if it was a foreign country.

"Why do we have to wait for a truck?" I asked Lili.

"So it can take us back to the car."

What!? I was stunned.

It was near midnight when a pickup truck with a small crane swung into the car park and screeched to a halt on the gravel. At the wheel was what looked like an apprentice yakuza, clearly not amused at having been called out on a Saturday night. We grabbed our luggage, at which point he yelled out, "Only one." Surely he was joking? He made it clear he was not. "Okay, I'll get in the back with the crane," I said.

"*Da-me, da-me*" (no good), he said irritably.

"Okay, then, she can sit on my lap," I told him.

"*Da-me, da-me,*" he repeated even more irritably, adding for extra effect, "Hurry up!"

Panicking, we had to decide quickly what to do. I didn't have a Japanese license and it was possible the car needed to be driven, so barely a minute or two later Lili was off, and I was left with the luggage and no idea where I was. It was nearly one in the morning, and Lili had been driven off into the mountains by a mad truck driver. Even worse there was no signal and she would not be able to contact me.

It was four in the morning before we finally got to bed.

"AKITA" SOUNDS THE SAME as *akita,* Japanese for "fed up." That was pretty much how I felt after arriving by train from Aomori, as the weather was unfriendly, the information office unhelpful, and I got undue "micro-aggression" for being a gaijin. Communication was hampered by the local dialect, which twists *so desu ne* into *un da.* Nor did I care for the town's "famous dish," *kiritanpo,* a hotpot with mashed rice on cedar sticks. It is grilled and boiled in a soup or stew containing something my dictionary translated as Japanese water dropwort. I did not take to *mekabu* either, which is kelp taken from near the stalk with knobs on. Good for the digestion, but not for the tastebuds. Sorry, Akita, your green-pea slime was not for me.

For dinner I reverted to a reliable standard—*aji furai teishoku* (set meal with fried horse mackerel). This came in the kind of generous serving you get in the provinces, with the main dish augmented by fried oysters on a bed of cabbage and accompanied by miso soup, boiled rice, pickles, and a small square of tofu topped by salmon roe. It was more than filling, all for a mere 880 yen (about eight dollars). You could hardly ask for more—but I did. The Tohoku region prides itself on the quality of its sake, but nowhere quite as adamantly as Akita. I chose one of premier quality, which mills over fifty percent of the grain, hoping to savor something of Akita's pure mountain streams. It slipped down like the proverbial melted snow.

At the information office there were three women ready and waiting to answer questions, and when I asked for something unique to Akita, one of them handed over a leaflet inviting me to pet an Akita dog. These large husky-lookalikes, considered dangerous in some countries, are intensely loyal as exemplified by Hachiko, who for nine years waited at Tokyo's Shibuya Station for his owner to return. Much as I like dogs, I was already on petting terms with an Akita in Kyoto, so I asked for something else. How about Akita Zoo suggested another of the women, pointing to a poster of a giraffe. Too tall to pet, I joked, then regretted it as it was explained to me that petting was not allowed.

Next to the giraffe another poster showed three young women under the heading "Akita *Bijin*" (Akita beauties). Were they available as guides, perhaps? No, came the answer. So what was the point of the poster? This caused a lengthy discussion, resulting in a senior staff member being summoned to explain that in Japan women from Kyoto, Hakata, and Akita were renowned for their beauty. I see, I said, but why make the poster? Is Akita promoting its women as a tourist sight? "Yes," came the answer, "please admire them."

IMAGINE A GROTESQUE RED face, straggling thick hair, pointed horns, and a creature enveloped in straw that hangs down to the waist. Straw armbands and straw sandals complete the clothing, and in its hand is a staff. Pierced cheeks and saber teeth suggest something half-human and half-monster, and from out of this bizarre assemblage come deep roars. Imagine too an infant secure in the family house being suddenly confronted by such a creature. Terrified, the child bursts out crying but the parents look on proudly and beam happily.

Such is the Namahage Festival, peculiar to the Oga Peninsula about an hour's distance from Akita City. By tradition it was held in villages on the first full moon of the new lunar year, but with the introduction of the Gregorian calendar in 1873, it was moved to New Year's Eve.

The festival is very much a village affair, but the Namahage Museum is intended for the public, so it comes as a surprise to find that at Oga Station there is no bus connection. In fact there is virtually no transport on offer but a two-hour "taxi tour" that cost more than my hotel room. At least there will be some local chat, I consoled myself, but the driver was unusually taciturn and clearly not enamored of his job. Either that or, in Bruce Willis style, he was having a very bad day.

The main exhibit at the museum is the costumes, made anew for the festival every year. In the past, masks were shaped from anything to hand, such as clay, plywood, and even tin, though nowadays they are all wood. The straggly hair is made from hemp fiber, horsehair, or matted human hair. Rather than evil beings, the ogres are seen as friendly, bringing the promise of health and a good harvest. Videos show how the costumed strangers are welcomed by parents, who offer them food and drink. "Are there any children here who don't do their homework?" demand the demons. By this time terrified toddlers are in tears.

For Westerners this looks like a clear case of child abuse, but in the Far East it is part of a shamanic tradition that privileges the life force. Babies that cry loudly show vigor, thereby promising a healthy future. A similar notion underscores festivals with Chinese dragons, when parents offer babies to be "bitten" for good luck. Should the baby burst our crying, it is a good omen. There is even a contest called Crybaby Sumo (Nakizumo), when babies held by sumo wrestlers compete to be the first to cry. One big squeeze is all it takes.

Namahage's origins are unknown, but it could have originated with mountain ascetics emerging unwashed from the woods and visiting houses to pass on the spiritual merit they had acquired. True or not, the festival has won recognition from UNESCO as an Intangible Cultural Heritage, ensuring it will not die out. For children on the Oga Peninsula, even if Father Christmas does not appear, the Namahage surely will.

On the little train back to Akita I was seated just behind the driver, which afforded me a close-up of his actions. To his right at eye level, he had the itinerary printed out with scheduled times written on a long strip of paper, and before arriving at a station he would run his finger over the name and check the time next to it with his clock, then double check again with the schedule. Approaching a signal, he would point at it while saying out loud the name.

Though it was only a local train, the place for doors to open was clearly marked on platforms, and the train pulled up inch perfect at the designated spot. At each station he would stand up and stick his head out to check for anyone getting on or off. All in all he was a busy man, and the busyness kept him alert. In its way watching him was as fascinating as watching the chefs in the Otaru sushi shop. The punctiliousness was after all what makes Japan special—that and the Namahage.

AKITA WAS THE FIRST of the castle towns on my journey. In the Edo period such towns were the seat of a feudal lord (*daimyo*), who had complete and absolute power within his domain. The towns date from the beginning of the seventeenth century, when the Tokugawa sought to impose stability by insisting on a "one castle, one domain" rule. It meant the *daimyo*'s resources were concentrated on one site, and the grandeur of the building reflected his status.

Typically the castle stands on a hill, around which are clustered the houses of samurai. The upper ranks were closest to the seat of power, with lower ranks spread below. Further afield were districts for merchants and artisans. The towns were arranged to slow down attackers, and in some cases the approach to the castle resembles a maze.

Within the town were gathered the domain's creative talent, and still today the towns act as regional hubs for arts and crafts. In terms of my journey, the castle towns made convenient stepping stones: Akita–Niigata–Toyama–Kanazawa–Fukui–Tottori–Matsue–Hagi–Hakata–Imari–Hirado–Nagasaki–Kumamoto–Kagoshima. In this way I could skip from the north of Honshu to the south of Kyushu via many of Japan's most attractive towns.

Akita is an example of a castle town without a castle—or rather with a ruined castle. Following the Meiji Restoration, the modernizing new government saw the castles as bastions of feudalism and ordered their demolition. Only after World War II were they reassessed as cultural treasures. Castle connoisseurs will tell you with great glee that there are only twelve genuine castles left in Japan, and that the others are mere reconstructions. Some—perish the thought—are replicas in ferroconcrete.

Kubota Castle in Akita exemplifies this historical development. Following its abandonment in 1872, the moats were filled in and the materials used for scrap. A large conflagration ravaged the rest, and the site ended up being donated to the city for use as a park. Shinto shrines were added, over a thousand cherry trees planted, and gardens laid out. There is even a relocated samurai house. The result prompts Ozymandias-like reflection—swords converted into ploughshares, castles transformed into parks.

Walking the ruins gave me an appetite, and I went in search of lunch. Across the counter sat two smartly groomed women communing in silence, and I thought of the poster at the information office. Like other areas in Tohoku, Akita prides itself on the quality of its rice, because of the crystal-clear streams that come pouring down from the mountains. It is said to be why the women are so beautiful. Perhaps that information office poster had a point after all.

On Track ||||||||||||||||||||||||||||||||||||||||||||||||||

Akita Station first opened in 1902, and was last rebuilt in 1997. Unusually, it services both regular and Shinkansen trains. The Tsugaru limited express from Aomori takes two and a half hours. The Akita Shinkansen Line from Tokyo was converted from regular tracks, and trains are limited to 130 kilometers per hour for part of the way. As a result the 670 kilometers take roughly four hours.

Train enthusiasts from Tokyo enjoy the contrast of high and slow speed that Tohoku offers by first taking the Komachi Shinkansen to Kakunodate. Transfer to the private Akita Nairiku Line provides access to a two-carriage train that winds its leisurely way along a single track through mountainous countryside, offering picturesque views of ravines, forests, and rice fields.

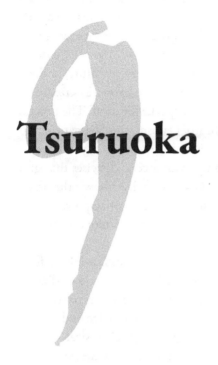

Tsuruoka

TSURUOKA FOR ME WILL always mean self-mummification. Not of myself, of course, but of Buddhist priests. Many years ago I visited the town to research an article I was writing about *sokushinbutsu* (accelerated Buddhahood). The practice involved gradually reducing the intake of food until the diet only comprised nuts, corns, and bark. After a thousand days of this, the priests entered a grave in which they sat in the lotus position and were covered with soil, breathing through a narrow bamboo tube while ringing a bell and chanting Buddha's name. Three years and three months later, they were dug up and revered as saints, able to bestow on others their accumulated merit. A few are on public display, with their wrinkled, leathery faces still eerily intact. The small town of Tsuruoka is home to four such mummies.

This time I was focused on something else—mountain asceticism. Japan is rich in religious expression; as well as several Shinto sects, there are varieties of Buddhism of which Zen, Pure Land, and Nichiren are the most well known. In addition, there is a rich folk religion, and an array of new religions. But of all the various groupings, Shugendo is in many ways the most appealing and in my opinion has the potential to be an even greater gift to the world than Zen.

The Japanese pride themselves on their closeness to nature, and you can hardly get closer than Shugendo. Its followers are known as *yamabushi*, or one who sleeps in the mountains, which speaks for itself. The practice draws on elements from Buddhism, Shinto, Daoism, and Shamanism, but the basic concept is simple. By entering into the mountains, you leave the mundane world behind, and through rigorous ascetic exercises the ego is broken down and a new self is fashioned by nature. In this way the practitioner returns to the everyday world with enhanced spiritual power, which can be used for the benefit of others. It is thus an acting out of the universal motif of death and resurrection.

The austerities carried out include mountain walks, minimal food, cold water bathing, sleep deprivation, prolonged chanting, and meditation in caves. At Mt. Omine, in Nara Prefecture, novices are confronted with imminent death by being dangled headfirst over a cliff edge and asked if they will strive to be virtuous. No prizes for guessing their answer.

The *yamabushi* costume is white, the color of death (white signifies the pure world of spirit). On their forehead they wear a small round black cap, which can double as a cup, and on their back hangs a piece of animal skin, usually goat or deer, which keeps the backside warm when sitting on cold, wet surfaces. Some carry a conch shell, the sound of which, ringing out through the woods, announces their presence.

The legendary founder of Shugendo was an eighth-century ascetic called En no Gyoja, and throughout Japan are sacred mountains on which he allegedly practiced. Local groups were attached to particular mountains, then in the Edo period the government mandated that everyone should be enrolled with a Buddhist temple, so the Shugendo groups were assigned to Shingon and Tendai sects. In 1868 came a stunning shock: Shugendo was banned by a modernizing new government, which found it embarrassingly primitive. Only after World War II was the practice resumed, and Dewa Sanzan, near Tsuruoka, is home to one of the oldest and most prestigious groups.

I had the evening free and set out to find what the little town could offer in the way of specialties. There was a likely looking restaurant near the station, and in response to my question the waiter pointed to *dacha-mame*. "King of edamame," the menu said. It was a touch sweeter than your usual bean, but tasty for sure. I needed something more substantial, however. How about Tsuruoka-style udon, suggested the waiter. "The noodle is finer and the *dashi* stock more delicious than usual," he said. To me it tasted much the same as elsewhere, but it was warm and satisfying. So, mindful of local pride, I told the staff it was the best udon I had ever had. That put a smile on their faces.

Food lovers with time to spare in Tsuruoka usually have a smile too, for in 2014 it was declared, rather grandiosely, a UNESCO Creative City of Gastronomy. "Surrounded by nature and pristine seas, Tsuruoka City is a gem virtually untouched by foreign tourism, and blessed with a multitude of seasonal ingredients throughout the year," runs the PR material. Gourmets might take note.

SANZAN MEANS THREE MOUNTAINS, in this case referring to Mt. Haguro (414 meters), Mt. Gassan (1,984 meters), and Mt. Yudono (1,504 meters). Dewa is the historical name of the province. The three sacred mountains are said to represent the past, present, and future, but practically speaking the small hill of Mt. Haguro acts as entry point for Mt. Gassan, where ascetic exercises are performed. The more remote Mt. Yudono, only accessible by foot, serves as holy sanctuary, and in the past worshippers were required not to speak of what they saw there.

According to tradition, Mt. Haguro grants happiness, Mt. Gassan consolation, and Mt. Yudono rebirth. Since I was not looking for rebirth, nor did I feel in need of consolation, I decided the gentle slopes of Mt. Haguro would suit me just fine. In fact I had visited once before and remembered fondly the magical sight of its five-storied pagoda—a work of art in harmony with the surrounding cedars. Santoka, the wandering poet, wrote of Westerners conquering mountains whereas Easterners contemplate them, while he himself "tasted" them. I knew what he meant, for the fine taste of Haguro lingered on my lips.

The bus from Tsuruoka emerges into a timeless landscape in which tiny figures in farmer's clothing are dwarfed by misty mountains, as in a Chinese ink painting. When we reached the foothills, a large *torii* straddling the road announced we were entering the realm of the kami, and to either side were conspicuous signs of religiosity—shrines, Buddhist statues, and *shimenawa* (rice-straw rope denoting sacred objects). Most striking of all was an enormous oversized purification stick that looked like a relic from the Age of the Gods, when heroic figures and giant ogres strode the countryside.

At the entrance to the trail up Mt. Haguro stood a run-down public toilet, placed strategically for the relief of visitors to the realm of the sacred. Despite its mosquito-ridden condition, someone had taken the trouble to place social distance markers on the floor. It was impressive. Even here, alongside the ancient traditions, modern hygiene prevailed.

Immediately on entering the woods the fresh fragrance of cedar became apparent, and it was noticeably cooler, welcome relief on such a warm day. Noticeboards announced with a concern for precision that the pathway had 2,446 steps, and that lining the righthand side were 281 trees, while lining the left were 301. This was thanks to the fiftieth head priest, who had laid out the approach over a period of thirteen years in the seventeenth century.

The pathway into the woods begins with a gentle descent, accompanied by the refreshing sound of water running down either side. Since my last visit there had been a significant change in that signs were bilingual for the benefit of tourists, and in front of a small wooden shrine was an announcement in English: "Presiding kami: Amenotajikarao no Mikoto. Divine virtue: Proficiency in arts and sports." It seemed an invitation to pray, and praying in Japan means paying, so I tossed a coin into the offertory box and prayed for proficiency in arts. The sports I was willing to forgo.

Further along the trail, the outline of a pagoda became apparent. From a distance it was barely discernible among the trees, for though it is an impressive twenty-nine meters high, it nestles beneath the canopy of the surrounding cedars. The result is a harmonious blending of art and nature. The impossibly tall trees have slender trunks stretching skywards as if reaching for heaven, while the pagoda exhibits elegance combined with stunning craftsmanship. If you stand below it and try to work out how the joints fit together, your brain is sure to get scrambled. And all that interconnecting complexity is done without the use of nails.

At this point, covered in a film of sweat, I decided I had had enough. Foolishly I had not brought any water, and my back was aching. I had intended to press on to the thatched buildings of Haguro Shrine, but I knew the kami would forgive me if I turned back. On the bus to Tsuruoka, I watched the mountains recede into the distance and thought of Basho. Trained in Zen, he was open to all forms of spirituality as is the Japanese way, and he had managed the full course at Dewa Sanzan, austerities and all. But then, I consoled myself, he was a mere forty-five at the time. Like myself, he had visited on a warm day, and he wrote of relief from the summer heat.

> The coolness
> And a faint three-day moon—
> Mount Haguro

After a week at Minamidani (South Valley), Basho climbed the more demanding Mt. Gassan and did ascetic exercises before proceeding to Mt. Yudono. Given the taboo on revealing what happens there, he cleverly wrote of it by not writing of it.

> Yudono
> of which I may not tell—
> sleeves wet with tears

The mountain experience stimulated the poet's imagination and brought out his playful side too. The "De" of Dewa Sanzan means exiting or emerging, and Basho used this in a haiku that sees him emerge from the mountains not to some great spiritual insight, but to vegetables. The first-of-the-season eggplants were prepared specially for him by his pupil, Nagayama Juko.

> How unusual—
> emerging from Dewa
> to first eggplants

From Tsuruoka I planned to get one up on Basho by heading for the island of Sado. The poet had viewed it from the coast, but never visited. As he watched, the surging sea and sound of waves made him melancholic, and mindful of it as a place of exile, he wrote a *haibun* essay about pushing open the shutter of his room to see a rising moon. The Milky Way (a.k.a. "heavenly river") led his eye to the distant island, sixty-five kilometers offshore.

Stormy sea—
stretching out to Sado
"heavenly river"

A later wanderer, the Zen monk Santoka, also visited the coast and like his predecessor looked out towards the island. Poets talking to poets down the passage of centuries is one of the great joys of literature, and haiku is particularly rich in the timeless interchange between masters. The more one immerses oneself in the genre, the more one appreciates listening in to the discourse between the living and the dead.

Sitting on a sand dune
today again
no sign of Sado

What was it about Sado that was so alluring? I had not originally included it in my itinerary, but now, following a brief stop in Niigata, I was excited at the prospect of a detour. Much as train travel attracts, even more appealing are ferries, islands, and the smell of the sea. Sado is also host to Japan's most famous drumming group, called Kodo. What is more, there are close connections with Kyoto, and anything to do with the ancient capital is of interest to a Kyo-centric like myself. In fact, I had long wanted to visit the island, and now there was a golden opportunity. It was the perfect occasion to take time out. Time, as it were, to de-rail.

On Track ||||||||||||||||||||||||||||||||||||||||||||||||

Tsuruoka Station is served by the Uetsu Main Line, which runs between Akita and Niigata. (Uetsu refers to the two ancient provinces in which it operates.) Although it started in 1912, even today only half its length is double track. From Tsuruoka the limited express to Akita takes an hour and forty minutes, and almost the same to Niigata. The small station caters to a population of just 125,000, so it comes as a surprise to learn that through amalgamation of neighboring villages the municipality is the largest in Tohoku.

Japan's train tourism is evident in the Kairi express, which runs from Niigata to Sakata and stops at Tsuruoka. Designed to showcase the scenic coastline, it has plush reclining seats, large viewing windows, and a dining car with regional cuisine.

Sado Island

THIRTEENTH-CENTURY EMPEROR JUNTOKU; NICHIREN, apostle of the Lotus Sutra; Zeami, perfecter of noh. What do the three men have in common? Exile to Sado. For centuries, banishment to Japan's sixth-largest island was the equivalent of being sent to Siberia. Like Alcatraz, it was considered a place from which it was impossible to escape.

There was a scorching September sun when I arrived, but Takayuki Tsukakoshi whisked me into his air-conditioned truck and away we sped. Raised in Tokyo, his Sado-born mother had taken him to the island for summer holidays. After graduating in mechanical engineering, he was transferred to work in Kentucky at a time when American car companies were eager to hook up with Japan. Fate intervened in the form of 9/11, after which the Homeland Security Act came in and foreigners were out. Instead of an American Dreamer he became a Sado Dreamer, working as a freelance translator and guide. Had it been a good move? "Yes, yes!" he said emphatically.

With little work because of Covid, Takayuki had set aside time to show me around. His time in America had made him easygoing, friendly, and flexible. When he asked what I wanted to see, I mentioned four things for which Sado is famous: exile, gold mines, noh, and taiko. If I could fit them all in, I would be more than happy. "No problem," he said.

We had not been driving long before we passed a copse-encircled Shinto shrine. The *torii* gateway was in the syncretic Ryobu style, indicating Buddhist connection, and the rundown condition of the buildings spoke of a former grandeur. Spiders' webs covered the doors, and to me the faded glory exuded a melancholy air, as if seeing a friend succumb to old age. I asked about depopulation. "When I came here twenty years ago, there were seventy thousand people," he said. "Now there are only fifty thousand. If we continue like this, there will be no one left in fifty years. It is very, very sad. People have been living here since Jomon times."

Our next stop was Seisui-ji, a temple founded in the ninth century on orders of Emperor Kanmu, who was concerned that the islanders were cut off from worship. The main hall was modeled on Kyoto's famous temple Kiyomizu-dera, and the complex had some fifteen buildings in all, many of which were dilapidated. Faded glory was becoming a theme. The only well-maintained structures were two *kura*, freshly painted in white, so it did not take much thinking to figure out where the temple treasures were kept.

The temple was as grand as the aristocratic villas of the Heian period (794–1185), and it seemed a shame to leave it to rot. Takayuki pointed out that rather than renovate, it would be cheaper to knock down and rebuild. One of the priests had apparently run away from the debts, and on the door of the abandoned house was a handwritten sign in English saying, oddly, "No asking of identity." Perhaps it was not debt he ran away from, but foreign tourists.

In the small graveyard the stone markers were in the familiar *gorinto* form, referencing the Chinese system of five elements in their five different shapes. At the bottom was a kind of drawer that could be pulled open for the bones of the deceased to be added to those already there. Family names were displayed, though some of the graves simply said, "For our ancestors."

Takayuki told me his family grave had been moved to the mainland, so his cousin could maintain it.

"He has a young family so he cannot travel to Sado two or three times a year."

"But why not leave it where it was?" I asked. After all, Takayuki was living on the island so could easily maintain it himself.

"My cousin is the oldest son of the oldest son," he told me, "so it is his responsibility. Tradition says it is his duty to keep in good order and pay the temple fee." Instead of going to visit the grave, the grave had gone to him.

"So how about you?" I asked. "Where will you end up?"

"My mother is in the family grave of her husband," he said, "and I will join too."

For a while we stood contemplating the scene, and I thought of the graves of my grandparents, the whereabouts of which I was barely aware. Ancestral ties are taken more seriously in Japan. After the 2011 Tohoku tsunami, for example, the main concern of desperate relatives was to find missing bodies so that the dead could be at rest.

EMPEROR JUNTOKU (1197–1242) LIVED in an age when power resided in Kamakura, with the shogun. Following his father's failed attempt to win back power, he was sent into exile and spent the last twenty-one years of his life in Sado. The place where he lived is marked now by a few ruins among tall pine trees by a stream. Withered flowers lay at the entrance, and inside Japanese visitors with hands in prayer paid respects to the former emperor. The poet Suzuki Shigenu (1814–98), last of a long line of governors appointed to oversee the exiled, captured the atmosphere in the following short verse.

> In ancient pine trees
> the murmuring wind
> fills the air with sadness
> recalling the emperor
> and his house here in exile

Another famous exile, Nichiren (1222–82), was only on the island for two and a half years before being pardoned. On the site of his residence stands an ornate temple with large thatched roof set in picturesque grounds.

No faded glory here. Takayuki suggested that Nichiren followers maintain it in good condition to honor their founder, because he had brought good news. The Lotus Sutra, Nichiren claimed, was so holy that chanting *Nam myoho renge kyo* (All hail the Lotus Sutra) was enough to secure salvation.

A statue of the man stood at the altar. He was an abrasive and divisive figure, not afraid of confronting other sects, and his legacy is a massive following, who themselves are sometimes at odds with each other. Apart from two religious sects (Nichiren Shu and Nichiren Shoshu), there is a powerful lay group called Soka Gakkai, who chant for material as well as spiritual benefits. Linked to them is an influential political party, Komeito, currently part of a government coalition. Takayuki told me he was not a believer, but I noticed he prayed at the altar. It exemplified why scholars find it difficult to decide if the Japanese are religious or not.

The third of the famous exiles was Zeami (1363–1443), founder of noh. Despite his status, he fell out with a shogun and in 1434 was sent into exile, where he is thought to have remained until the shogun died seven years later. His legacy, remarkably, is some fifty plays and treatises which spell out the aesthetics of noh. The slow and dreamlike atmosphere is so far removed from the busy life of modern Japan that it is a wonder the art form still survives. In Sado it is deeply enmeshed in community life. Or was. There used to be well over a hundred stages on the island; now there are "only" thirty, which given the small population is extraordinary.

Takayuki explained that the popularity had little to do with Zeami as such, but originated centuries later when the country was in Edo-period lockdown. The plays were introduced by samurai officials running the gold mine, and the isolated islanders took to the upper-class entertainment. And so it was that uneducated farmers sat entranced as ghostly figures moved with eerie slowness to the otherworldly sound of musicians. Performances became a measure of a village's worth, and the stage a measure of its standing.

All that is now left of Zeami's stay on the island is a small rock on which he stopped to rest. Not so much a case of Zeami lived here as Zeami sat here. Since there was no one around, I started to imagine the scene as the setting for a noh play. A local farmer planting rice is approached by a robed figure who asks the way, and the farmer tells him of a famous man who was exiled here. He sits on the rock and discloses to the stranger that he is in fact the spirit of Zeami, unable to rest because of the injustice done to him. In the second part of the play the stranger takes a nap, and in his dream Zeami appears and does a stately dance reenacting his wrongful exile. The play then ends with the stranger awakening and the "hungry ghost" pacified.

I tried to tell Takayuki the story, but he had little enthusiasm and said he did not care for noh. His tastes were all American, he confessed. Cowboys and Disney and pop music. It was a case of mirror images: the Japanized Westerner face-to-face with the Westernized Japanese.

MY HOTEL FOR THE night boasted a hot spring bath that used ocean water from 232 meters deep—an intriguing statistic to contemplate while soaking. A notice claimed the water was superior to that from the Pacific, because the temperature was warm enough to prevent bacteria. Another notice promised refreshment, smooth skin, moisture retention, and "keep odor eliminating."

Sado was once dubbed "the golden island," and the next day with Takayuki at the wheel, we set off for Aikawa and its famous gold mine. On the way he told me his son was in Tokyo, his elder daughter in Osaka, his younger daughter in Niigata. "All of them are overseas," he joked. The long drive gave me a chance to learn more about the island, especially the climate. In popular culture the coast along the Sea of Japan is dark, cold, and uninviting, but Takayuki said the Tsushima current from the south makes for mild winters, and there is relatively little snow because clouds are driven inland by the prevailing wind.

Along with the benign climate goes a rich heritage, for exiled aristocrats and artists had brought Kyoto's court culture to the island. In later times, Tokugawa officials administering the gold mine introduced samurai culture, and the prosperity led to an influx of enterprising merchants and sailors. The result was a fertile mix that gave rise to some unusual folk songs and festivals.

We arrived at the mine to find the tunnels were closed, but were offered a private tour of the exhibits instead by the museum's curator. The site had begun with silver mining, he said, but awareness of the gold went back a long way. The earliest mention was in the thirteenth-century *Konjaku Monogatari*, which said, "Sado is a country where golden flowers bloom."

"Not many people know that in the seventeenth century, Aikawa was the largest producer of gold in the world," said the curator with understandable pride. Throughout the Edo period, in fact, the Aikawa gold and silver mine had been a major pillar of the Tokugawa economy, producing the *koban* gold coins on which it depended. Small wonder then that the island was put under direct rule for safekeeping.

"There were traditional mining techniques here that did not exist elsewhere," continued the curator, "and the mine continued operating until 1989. Now we are aiming for World Heritage status." What he did not tell us was that Korean forced labor was employed from 1910 to 1945. It was failure to mention this that led South Korea to object to recognition by UNESCO.

There were two means of production. One was underground mining, and picture scrolls from the eighteenth century show the dark and dangerous tunneling involved. Conditions were atrocious, accidents common, and progress painfully slow—just five to ten centimeters per day. The handmade tools simply made little impression on the subterranean rock.

Placer mining on the other hand involved scraping rock soil and flushing away the sediment. There followed a month of processing, which the curator explained in laborious detail, though it was impossible to follow the mind-numbing complexities involved. How did anyone come up with such a procedure? Figuring it out must have taken a team of geniuses.

Around the mine there developed a unique subculture. Shrines held special rituals to promote safety; red soil from the mines was used for pottery; there were original dance, song, and drum performances. Governors had well-appointed residences, and in the Meiji period foreign experts added a Western touch. Although Mitsubishi took it over for a while, a drastic downturn in productivity forced the closure of the mine in 1989.

On the way back, conversation turned from gold to a Japanese film with which Takayuki had been involved.

"Do you know, John-san, a film called *The Night My Number Came Up*?"

I confessed I didn't.

"It's a British film. Very famous in Sado."

"Really?"

"It's about a man who has a dream that a plane will crash."

"And does it?" I asked.

"Yes. In Sado."

"When was this?"

"In 1946," he said. "Just after the war."

"Oh? What happened?"

"Everyone on the plane survived, and the Sado people helped them. They could repair the plane and take off again."

I looked it up: an Ealing drama of 1955, starring Michael Redgrave and a young Denholm Elliott, with a rating of 7.1 on IMDb. It was based on a true story of a man who foresaw a British military plane crash on a beach during a snowstorm. Though it was only six months after the end of World War II, the villagers took in the survivors, helped repair the plane, and built an *ad hoc* runway.

The film Takayuki had helped with was a Japanese follow-up, called *Fly Dakota Fly*. It focused on events after the crash, and like *Whisky Galore* was a heart-warming story in which a whole village turns out to brave a wild sea.

"Do you know John-san, we used three thousand people for making the film. They built a runway, but instead of real stones they used *papier-mâché*."

I laughed. "And was it a success?"

"Yes. Famous actors. And some foreigners. I was translator."

"Interesting work."

"Yes," he said, nodding. "Some islanders could remember their parents talking about the crash. And one old man could remember seeing it as a child."

"So the film was shown in cinemas?"

"Yes. I think it was popular."

Again I looked it up. A slightly higher rating than the original, with a respectable 7.3. It had come out in 2013 to mark four hundred years of friendship with the UK (the first English ship arrived in Japan in 1613). "Because of the crash, we feel a special tie with England," Takayuki said. It was good to know that in Sado at least Anglo-Japanese relations were still flying high.

FOR MY LAST DAY on Sado, Takayuki took me to the headquarters of Kodo, Japan's most famous taiko group, known for their dedication and community lifestyle. Group bonding, exercises, and rigorous training are part of the daily regime. When we arrived, a couple of members were teaching basics to school children inside the custom-built hall. We used the time to look through photo albums cataloging tours and concerts, and I found to my surprise they had performed at England's WOMAD Festival the year I attended. Thinking back, I could just about remember some astonishing drumming—by the drummers of Burundi!

When the lesson finished, we chatted with the band members for a while, and I was invited to try my hand at drumming. Who could resist the biggest drum of all? In live performances bare-topped men stand before it in heroic pose with sweat running down rippling muscles as they pound it with all their might. My pusillanimous pummeling was nothing like that, however, and the tautness of the leather hurt my wrists. It was not surprising, for the only thing I had ever drummed was the keyboard of my computer.

It is said that taiko drums are imbued with the spirit of the trees from which they are made, in keeping with the animism that runs through Japanese culture. In this sense the drums "animate" the audience in a very real way.

"We believe the spirit of the tree from which the wood came enters into the drum," one of the Kodo members told me. "We see it as living, so we must look after it and treat it well."

"How about when you hit it?"

"It likes to be hit, because that is its purpose. It is happy to be a drum."

"How about the spirit of the person playing it?" I asked.

"Yes, that person's spirit can enter into the drum. There is a special connection."

It brought to mind swordsmiths, who invite spirits to enter into their swords. As a result, the bond of samurai with his sword was intensely personal, for the life of one was bound with that of the other. Similarly the masks of noh are treated as having a spiritual presence; when you put on the mask, you put on the persona that comes with it. Because the material world is infused with spirit, the result is a greater reverence for everyday objects and a recognition that the "inanimate" is not a separate entity. "Rocks are not dead," as Alan Watts put it. "Where there are rocks, watch out," he said, "for life will surely follow."

I was booked on the afternoon ferry, and on the way to the port Takayuki offered to show me one more place. By now I had a good idea of just how large Sado is, for we had crisscrossed the whole of the island, over forested mountains and across the large plain that divides north from south. I was more than grateful: I don't suppose he will ever read this, but should he do so, thank you, Takayuki!

The place we were headed for was a slope of Jizo statues set in a grove before a small Buddhist shrine. It was a remarkable scene. Big and small, quirky and sorrowful, there were statues of all types, dressed in character- istic red bibs. The bodhisattva guides the dead in the afterworld, and the statues were donated by the family of those who had died. Takayuki demon- strated how during the Obon holiday the islanders hold a Jizo behind their back and dance with the dead. Could there be a more graphic image of the bond Japanese feel with ancestral spirits?

My short time on the island had been enriching, for in Sado the past lingers in ways not evident in Japan's big cities. I could hardly have asked for a better last day—drums imbued with spirit, statues representing the dead. Animism and ancestor worship are the very bedrock on which rests Japanese spirituality, and they emerged in ancient times when nature and ancestor were seen as one. The supreme example is Amaterasu, at once sun goddess and progenitor of the imperial lineage. The divinity of the emperor was Japan's response to the mystery of existence.

On Track ||||||||||||||||||||||||||||||||||||||||||||||||||||

From Tsuruoka the limited express takes one hour forty-four minutes to Niigata. The line with its picturesque coastal views was the setting for a rare train crash in 2005, when the Inaho express bound for Niigata derailed shortly after being hit by strong winds while crossing a bridge over the Mogami River. With a population of nearly eight hundred thousand, Niigata is the biggest town on Japan's west coast, and its station-cum-shopping mall is suitably large, handling some thirty-seven thousand passengers daily.

There are two main ways of getting to Sado Island. From Niigata port the Sado Kisen car ferry takes two and a half hours to Ryotsu, the largest town on the island. Alternatively there is the jetfoil, for a speedy one hour. The other route is the seventy-five minute jetfoil to Ogi from the port of Naoetsu (not operating in winter). Niigata port is accessed from Niigata Station by a fifteen minute bus ride, and Naoetsu port is a six-minute ride from Naoetsu Station.

Niigata and Joetsu-Myoko

THE TRAIN JOURNEY FROM Tsuruoka to Niigata had been delightful, at least on the stretch to Murakami, with views of rocky headlands, small islands, and inlets where the incoming sea has carved bites out of the landmass. Here and there were fields peopled by scarecrows wearing traditional *monpe* trousers and straw hat, interspersed by long tunnels and a reminder that the mountains had not gone away. They never do in Japan.

For much of the way the track runs close to the sea, passing by fishing villages huddled together for comfort. Shinto shrines spoke of sea spirits, and *shimenawa* were draped between rocks in picturesque fashion. Old women bent double scoured for seaweed, while out at sea their menfolk bobbed up and down in distant boats. Basho had walked this route, and he apparently appreciated the seaside scenery.

Niigata, from where the ferry to Sado departs, is an industrial port of importance but not noted for its tourist attractions. The town exemplifies modernization, when much of Japan's heritage was jettisoned in favor of industrial catch-up. Will Ferguson, hitchhiking through here in *Hokkaido Blues,* described it as "sullied and soiled and worn-out." *The Rough Guide* is more generous, calling it "a likeable but unexciting city." *Lonely Planet* dismisses the town altogether, saying, "There is little to see in Niigata."

In 1879 Isabella Bird had a very different impression. Bird's Niigata is a "handsome, prosperous city" with beautiful tea houses, excellent theaters, attractive houses, and miniature gardens at the back of long narrow buildings. It is an Oriental Venice in which life centers around canals, and goods are delivered by boat. The town is picturesque, Bird tells us, but then adds an ominous note: "The Niigata of the Government, with its signs of progress in a western direction, is quite unattractive-looking as compared with the genuine Japanese Niigata." Here we have surely the earliest expression of the Lost Japan sentiment, which was to color the writing of Lafcadio Hearn and later commentators.

At the time of Bird's visit, the population was around 50,000. Now it is 797,000, which speaks for itself. The city is split in two by Japan's longest river, the Shinano, and there is a marked difference between the east and west sides. This owes itself to a massive tidal wave, five meters high, which in 1964 destroyed over ten thousand houses and led to a devastating conflagration. The result was the almost total demolition of the east bank, on which now stand shopping plazas and arcades. To the west, however, there is still a feel of how things used to be, with narrow streets hosting two-story houses, temples, shrines, and an entertainment area.

Like other coastal towns, Niigata prides itself on seafood and sake. Especially sake. Though officially it belongs to the Chubu region, for tourist purposes Niigata is bundled in with Tohoku in which nearly every area boasts of fresh mountain streams. Niigata more than most. Not only is its water supposedly the freshest, but its rice is the best, and its sake the most delicious. There are more or less one hundred breweries, and in March every year the city holds a grand festival with performances, seminars, and over five hundred different varieties to sample. This is the Oktoberfest of the sake world—except it is held in spring.

In a likely looking *izakaya* I asked about local specialties and was told sushi and soba. Anything else, I inquired? "Maybe, but the fish here is fresher than any other fish, and the soba here has a *dashi* stock better than any other." It seemed I would have to choose one of them, but then my eye caught sight of a notice pinned above the counter saying, "Niigata special Noppe stew." A quick internet check identified it as soy-flavored *dashi* thickened by starch and containing an assortment of vegetables, with salmon roe, chicken, or potato. That would have done nicely, but, alas, the lack of visitors meant it was no longer available. It was a rare occasion when I wished there were more tourists.

And so I stuck to good old soba, which turned out to have a local touch after all, for *hegi* soba comes in snake-like coils mixed with *funori* seaweed. Afterwards I got to enjoy *sasadango*, a Japanese sweet colored dark green by mugwort, filled with red bean paste, and wrapped in bamboo leaves. Natural ingredients, nice aroma, and definitely *oishii*!

FOR THE RETURN FROM Sado I chose the ferry that runs south to the port of Naoetsu, part of Joetsu City. I planned to stay overnight in the area, handy for the rail connection to Toyama. A quick surf of the internet told me the small town of Joetsu hosted a huge thermal power station and once held the record for Japan's heaviest snowfall. Takayuki had told me it had formerly been of importance to Sado, because the feudal lord there owned the island. It seemed promising enough.

It was already dark when the bus from the port drew up in front of a small station building. It was dwarfed by a massive complex, which had swallowed the little station whole. The scale of one had no relation to the other, and oddly enough the juxtaposition was mirrored in the station sur-rounds, where a handful of high rises towered over rural shacks. Strangest of all, from what I could see there was no town.

My hotel was close by, and I asked the receptionist why there was such a big station and no people. She seemed as surprised by the question as I was by the situation.

"There are people when the Shinkansen train arrives," she said.

"But why build such a huge station without a town?"

"Maybe because the land was cheap," she replied.

"I see, but how can you get passengers if there is no town?"

"Mm, it is difficult. Our hotel only started last year. We were unlucky because of Covid, but at Obon we had many guests."

I ordered a shiatsu massage, and in between pressing my acupressure points the masseuse told me of the infamous Kakuei Tanaka. A Niigata man, he dominated national politics from the 1960s to 1980s, trailing behind him the whiff of corruption.

Suspected of ties to the yakuza, Tanaka was known for "pork-barrel politics," winning a string of industrial contracts for his hometown. Factories, hospitals, and road and rail projects rained down on the city. Not surprisingly, voters re-elected him with enthusiasm, considering him a *kamisama* (god). The cozy arrangement came to a head in the great Lockheed scandal, involving massive bribery payments. Sentenced to four years in prison, he never served time, dying before an appeal could be heard.

The Hokuriku Shinkansen line on which the Joetsu-Myoko Station stands opened in 2015 and at the time of writing terminates in Kanazawa. It has proved the most expensive line so far, with almost a third of the length tunneling through mountains. Objections to the station's location were waved away with the claim that urbanization would soon follow. In other words, instead of building a station for a big town, a big town would be built for the station.

The project can be seen as a microcosm of Japanese politics. Since 1955 the country has been almost exclusively controlled by the conservative-minded Liberal Democratic Party (neither liberal nor democratic, as is often pointed out). The result is a virtual one-party system, which draws on elderly voters in rural areas, who have a disproportionate weight in electoral terms. The arrangement fosters large-scale projects of dubious worth, and as a consequence there are roads leading nowhere, huge bridges to tiny islands, and fine art museums in places with few art lovers.

And so it is that at Joetsu-Myoko rice fields are more evident than houses. Walk just a couple of minutes from the station, and there is a noticeboard at the edge of extensive rice fields stating that they produce the Koshihikari variety, regarded as Japan's finest. And where there is fine rice there is fine sake, which is why the area lays claim to Japan's best.

On the other side of the station from my hotel was a statue of a mounted samurai, dressed for battle. Local hero Kenshin Uesugi was a commander in the Sengoku (Warring States) period (1476–1615), celebrated every year in a festival in neighboring Joetsu. A popular figure in television dramas, he is noted for his adherence to justice. Now, ironically, he stands guard over a monument to political corruption.

At the information office there were brochures that told of nearby ski resorts, hot springs, and mountaineering, but I was happy to forgo all that and take a break from the constant traveling. Rice fields would do nicely. And so here with nothing but a Shinkansen station, I holed up for a few days, only emerging to cross the tracks to get to the convenience store. There was little distraction. A few scattered buildings and a large car park on one side, a couple of business hotels on the other.

My route to the convenience store took me along a straight, immaculately clean corridor which crossed the station, at the end of which was a grand piano. On one occasion it was being played with great gusto by a high school student. It was seven thirty in the evening, when major stations are packed with commuters, but here there was just one other person visible in the whole edifice. With its fluorescent lighting, the corridor could have come straight out of a Kubrick movie.

Mine was the tallest of the business hotels, with a what-were-they-thinking eighteen floors, which offered panoramic views of nothing very much. At this point let me make a confession. Unlike Alan Booth and his catalog of cheap *ryokan*, I was using a standardized chain of business hotels called Toyoko Inn. They offer convenience at a cut-rate price, and I like to think of them as the Uniqlo of business hotels—cheap but dependable, customer friendly, and efficient. In short, value for money. Most importantly for a train traveler, and this is key, they are almost always located a few minutes' walk from the main rail station. And where there is a rail station, there is invariably an information office and buses that run to all parts of the town.

The first Toyoko Inn was erected in 1986, and now there are 270 with the beginnings of expansion abroad. You wonder if they will ever stop. Every Japanese town has one, and large metropolises have several. The rooms are cramped but kitted out with everything a traveler might need. The hotels provide *yukata*, plenty of hot water, and even a free breakfast.

The staff are almost exclusively female, and so is the company head, Maiko Kuroda, daughter of the man who started it all. "Feminine hospitality" is the concept. In pre-Covid time the hotels were often booked out, and the company holds the Guinness world record for the largest hotel chain to be fully occupied—48,831 rooms in 249 hotels on May 2, 2015. As always in Japan the staff are hardworking. The receptionist told me she worked a twenty-five-hour shift, then two days off. "It is okay for me, but I think it is better for young people," she added. "Sometimes we cannot sleep very much."

Close to the hotel was a hot spring bath, doing a busy trade. I presumed it was because there was nothing else to do. There was an *inaka* (rural) feel to the clientele, and I was aware of eyes fixed on the unusual sight of a foreigner. Aware of the responsibility of representing gaijin as a whole, I made a special point of doing things the proper way by lathering up and double washing every single inch of my body. Meanwhile, someone had come in and sat on the floor behind me. He was splashing himself with water, and I could feel some of it on my back. It was a shocking breach of etiquette, and I showed disapproval by tutting as I stepped over him. It was at this point I noticed he had tattoos all down his back. Whoops! I had crossed a yakuza.

In the communal bath I made myself as small as possible, but he got in and turned his back towards me, spreading himself in such a way that I was squeezed in a corner. He looked round and eyed me in a way I can only describe as a glare. I smiled back, sheepishly. There was no way out without passing him at very close quarters, so I remained stuck in very hot water. Everyone else was very deliberately not noticing this at all.

When I arrived in Japan, the yakuza were easy to recognize, as they wore punch perms and badges showing their affiliation. However, in 1991 it was made illegal to belong to "violent gangs," after which they camouflaged themselves as salarymen. A missing finger could still mark them out, as would their tattoos, which is why swimming pools and some public baths ban them. (My American friend, who had a butterfly tattooed on her shoulder, was once asked to leave a water park.)

The closest I had come to crossing a yakuza before was, ironically, on a pedestrian crossing. As I stepped off the pavement, a car came speeding around a bend and nearly cut me down. "*Bakayaro*" (stupid idiot), I inadvertently yelled out, which is about as rude as it gets in Japan. The car screeched to a halt and a sumo-sized man got out in a rage and, digging into his tracksuit pocket, took out a handful of coins and threw them at me. They flew harmlessly past, which prompted me to say, "Not very good, are you," at which he went apoplectic and unleashed a tirade of incomprehensible Japanese, the gist of which was clear enough. He was overweight, so I did a pretty good Forrest Gump impression by running like the wind all the way to the university. And so it was that at full speed the visiting lecturer in English was seen racing across campus and disappearing into his study room, leaving a trail of bewildered students in his wake.

Following my close encounter in the hot spring bath, I felt it was time for me to leave Joetsu-Myoko and press on with my journey. The ticket office urged me to take the Shinkansen to Toyama, but the little private line that ran along the coast looked more appealing, and the enterprising company, Echigo Tokimeki, offered an excellent station-by-station brochure. Many of the hamlets through which the line runs have little to offer, but the pamphlet tries its hardest to promote them. Hats off to the PR team! The main attraction of Omi, for instance, is a derelict switching yard, relic of its manufacturing days. Worth getting off the train for? I don't think so. Nice to know as you pass blithely by? Sure.

At one point the train stops at the place where skiing was introduced in 1911 by the splendidly named Major Theodore von Leerch of the Austro-Hungarian army. Imagine the reaction of the locals as a crazy foreigner went hurtling down slopes they had spent their whole life gazing at in trepidation. Von Leerch is honored now at the Japan Ski Memorial Museum, another instance of the strong sense of gratitude felt by Japanese to foreigners who have contributed to their culture.

As the train rumbled along, rain and mist obscured views of the coast, where shrouded shapes loomed into view then faded into the distance. Bays appeared briefly but were quickly enveloped again. Stations were small and, perhaps because of the weather, deserted. At one unmanned station there was only a lone crow waiting.

At Ichiburi we had to change trains, which was apt since it marked the Edo-period checkpoint between the ancient provinces of Echigo and Etchu. Basho and Sora would have checked in too as they wandered their way along this coast, clambering over boulders and negotiating cliffs. Intrepid souls. What on earth would they have thought about the huge concrete pillars sunk into the ocean bed to carry cars along an elevated highway? What kind of haiku would that inspire?

Along the way the pair of poets encountered two prostitutes on a pilgrimage to Ise, but the men made it plain they were more interested in poetry than company. I wondered if they would have walked on stormy days like this, when even the train seemed happy to take shelter? One of the tunnels extended for long minutes on end and contained a station midway, like something out of Harry Potter. It felt as if a portal had opened into a different dimension, and in a way it had, for I was being transported back into the past, back to my old stomping ground of Hokuriku. Clouds, rain, and wind—it was appropriate weather for the region too.

On Track ||||||||||||||||||||||||||||||||||||||||||||||||||||

The Joetsu-Myoko Station opened in 2015 as part of the Hokuriku Shinkansen, which connects Tokyo with Kanazawa. From Joetsu-Myoko it takes one hour forty-eight minutes to Tokyo and one hour to Kanazawa. The station also houses the Echigo Tokimeki company, founded in 2010. It operates two lines with a total of twenty-three stations. At weekends it runs a smartly decorated two-carriage resort train with the poetic name of Setsugekka (Snow-moon flower).

Niigata has been a leading promoter of train tourism, boasting a selection of gastronomic trains, steam trains, and art trains. They are fitted out with specially designed carriages, large viewing windows, and luxurious seating.

Confusingly there is a Joetsu Shinkansen, which runs directly from Tokyo to Niigata but does not stop at Joetsu. It was first proposed in 1971 by the infamous Kakuei Tanaka, who is said to have used a red pen to draw his preferred route on a map. In 2004 the line suffered the Shinkansen's first ever derailment, due to an earthquake. Thanks to the emergency braking system, there were no fatalities or injuries.

Hokuriku

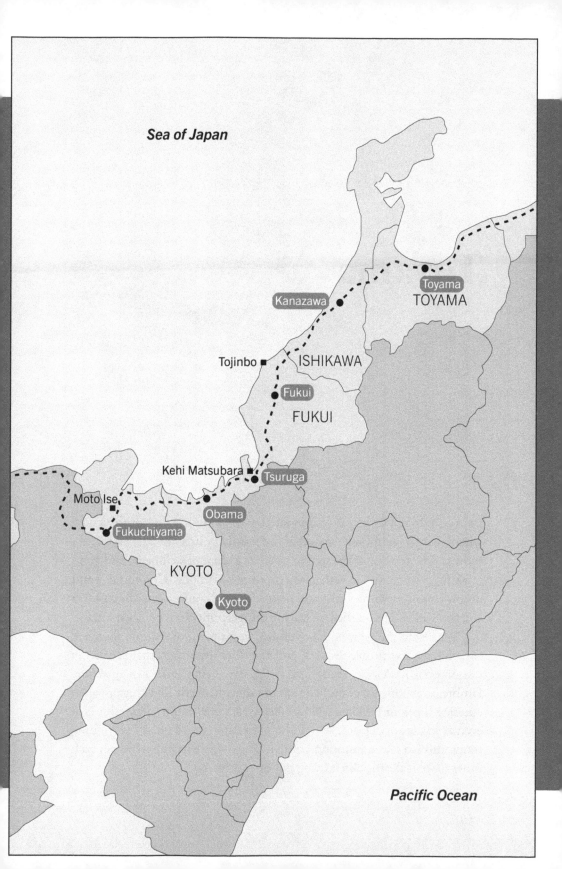

Sea of Japan

Toyama
TOYAMA

Kanazawa

Tojinbo
ISHIKAWA

Fukui
FUKUI

Kehi Matsubara
Tsuruga

Moto Ise
Obama

Fukuchiyama

KYOTO

Kyoto

Pacific Ocean

Toyama

OF ALL THE MANY places I have visited on my travels, I cannot recall anywhere that so completely embodies the word "bourgeois" as Toyama. As soon as you step out of the station, there is a sense of well-being and good taste. Everywhere you look there is a pleasing orderliness. Comfortable and deeply conservative, it exudes middle-of-the-road conformity. Touch a taxi and you will be admonished for leaving a fingerprint on its polished surface.

Where are the crowds, you wonder? For a town of 418,000 there are surprisingly few people around, and the cute little tram that serves the station even has empty seats. This is the easy-living town *par excellence*. Umbrellas are opened at the first hint of rain, and neatly folded again when entering buses or buildings. No homeless, no graffiti, no vandalism. Not even a bicycle out of place. With its litter-free streets and smoothly running trams, this is a self-monitoring Truman Show where neighbors watch each other to see if the rubbish is being put out correctly.

Consumerism is the name of the game, and high-end department stores boast toilets as plush as those of a Hollywood mansion. Non-threatening artwork pulls in well-heeled customers, and brand names scream from every corner. You have the feeling everything here is tightly controlled. Formulaic politeness eases social interaction, and spontaneity can be unsettling.

In surveys about the quality of life, Toyama Prefecture is always near the top, thanks to the prosperity and pleasant environment. The town is located by the side of a bay, with spectacular views of the Japanese Alps. The combination of sea and mountains means the fish is fresher, the air cleaner, and the water clearer than pretty much anywhere in Japan.

There are any number of well-endowed art galleries and culture halls, which owe themselves to a generous level of funding derived from the prefecture's industries—pharmaceuticals, electronic parts, and metal products. The town's leading attraction is a glass-art museum, housed in a light and airy building worth seeing in itself. Designed by famous architect Kengo Kuma, the building is shared with the city library, which explains the number of visitors who carry books and never show up in the museum. The exhibitions can be dazzling, but the highlight is invariably the spectacular glass-art garden by master artist Dale Chihuly. Even those uninterested in glass are wowed by this.

The prefecture's Tateyama is one of Japan's "three holy mountains" (together with Fuji and Hakusan). At the top, a Shinto priest waves a purification stick over bowed heads. In my early days in Japan this was puzzling to me, so I asked the priest to explain.

"You pay me money and I purify you," he said.

"I see," I replied, "but is there something more? For example, rules on how to behave in everyday life." There was a short pause.

"Yes," came the answer, "you pay me and I purify you."

At the time I thought the answer amusing. Later, as I came to understand more about traditional religions, I realized he was right. The concern is not with morality, but with harmonizing with the spirit world. Whereas the material world is characterized by unease and decay, the spirit world is free of taint. Pure purity, in other words. The waving of the magic wand is the Japanese acknowldgement of what Arthur Koestler called "the ghost in the machine," the animating spirit that lies within the physical body. Here at the top of the mountain the priest was evoking oneness with the universe.

IT WAS POURING WITH rain when I arrived, and despite being familiar with the Hokuriku proverb, "You can forget your lunch box, but don't forget your umbrella," I had not bothered to bring one. No matter, I thought, the hotel is just five minutes' walk away, but such was the downpour that I arrived completely drenched.

The rain clouds of Hokuriku are linked in the public mind with the insular character of the populace, different from the sunshine smiles of those in southern regions. My connection with the region went back to my earliest days in Japan and a private student called Terada-san. As is often the case, she felt able to say things in English that she would be too embarrassed to say in Japanese, and the lessons were more akin to therapy than language learning.

Daughter of a bank manager, Terada-san had unexpectedly opted for an arranged marriage on graduation. It was the late 1980s, and arranged marriages were on the way out in favor of "love marriages." All her friends were determined to choose for themselves, but Terada-san was happy to tread the traditional path.

For the older generation, arranged marriage had been common practice, and one of my university colleagues confessed that he had only seen his wife for fifteen minutes before agreeing to marry her. Nonetheless, he said, they had enjoyed forty-five years of marital happiness. "You grow to love each other," he explained, "and if you don't you grow to hate each other. Either way, you stay together."

It was some time since my last meeting with Terada-san, and in response to my suggestion that we meet, she had chosen a typical Toyama restaurant called Gomangoku. The name derives from *koku*, a traditional measurement of rice, roughly the amount a single person needed to survive for a year. Feudal domains were estimated in size according to how many *koku* they generated. Toyama rated a modest *gomangoku* (fifty thousand *koku*), whereas its mighty neighbor, Kaga, was valued at one million.

However, it is not bushels of rice on which modern Toyama prides itself, but on the seafood from its abundant bay. Most famous is the firefly squid (*hotaruika*), a luminous little creature considered a spring delicacy. They are either eaten dried, or the intestines are fermented and served in a small cup.

Sadly the firefly squid was out of season, but our set meal included one of Toyama's most famous products—white shrimp (*shiroebi*), considered "the jewel of Toyama Bay." Small, soft, and sweet, it was served in a mouth-watering clump and deserved its place of honor. Along with this was another local specialty, *kobujime*, which is fish preserved between strips of *konbu* seaweed. Such was the presentation that one fancied it would not disgrace banquets at the imperial palace, yet this was standard fare for the goodly citizens of Toyama.

Seafood might have taken pride of place, but there was plenty of variety, for along with *chawanmushi* (steamed egg) were small servings of bamboo shoot, okra, and *namafu* (gluten), as well as a potato cube and a neat square of tofu. Each item, less than a mouthful, was prepared so as to draw out the natural flavor. The result was that for a satisfying half an hour all the cares of the world no longer existed—climate change, overfishing, unsustainability, plastic pollution, the end of life as we know it—all dissolved in one exquisite taste after another.

In between eating, Terada-san and I had time to catch up with each other's news. I remembered talk of her childhood and the way the family had to move every few years, whenever her father's job demanded it.

"How long before moving did you know where you would go?" I asked.

"Mm, about a week or ten days," she replied.

"Wasn't that a problem?"

"Not really. We knew it would be like that."

"So where did you live?"

"We moved about every three years. I was born in Toyama, and from three to six we lived in Saitama, then back to Toyama. Then when I was nine we went to Osaka, after that Hokkaido. When I was sixteen, we were based in Kanazawa."

"Did you mind moving? Was it troublesome?"

"Not really. I quite liked it. We could know different places."

"Which did you like best?"

"Osaka. There were many things to do. It was fun."

"At university I remember you were living on your own."

"Yes, at first I lived with my parents, but I didn't like it. They scolded me if I came in late."

"You had a curfew?"

"Yes, ten. It's too early," she laughed. "So I often broke it."

Beneath her modest demeanor lurked a rebellious spirit.

Mindful of my request to try something local, Terada-san had ordered *genge*, a fish found in deep water in Toyama Bay. "It can be eaten dried, or fried, or put in miso soup," she told me. "It is full of collagen, so women like it." Though I had visited Toyama several times, the fish was completely new to me, but keeping up with varieties of fish in Japan is a taxing proposition, for ten percent of fish caught in the world is consumed in the country. There are over four thousand varieties in the waters round Japan, of which, remarkably, some three hundred can be eaten.

"At university I remember you studied geography," I continued. "Why did you choose that?"

"Because my teacher at high school was friendly. And he was good looking."

"Hah, that reminds me that you joined the Yacht Club because of the boys, even though you didn't like sailing."

Terada-san laughed. "Yes, I was manager."

"Manager? You had to coach people how to sail?"

"No, I had to cook when they had meetings."

"But doesn't the manager have to manage the sailing?"

"No. Just cooking."

"Wasn't it a lot of work?"

"Yes. But I like cooking."

"What kind of things did you make?"

"Curry rice, miso soup, salad. Boiled things like hot pot."

After the meal the conversation drifted back to the time of Terada-san's arranged marriage, for many of her English lessons had centered on the topic. The idea had been suggested by an aunt, who took the role of go-between and made tentative enquiries among her acquaintances. The first step involved a formal photograph, presented with information about the young man's background. If both parties agreed, a meeting would be set up with the go-between in attendance.

In Terada-san's case the first attempt had not worked, for there was a mismatch between the photo and the disappointing reality. The second candidate was more pleasing and a good listener. After the initial pleasantries, the aunt withdrew to let the couple chat, and both sides subsequently reported a wish to continue.

The second meeting was a "car date," fashionable at the time and typically involving a drive to a scenic spot with a break for refreshment. A further ten dates followed, after which the couple agreed to meet their prospective parents-in-law and ask for their blessing. There was one problem. Sex. Or rather the lack of it. The couple had not engaged physically, which raised in Terada-san the very real concern that her partner might be homosexual. Gay men in the 1980s often hid their sexuality in order to conform, and this was particularly true in conservative areas like Hokuriku. It was such common practice that my university students genuinely thought that homosexuals did not exist at all in Japan.

So concerned was Terada-san that her friends suggested to her that she should try a love hotel. "I couldn't do that," she told me, "because he might be shocked and cancel the marriage." But as the wedding day approached, she mustered enough courage to confront him and get a confession that he was simply nervous of what her parents might think. Post-marital consummation followed, and a daughter was born.

This was all thirty years ago, and much in Japan had changed since then. Arranged marriages still exist, though few in number. My friend Hirota-san had tried three times with no success. How did Terada-san feel about it in retrospect? Had it worked out well? She had a secure life and was close to her daughter, she said. I noticed, however, she was not wearing a wedding ring. How were things with her husband? "I don't dislike him," she said.

Afterwards talk turned to her teaching job. When her daughter had reached seventeen, Terada-san had sought work outside the house. Japan does not offer the flexibility of some countries in terms of jobs, but being a graduate meant that she was able to work as a teaching assistant, though with little pay. "It's like volunteer work till you can get a contract." she said. High school teachers are known to have a heavy workload, so I asked what duties she had.

"I have to manage a class," she said. "There are about a thousand students in the junior high, and they are divided into three years. Students are aged thirteen to fifteen. But there are also many chores to do outside the class. Paperwork, for instance. Now I have to address envelopes for reminders to parents to pay the school fees. Also I have to calculate expenses and get the forms signed by five different people—head, deputy head, admin officer, and two grade supervisors. It is very troublesome."

"I've heard clubs and circles take up teachers' time too."

"Yes. I'm manager of basketball. Actually I don't know anything about the rules of basketball, but I just watch in case of injuries or problems. It's my responsibility on behalf of parents. It's called *sabisu zangyo* [unpaid overtime]."

"How much time does it take on average?"

"Usually I have to be there five times a week. Maybe two hours, or an hour and a half. It's okay for me, I like the students. They are cute. And I'm lucky because my husband helps with housework."

Given her rebellious streak, I couldn't help wondering how she felt about a life spent in Toyama, tied to family and teaching. Her answer, though, did not suggest dissatisfaction. It was an easy place to live, no crowds, no queues, the environment was good, the food delicious, there was mountain scenery. On the other hand there was nothing very exciting, the winters were long and cold, there was small-town gossip. And one more thing:

"There were few Covid cases here. So we were lucky. But there was one big outbreak. A student in Kansai caught the virus and brought it home to Toyama. Her family was harassed because of that and had to move house. And she got a mental problem. It's also a small-town problem, I think."

The reunion with Terada-san had proved heartwarming, and not since the meeting with Lily had I had such a frank conversation. It is said that it is difficult to make close friends in Japan, because the tendency is to keep one at arm's length. No idle chat at the cashier desk, no befriending of strangers. Those who associate with gaijin are often rebels, misfits, or have spent time in the West. Others are unfailingly polite, there is never hostility, yet somehow there is a distancing and the foreigner remains forever representative of a different culture.

The frequency and intimacy of English lessons serve to bridge the social distancing, and Terada-san was a case in point. As she herself confessed, she would not have been so open even with her friends. Speaking a different language is the linguistic equivalent of donning a mask, as it allows freedom from the usual restraints. Some of the best insights into the culture come from private lessons, yet ironically it is the teacher who gets paid.

During my early years in Japan I learnt all about the business world from a company chairman who took me to restaurants and hostess bars way out of my budget range. I learnt a lot about the medical system from teaching a university doctor and his wife, with the benefit of free medical advice. And I learnt a lot about politics and how the justice system works (and does not work) from a human rights lawyer active on behalf of the Communist Party.

But it was my very first private lesson that opened my eyes to the hidden depths of Japanese society. The students were three middle-aged women, conventional, polite, and well-mannered. But as the weeks went by, it became apparent that beneath their outer conformity they were leading unusual lives. One was married to a doctor in whom she had little interest. Another was a forty-year-old virgin, worried that her lack of sexual experience was restricting her art. And the third was a lesbian married to a gay man with whom, after one attempt at making love, she had agreed to share her life but seek satisfaction elsewhere.

Outwards conformity masking a rich inner life is something that struck Pico Iyer at West Point, the US military academy. He devotes a section to it in *A Beginner's Guide to Japan,* describing how he found that in the subjugation of the self lay a framework that fostered remarkable individuals. The courtesy, the self-discipline, the uniformity, and adherence to rules—what do the regimented individuals remind him of? Yes, indeed, Japan.

On Track ||||||||||||||||||||||||||||||||||||||||||||||||

Toyama has a reputation for being a user-friendly "train town," with trams and private companies in addition to JR. Toyama Station, first built in 1899, hosts the Hokuriku Shinkansen, which was opened in 2015. Also serving the station is the Takayama Main Line, completed in 1934, which runs from Gifu and takes in tourist attractions such as Gero Onsen, the mountain town of Takayama, and the World Heritage site of Shirakawa-go.

Adjacent to the JR station is the Dentetsu-Toyama Station, operated by the Toyama Chiho Company. As well as trams, it manages three lines, which access Unazuki Onsen, Kurobe Gorge, and the Tateyama Cable Car. It also runs scenic viewing trains such as the Alps Express, with bar, wide windows, and spacious seating, as well as a retro train harking back to 1965, notable for its gleaming woodwork.

Kanazawa

AH, KANAZAWA!

City of my rebirth, of my second childhood, when illiterate and uncomprehending, I found every day brought a new wonder, a learning experience, a fresh insight. A city with which I fell heavily in love—and then heavily out. Kanazawa is forever stamped on my heart.

Thirty years ago foreigners were registered as "aliens," and it did indeed feel as if one had landed on a different planet. I knew little of the country, less of the culture, and nothing of the language. In Britain I had been struggling to survive by writing textbooks, but far from keeping my head above water I was slowly drowning. As is often the way, a chance encounter determined the rest of my life, and before I knew it, I was on my way to a town in Japan of which I had never previously heard.

Of all Japan's "little Kyotos," Kanazawa is the biggest and best. The epithet refers to towns that in the past drew on the culture of the imperial capital. In the case of Kanazawa, the legacy owes itself to an influential *daimyo* called Maeda Toshiie (1538–99). As a result the town of 440,000 punches well above its weight. Geisha district, gold leaf, Kutani pottery, *yuzen* dyeing, noh theater, lacquerware, and one of Japan's "top-three landscape gardens." Add to that a ninja temple, samurai house, reconstructed castle, and the highly popular 21st Century Museum of Contemporary Art, and you can see why it has become a top tourist destination.

Compared with Toyama, there is a buzz to Kanazawa. People walk faster, there is a more purposeful feel, a greater sense of activity. Views of the Northern Alps may be enough for Toyama, but Kanazawa makes greater effort. After the Hokuriku Shinkansen was completed in 2015, few got off at Toyama, but at Kanazawa the platform was crowded.

The town has rich literary associations. Basho wrote haiku here, and it is the birthplace of Zen proselytizer D. T. Suzuki (his home is now a museum). The town's two rivers also have celebrated connections, for fantasy writer Izumi Kyoka grew up near the Asano River, while the poet Muro Saisei wrote of his fondness for the Sai River.

> This beautiful river
> Near which I lived
> Seated on its bank, home to
> Spring flowers in spring,
> Summer flowers in summer,
> Attentive to books of love and compassion
> Still now the river flowing—
> Beautiful breeze
> Rippling blue waves

Japan in the 1980s was very different from today. The country was on a roll, and books spoke of it as Number One. It acted the part by buying up prestigious real estate, leading to resentment and disparaging descriptions. "Workaholics living in rabbit hutches," was an often-heard phrase (attributed to an obscure EU bureaucrat). Western media portrayed the people as exotic and bizarre, typified on British TV by a program called *Gaman*, little known in Japan, which tested how long participants could endure conditions such as being locked in a room with no toilet.

By the late 1980s, the "bubble economy" was full-blown and money was being thrown around like confetti, some of which to my good fortune landed on me. I prided myself on being a seasoned traveler—close encounters with the KGB; three months in a German hospital; three years in the Middle East; marriage to a Yemeni; ten months doing the hippie trail; a night in a Saudi jail; mugged in Sri Lanka; a bad trip in Kathmandu; stranded on a Javan volcano. Little could faze me, I thought. Then I arrived in Japan and was hit by a cultural tsunami.

It struck me the very first morning, when a taciturn professor told me to take breakfast while he went to a meeting. A tray set before me held fish, an egg, chopped cabbage, miso soup, and rice. I seized on the egg and cracked it open against the side of the table. A slimy glob oozed down to the floor, followed by the yellowish yolk. Of all the stupid things, I thought, they forgot to boil it.

Seeing what had happened, a waitress cleared up the mess, brought another egg and showed me how to crack it over the warm rice. Out of gratitude I tried to pass her a tip, but she refused, and in the commotion the money fell to the floor. Heads turned. I felt that I had been caught in the act, though what act I was unsure. I never tried to tip again.

Over the next few weeks new experiences rained down on me. When I entered shops, people yelled out something unintelligible, and the bottle of mayonnaise I bought, when poured onto a salad, turned out to be shampoo. I could not distinguish a restaurant from a shop, and if I asked a question the answer would invariably be "Maybe." The market was so full of mysterious items that I came away empty-handed, and though I learnt the phrase for "no meat" waiters would nonetheless bring me something with pork or chicken. It was all very baffling, so when I came across Lafcadio Hearn's initial impressions of Japan in the 1890s, they resonated with me.

> Food-stuffs of unimaginable derivation; utensils of enigmatic forms; emblems incomprehensible of some mysterious belief; strange masks and toys that commemorate legends of gods or demons; odd figures, too, of the gods themselves, with monstrous ears and smiling faces.

The famed drinking district of Katamachi (three thousand bars set around a couple of crossroads) was ten minutes' walk from my apartment, and on my first outing there I was befriended by an amiable drunk who took me to a small bar where we sat at the counter in front of "Mama-san." My companion had limited English, but one phrase he knew was "sex friend," which he repeated over and over as he pointed at Mama-san. She waved a hand dismissively and made sure to pour us generous amounts from his "bottle keep" of quality whisky. The next day at the university I told the departmental secretary about it and pulled out a name card. "Ah," she said, "he is head of a famous temple." It was my introduction to one aspect of Japanese Buddhism.

In those early days it often seemed I was living in a Wonderland, and some of the conversations conjured up the spirit of Lewis Carroll. Even attending a student party could lead to utter confusion.

"Please give me ticket," said the student at the front desk.

"What ticket?" I asked.

"Pardon?"

"Do I need a ticket? I don't have one."

"Eh?"

"How much is the ticket?"

"Twenty-five hundred yen."

"Okay, so I will pay twenty-five hundred yen." I fished the money out of my pocket.

"Thank you. I am sorry."

"No need to be sorry. How about my ticket?"

"Eh?'

"I paid twenty-five hundred. Do I get a ticket?"

"You want ticket one more?"

"No, not one more. I want the ticket I paid for."

"No ticket."

"You mean I don't need a ticket?"

"No," said the student emphatically. I was confused. Was that "No, I don't need," or was it, "No, you do need?"

"So I can go in without a ticket?" I tried to clarify things.

"Maybe."

"Okay, I will try without a ticket."

"Without ticket no good."

"But I just bought a ticket. Can't you give me one of those?"

"It is rainy day."

"Sorry?"

"It is ticket for rainy day."

My attempts at Japanese were equally haphazard, and learning the language was full of challenges. Many words sound similar, so it was easy to mix up *ninjin* (carrot) with *ningen* (person) and ask how many vegetables live in Kanazawa. Once you input a word mentally, it is difficult to erase, and still to this day I am prone to confuse the mating habit of pigeons (*hato*) with flags (*hata*). Worst of all, I once embarrassingly enquired of a sophisticated lady if there would be any excrement to sit on at our picnic spot, mistaking *kuso* (shit) for *kusa* (grass).

For an English speaker, the Japanese language has some daunting differences. There are no plurals; a single sound can have multiple meanings; there are three written scripts; you need two thousand kanji to read a newspaper; seventy percent of spoken sentences have no subject; and there are different ways of counting depending on the size, shape, or type of what is being counted. Those are just the basics.

Language difference also opens up a gap in humor, for jokes that work in one language may not in the other. I suggested to Lili once that Japanese suffer from inferiority (*rettou*) because they live in an archipelago (*rettou*). She was not amused. Written in Roman letters the words read the same, but in Japanese they are differentiated by the use of kanji. The joke thus seemed childish, for only a child unable to read would find the similar sound to be amusing.

On the other hand, there are rewarding moments that greatly enrich the learning process. Almost at the start, with mastery of the phonetic scripts (hiragana and katakana), there comes the realization that mysterious items on the cafe menu simply say *kohi*, *keki*, and *sando* (coffee, cake, and sandwich). And I still remember the thrill of coming across four different scripts in a short book title, *Poems of D. H. Lawrence*: Poems (kanji), of (hiragana), D. H. (Roman letters), Lawrence (katakana).

Loan words are a topic to themselves, and there are whole dictionaries devoted to them. "It has got to the point where if you do not know English, you cannot understand Japanese," said a commentator on television. The loan words make acquiring vocabulary easier, but they can be unrecognizable to a native speaker. Not only are they adapted to Japanese pronunciation, but longer words are shortened to make them manageable. Take *bodicon, eacon,* and *mazacon* for instance, where the first "-con" stands for "conscious," the second for "conditioner," and the third for "complex."

The language divide means that blind spots occur on both sides. The l/r problem is well known, though it is still startling to see grass wine on a menu, or to be told by a friend she has "a lusty bicycle," or indeed to hear a flight attendant tell you to "Have a present fright." For their part Westerners have trouble differentiating the short and long vowels that occur in Japanese, and I was once taken aback when a student told me she had a job at Sexy House—it turned out she was employed in a construction company called Sekisui House.

WHEN I LANDED IN Kanazawa, there were just eighty Westerners in a city of 460,000. I did not know any of them, and for my first year I felt pretty much isolated, apart from a German colleague equally at sea, whose mantra was, "What the hell is going on?" He told me one day that because of confusion about the floor number he had gone to the wrong classroom (European "ground floor" is the Japanese first floor). For fifteen minutes he had been trying hard with beginner's German: "Ich komme aus Deutschland. Woher kommen Sie?" The students were all attention, but no one answered. Suddenly a knock came at the door. Outside was a nervous looking Japanese professor. "Excuse me, but I think it is my class," he said. "I am teaching Japanese history." For fifteen minutes the students had sat silently, perplexed by the intimidatingly tall gaijin talking in a strange language. What the hell is going on, he wondered. Why did none of the students tell him?

The paucity of gaijin meant we were treated as minor celebrities, and as a redhead I found that I was not just an honored guest but an object of fascination. A little boy once asked if he could have a piece of my beard to show his mother, and if I showed up for a tennis match it would automatically become an "international" tennis match.

As a visiting lecturer, I was told my purpose was internationalization, though no one could explain what that meant. It had something to do with the "gaijin complex," which was explained as nervousness around foreigners. It may be hard to imagine now in an age of mass tourism, but things were very different thirty years ago when it was not uncommon to meet people who had never spoken with a foreigner before.

The full extent of the complex came home to me one day when there was a knock at my office door. "Come in," I shouted. Nothing happened. Again there was a knock. "*Ohairi*," I called out. Silence. I walked over to the door, and there in the corridor was a student hyperventilating. I thought it must be asthma and got her a glass of water, but it turned out she simply wanted to ask if she could join my class. Such was her nervousness that she had a panic attack. I doubt such things happen these days.

At the time there was an assumption that all Westerners were American, a legacy from the Occupation. I was asked so many times which part of America I was from that I developed set responses—"The part with a Queen," for instance. The obsession was reflected in school textbooks, where every detail of Japanese culture was contrasted with that of the US, from baby care to body size, from food to relationships. This could result in some odd conversations, such as the taxi driver who asked me, "American?" And when I answered in Japanese that I was British, continued with, "In America, sky what color?"

There was a popular saying at the time, "University is a four-year holiday from the rest of life." I soon learned why. Student priorities lay with clubs and circles, part-time jobs, and dating. After all, they had studied hard to get into university and needed a break. It was still the era of "examination hell," when entrance was highly competitive. Now in an age of a falling birthrate colleges are virtually begging students to apply.

At first I tried teaching the way I had been trained in the UK, but soon ran into difficulties. Speaking out in groups was frowned upon as egotistical, so there was a reluctance by students to stand out by answering questions. A lot of effort went into not responding, and I came to understand why books said silence was the natural mode of communication. A common strategy was to turn and consult others, or pretend to consult. However long I waited, the student could wait longer. Another tactic for a student to avoid answering was to leaf through a dictionary, which I thought would eventually produce a result. It never did, for again the student was just pretending. And if I pointed at someone to answer, they would simply turn around and look at the person behind. To counter this I asked a student in the back row, but he stumped me by turning round and looking at the wall. It was so unexpected I felt like applauding.

It was soon apparent that I was fighting a losing battle, and I learnt to adjust my teaching to suit the classroom culture. I did not realize it at the time, but a similar pattern was happening in other walks of life. Unconsciously I was adapting to the culture around me; talking in a lower voice; bowing and not hugging; being on time; not jaywalking; waiting for others before eating; washing before getting into the bath. Like many before me, I had arrogantly thought I knew best and had wanted to change Japan. Instead, I found that Japan was changing me. Unlike Julius Caesar, I came, I saw, and I was conquered.

TO COPE WITH CULTURE shock, I embarked on an intensive reading program. Groupism, said Reischauer. The pursuit of harmony, said Buruma. Zen, said D. T. Suzuki. Emotional dependence, said Doi. Bureaucratic rule, said van Wolferen. Different brains, said Tsunoda. As pieces of the puzzle slotted in, the greater picture became clearer. Early insight concerned the emphasis on form and appearance, the way that presentation was more important than the present. It helped explain such oddities as why people with no interest in Christianity chose to marry in chapels with a fake Caucasian priest.

One time I was asked to be a judge at an English speech contest. The convention was for students to memorize a speech, the result being nervous contestants who struggled to remember their lines. On this occasion an older man stood up and said, "Good day, I have no prepared speech so I am just going to talk about anything that comes into my head," and he continued ad-libbing in good English.

There were two other judges, both Japanese, and we marked the participants independently. I placed Mr. Spontaneous at the top, the other two had him at the bottom. Why, I asked? "He did not show a good attitude," they explained. "He did not prepare or make an effort." It was a serious charge, for Confucian values still prevail. Sincerity, earnestness, endurance, rote learning, doing your best—these will win top marks.

One book that was particularly useful was Karel van Wolferen's *The Enigma of Japanese Power*, which portrayed Japan as operating on automatic pilot. It helped make sense of faculty meetings, which I was asked to attend. When I suggested I could be more productive elsewhere, an elderly professor advised me to sleep, saying that as a junior member I should sit up and nod occasionally. On the other hand, senior staff like himself could sit with head back and snore. It was amusing, but like many a joke conveyed a truth, for as van Wolferen noted in his book physical presence alone is enough to signal participation. No individual was responsible for decisions; we all were. By dozing, I was doing my job.

The relative homogeneity of Japanese culture leads to what E. T. Hall calls a high-context environment in which information is shared and does not need explaining. As a result, Japanese often say they can communicate without words and that they are good at "reading the atmosphere." In an influential book, former US ambassador Edwin Reischauer put it another way, stating that Japanese see themselves as a single great family, "a concept more frequently encountered among primitive tribal people."

The idea was taken up by Australian academic Gregory Clark in a book entitled *The Japanese Tribe: Origins of a Nation's Uniqueness*. It helped explain the remarkable social cohesion, which has baffled Western observers all the way back to the sixteenth century. Early missionaries, for example, noted the harmonious relations, and still today social problems like drug taking, vandalism, and alcoholism are relatively small scale.

The shared values lead to an insider-outsider view of the world, evident in two phenomena familiar to gaijin—"the empty seat syndrome" and "the waiter syndrome." In the first case the seat on a train next to a gaijin will be the last to be filled—and sometimes won't be filled at all. In the second case a gaijin dining with a Japanese friend might order food from a waiter in perfectly good Japanese, but the waiter will turn to the Japanese person for confirmation, as if true communication cannot be had with an outsider.

So it was that as the world around me fell into place, reality reared its disturbing head and the honeymoon enchantment abated. Japanese politeness no longer seemed charming but an empty formality. Innocent questions became irritating —"Can you use chopsticks?" "When will you go back to your country?" As Donald Richie points out in *The Inland Sea*, because there is less emphasis on individualism, foreigners are taken as representatives of their culture. "Ah, you are English, I think you like afternoon tea," for example.

Theorists of culture shock hold that adjustment to the host culture takes a critical turn around the three- and five-year mark, when there are "dips of antipathy." As the values of the host country are absorbed, the old personality clings desperately to its identity, resenting the changes. After seven years there is a significant transition—a seven-year itch—as a new self emerges. From now on you are forever changed, and if you return to your country, you will have reverse culture shock, all the more intense because it involves alienation from your own country.

Adjustment is thus a developmental process, much like the stages of childhood. It is surely no coincidence that seven, five, and three feature in the rite of passage known as Shichi-Go-San (7-5-3), when children of those ages dress up to be blessed at shrines throughout the country. Seven marks a major growth towards adulthood, and the seven-year itch indicates the urge for a new phase of life. It was after seven years that I left Kanazawa with the intention of seeking work in Britain, but fate steered me back to Japan. Man proposes, but God disposes.

IN REVISITING KANAZAWA, I realized how much Japan had changed in the past thirty years—as had I. It came home to me as I retraced my one-time walk to work, alongside ancient stone walls and over a bridge to the only university outside of Heidelberg to be located within castle grounds. I looked in vain for where my office used to be, but the whole precinct, all seventy-five acres, had been transformed. Where once were playing fields now stood the gleaming white walls of a rebuilt castle. Where once were classrooms was now a landscaped embankment. It was disorientating; my past had been erased.

At the entrance gate stood a volunteer guide, and when I told him I used to teach at the university he thought I was joking. I thought he was joking when he said he was eighty, for he looked nothing like it. He had studied English after the war, worked for a trading company, and now in retirement was trying to stay useful. Together we strolled around the grounds as I reminisced about teaching and he told me of wartime days of hunger and distant bombing. He was at pains to point out that the castle was authentic, for the reconstruction used only materials and tools which would have been employed originally. It was no mere replica, but a genuine fake.

Afterwards I visited Kenrokuen, a stroll garden laid out for the feudal lords of the early seventeenth century. I had rarely visited it though I lived nearby, put off by tour group guides announcing in deafening tones by loudspeaker that the garden is noted for its tranquility. And if that were not enough, there were school excursions and shouts of "Harro," or if particularly brave, "Harro, how are you? I am fine, thank you."

Now, however, in a time of Covid there was time to stop and stare, time to take in all the beauty. It was as if I was seeing the garden for the very first time. Before me lay an organic museum: rambling root and twisted bough; an awe-inspiring boulder; a tree trunk colonized by moss; thousands of irises set along a rippling stream; the vigor of cedar trees; the elegant stone lantern adopted as symbol of the city.

When Basho visited on his long-distance walk, he spent ten days in Kanazawa meeting with dignitaries and taking part in haiku gatherings. He may have been a wandering poet, but he was no solitary soul. It was late summer, and a haiku he wrote tells of the lingering heat.

Bright red sun
unrelenting, merciless—
yet an autumn breeze

Near a monument celebrating Basho's visit stands a larger-than-life sculpture of Yamato Takeru, mythological hero of the *Kojiki*. It was put up in the nineteenth century to commemorate soldiers killed fighting "the last samurai," Saigo Takamori. While I was looking at the puffed cheeks of the statue, a man approached me and asked in Japanese, "Don't you think it's *kirei*?" (*Kirei* can mean clean or beautiful, which is significant in Japanese understanding.) "It is made with a bird repellent," continued my interlocutor, "which is why pigeons do not sit and shit on his head."

As we walked, I realized my would-be guide was glad to have found a solitary gaijin with whom to share his love of the garden. "You see the cherry grove," he said, "there are 420 trees and 40 different types." It was impressive, but I was already punch drunk with facts and figures and fauna, so I invited him to join me for a green tea on the veranda of an ancient teahouse. Before us was a pond with the oldest fountain in Japan, and we sat together listening to the sound of falling water. Like the carp, we were immersed in nature.

To one side, three middle-aged women in traditional gardening gear were meticulously clearing away dead leaves from behind bushes, and I realized the garden must have been maintained in this way for four hundred years. The pursuit of beauty, awareness of transience, the seasonal round, attention to detail, the cultivation of tradition, harmony with nature—it was all here, compressed into a garden, and it was in Kanazawa that I first awoke to the aesthetics.

On Track |||||||||||||||||||||||||||||||||||||||||||||

Due to its remoteness, rail did not arrive in Kanazawa until 1898. The first station was a one-story wooden building amid rice fields. The second Kanazawa Station, built in the 1950s, was a four-story block of reinforced concrete with dozens of shops. The present station, completed in 2005, has been called by *Travel and Leisure Magazine* "one of the world's most beautiful." The entrance gate combines traditional grandeur with a modern twist, and inside the station are artistic touches to illustrate the city's rich cultural heritage.

The Hokuriku Shinkansen opened in 2015, and young people flocked to the city to see the much-praised 21st Century Museum of Contemporary Art. From Tokyo the fastest train takes two and a half hours, meaning a day's outing is possible. By contrast the little Hokutetsu-Kanazawa Station beneath the JR platforms is the terminal for the Asanogawa Line, which runs to the seaside town of Uchinada. It takes just seventeen minutes, with twelve stations.

Fukui

FUKUI CITY IS A small prefectural capital, with a population of some 260,000, traditionally known for two features—the Zen monastery Eihei-ji and the suicide cliffs of Tojinbo. So it came as a surprise as I exited the station to find not only the usual line of taxis, but dinosaurs. Model dinosaurs. And not just models but moving models. Giant lifelike creatures set in the grassy space between taxi stand and bus terminal, like an advertisement for *Jurassic Park*.

In fact, most of Japan's dinosaur remains were found in this region, and as a result the city has branded itself the Dinosaur Capital of Japan. There are forty full replicas and over one thousand items stored beneath the massive dome of the Fukui Prefectural Dinosaur Museum. In this way Fukui has come up with a unique theme: extinction of the ego in Zen, extinction of the self at its cliffs, and extinction of a whole species with the dinosaurs.

Next morning I was first at the information office, and I came away clutching a wad of maps, timetables, and charts. There was also an explanation of how to navigate the station, which is being revamped as part of the extension of the Hokuriku Shinkansen from Kanazawa to Kyoto. Since it was pleasantly sunny, I headed for the coast and Tojinbo. The dinosaurs could wait. After all, they were wiped out sixty-five million years before humans even arrived in Fukui.

THE STREET LEADING TO the Tojinbo cliffs is lined with the kind of souvenir shops you often see at famous shrines and temples. At the end is a terrace offering a fine panorama over the rocky coastline. From the terrace a path twists its way down towards the sea, alongside which people pose for photographs against the dramatic backdrop.

At the foot of the cliffs, little passenger boats maneuver into inlets while keeping a cautious distance from submerged rocks. Columns soar some twenty-five meters into the air. Geologically, the phenomenon is so rare as to be found in only two other places—Mt. Geumgang in Korea and the east coast of Norway.

The path down is steep, and the slippery rocks are alarming. According to legend, the cliffs take their name from a corrupt priest lured here by resentful villagers and hurled over the edge. Did the Buddhist ecclesiast have karma on his mind as he plummeted towards his rocky end? Whatever the truth of the story, the cliffs went on to become a notorious suicide spot.

The Jesuit missionaries of the seventeenth century, men of keen intellect, noted that Japanese faced death with greater equanimity than other races. This was true not only of the samurai who trained for death, but of the populace in general. People die as they live, we are often told, and I can't help feeling the subjugation of the ego is a factor in this. It is one that makes Japan so pleasant in terms of daily interactions.

In the Western mind suicide and Japan are closely linked, fostered by images of samurai committing *seppuku* (ritual suicide). The spectacular death of the author Yukio Mishima furthered the association. But proactive measures in recent years have lowered the number, and in 2019 Japan ranked twenty-fifth in *per capita* terms, below the US. The biggest category is of men who cannot support their family, either by business failure or losing their job. The forest at Aokigahara near the base of Mt. Fuji is noto-rious as a suicide spot, but sadly a more common means is throwing oneself in front of a train or subway. Apart from the emotional stress for drivers, it can also be a cause of hardship for families left behind, for they are respon-sible for debts caused by damage and disruption to services.

In recent years suicides at Tojinbo have shown a sharp decrease, mainly thanks to a former policeman, Yukio Shige. His job included pulling bod-ies out of the sea, and on retirement he set about tackling the problem by taking preventative action. At first on his own, then together with a hand-ful of volunteers, he patrolled the cliffs over eighteen years and talked to as many as 650 desperate people. As a result the suicides have been drastically reduced, testimony to the difference a single person can make.

FROM FUKUI STATION A forty-minute bus ride penetrates deep into the mountains, where one of Zen's foremost temples is located. The driver of our bus seemed intent on helping us confront the fear of death, and as we skirted the perilous slopes of cedar-covered mountains his driving grew ever more erratic. We ascended high enough for my ears to pop before we drove into a long tunnel, at the far end of which was a circular vision of a lush Shangri-la. In the valley before us were huddled houses, shops, and a sprawling temple compound.

There are two main sects of Zen—Soto and Rinzai. Both pursue enlightenment through meditation (*zazen*), though in historical terms they differed in development. Rinzai sought patronage from on high, whereas Soto spread among the common folk. As a result, Rinzai's strength is in the former power centers of Kyoto and Kamakura, whereas Soto's is more likely to be found in remote areas.

In spiritual terms Rinzai relies more on riddles (called *koan*) to trigger insights, whereas Soto emphasizes "just sitting." Enlightenment in Rinzai is likely to be sharp and sudden; Soto is more gentle and stresses contin-ual awakening. The simplest way to tell them apart is in their meditative practice: Rinzai groups face inward, while Soto faces outward, towards the wall.

Eihei-ji (Temple of Eternal Peace) is a Soto headquarters and a major seminary. I knew something of what went on there, for while in Kanazawa

I used to visit Daijo-ji, an attractive small seminary surrounded by a large cemetery. I remember facing the wall with half-closed eyes, aware of nothing but excruciating back pain. "All life is suffering," Buddhism teaches, and the prolonged sitting seemed to prove the point. Alan Watts called Zen "aching-legs Buddhism," and in my case it was aching legs, back, and pretty much everywhere else.

On one occasion there were four of us seated next to each other, and on the wall before us were four shadows. One of the shadows was gradually inclining towards me, and out of the corner of an eye I could see that my elderly neighbor had fallen asleep. While I was pondering what to do, an upright shadow with raised stick glided silently towards us. It paused behind me, bowed, raised high the stick, and gave me an almighty whack across one shoulder. And then the other.

All at once the shadow next to mine sat bolt upright. The whack had woken him up. Far from being resentful, I was rather grateful, for the blow released the tension in my muscles and sent a huge surge of warmth down my back, like a shot of whisky to the stomach. Afterwards my shadow and I did a much better job.

Eihei-ji is more than a seminary; it is a memorial to "the saint of Zen," Eihei Dogen (1200–1253). As founder of the temple, he established the lines along which it is still run today. He was someone who truly walked the walk, and you can't help but be in awe of a man so committed to a life of hardship. Born into the noble class, he embraced a life of poverty involving bitingly cold winters, low-level sustenance, and a ceaseless round of meditation, work, and sutra chanting.

For each aspect of monastical life, Dogen laid down strict rules. Take bathing, for instance, only permitted on days of the month containing a four or nine in the date (roughly every fifth day). Before entering the bath, each monk had to make three bows while reciting, "We bathe vowing to benefit all beings; may our bodies and minds be purified both inwardly and outwardly."

Along with such strictures Dogen had a knack for maxims, and he captured Zen's distrust of words by stating, "The more talking and thinking, the further from the truth." He had, too, a poetic side, and in Zen fashion cut to the heart of things in his verse.

In the spring, cherry blossom
In the summer, cuckoo
In autumn, the moon, and
In winter, the snow, clear and cold

Dogen's legacy is evident in every facet of the temple, and his presence continues to pervade the buildings. When haiku master Kyoshi Takahama visited in November 1949, he communed with the spirit of the founder.

Still now
at his reliquary shrine
maple tree viewing

The temple is dauntingly large. Dauntingly austere too. The whole site is set on a slope, and steps are everywhere. Perhaps after prolonged sitting, steps provide an antidote. There are moss-covered steps on the approach, steps to enter buildings, steps to the next room, and a long, long flight of steps all the way up to the main assembly room. Steps on the path to enlightenment too.

It quickly becomes clear that apart from religious training the seminary is a major tourist sight, for bustling confusion fills the reception area. Visitors are instructed to follow colored markers on the floor; choose the wrong color and you could find yourself becoming a sponsor. The majority head for a lecture room where, before a large map, a monk explains the layout. "Seven buildings represent the core of the monastery," he says. "Auxiliary structures total seventy in all."

Let loose on the buildings, visitors are steered by ribbons, ropes, and directional signs around the public face of the institution. The pleasing simplicity of the woodwork is largely bereft of decoration, save for the 230 paintings of birds and flowers on the ceiling of the reception hall. The monks' hall forms the heart of the complex, with its one-by-two-meter tatami mats. For those in training, the narrow confines comprise the limits within which they must eat, sleep, and meditate.

There is a tendency to romanticize monastic life as utopia, free of everyday concerns. For the reality you only need turn to the best-selling *Eat Sleep Sit* by Kaoru Nonomura, who left his job as a Tokyo designer for a year's training at Eihei-ji. What follows is a shock. Trainees are routinely slapped, kicked, and shoved down stairs. "When you passed a senior in the corridor," writes Nonomura, "failure to join the palms in respect was punished on the spot with a blow." Extreme stress and fear are compounded by exhaustion, hunger, and loneliness.

The military-style training conjures up the hierarchical world of Kubrick's *Full Metal Jacket*, and in either case the aim is similar—"to break down the self-centered ego." The group takes priority over the individual, and obedience, discipline, and subjugation of self are expected at all times. "Absolute submission was a must," writes Nonomura. Seen in this light, the connection of samurai and Zen makes perfect sense.

One time at Daijo-ji I stayed overnight with two friends, and at three thirty, when we were woken for morning meditation, we were ushered to a small room and told to wait. It was dark and perishingly cold, so we turned on a heater and innocently helped ourselves to some green tea. When one of the monks saw this, he exploded in rage and shouted at us in English: "What on earth do you think you're doing? This is not a holiday camp." He was visibly shaking with anger.

Later that morning we were given the task of sweeping leaves, and our angry monk came to apologize. "I used to be chairman of American company Shell in Japan," he explained, "so I am used to ordering people, you see. After retirement, I decided to become a monk. Already I'm training for four years, but still I can't control myself."

Ironically, our angry monk was one of the few at the seminary who was there out of conviction. Younger monks who were training to take over their family temple tended to have a far more relaxed attitude. One of them even invited us to join him after dinner in sneaking out for a hamburger.

Given all this, a quotation by Dogen pinned on a wall made for interesting reading. "There is a very easy way to become a Buddha," wrote the master:

Not to do any evil, not to have a mind that clings to birth and death, to have profound compassion for all living things, to respect those above us and to have compassion for those below us, not to have a mind that regards everything as loathsome, not to have a mind that is yearning for things, not to be anxious, not to be distressed.

Very easy? Dogen clearly had a mischievous sense of humor.

OPPOSITES ATTRACT, WHICH MAY explain the allure of Zen in the West. The subduing of the ego runs counter to the US style of individualism, which encourages self-assertion and self-expression. Fukui's tourist board is clearly aware of the appeal of Zen for Westerners and has crafted an English-language brochure that portrays sedate Fukui as a funky Zen kind of place. To emphasize the point, the word is written in capital letters. Bonsai is "a miniature ZEN world." Local food is prepared with "ZEN-like attentiveness." Traditional crafts are "an example of ZEN spirit." Soaking in a hot spring is "a precious ZEN moment." In short, "Find your ZEN here in Fukui."

Hungry after my tour of the complex, I wandered around to see what was available in the ZEN shops. Snow crabs were prominent, cherished for their rich, firm flesh. The vegetarian Dogen would not have approved, so to honor his spirit I chose "Eihei-ji soba." The handmade noodles came with seasonal mountain plants and a side dish of sesame tofu that was divinely creamy.

Close by stood some memorial rocks inscribed with haiku, one of them by wandering poet Santoka Taneda. Like Basho, he was trained in Zen, but whereas his predecessor fashioned the conventional haiku, Santoka was a modernizer who deliberately broke the rules. No 5-7-5 restrictions for a freethinker.

> In birth and death
>> snow falling incessantly

The verse was written at Eihei-ji after the poet had fallen into the snow, and given his fondness for sake, the likelihood is that he was drunk. Perhaps lying there in the snow, he had an epiphany. If so, it would lend depth to the few simple words and, in keeping with the best traditions of haiku, combine concision with universality.

Winter snow and the freezing cold is taken up in another of the inscribed haiku, this time by the poet Ito Hakusui. The image here is of a stone Buddha that has feeling, subtly suggestive of the way the figures are living beings to those who worship them.

In the deep snow
the Buddha too
enduring the cold

Basho too made it to Eihei-ji, but it does not feature in the haiku of
The Narrow Road to the Deep North. He had a contact in Fukui called
Tosai, whom he knew from the past and with whom he stayed for a couple
of nights. He left on the third day eager to see the full moon at Tsuruga,
reputed to be particularly beautiful. Tosai offered to show him the way,
comically playacting by tucking up the hem of his kimono in the manner
of a mountain guide.

I too was headed for Tsuruga, but where was my Tosai? And why
wasn't I aware of the phase of the moon? It was a sad indictment of how
detached from nature the modern world has become.

One of the virtues of Japan's traditional lifestyle, in Kyoto at least, is
that it is so in tune with the seasonal cycle. Lili is constantly aware of what
plants are in blossom, and of what festival or celebration is coming up next.
Should I show reluctance to view plum or hydrangea in bloom, she gets
upset, and if I were to suggest I had attended enough festivals, she would be
dismayed. Eating food in season, painting flowers in bloom, admiring the
phases of the moon—these are for her an essential part of what it means to
be alive. It was through her I understood how closely traditional culture
harmonizes with the seasonal round.

On Track |||||||||||||||||||||||||||||||||||||||||||||||||||

Fukui Station is jointly operated by JR West and the private Echizen Railway (named after the ancient province). It was first built in 1896, and
the present building with shopping mall dates from 2005. It is served
by the Hokuriku Main Line, which originates in Maibara (Shiga Prefecture). From Fukui, the Thunderbird express takes forty-eight minutes to
Kanazawa and thirty-four minutes to Tsuruga.

The extension of the Hokuriku Shinkansen from Kanazawa is due
to open in 2024, and in expectation of a higher number of tourists, an
eye-catching three-car train representing prefectural highlights has

been put into service. It has viewing screens, hand straps modeled after Echizen snow crabs, and seats made by a leading textile maker.

Echizen Railway operates two local lines in Fukui Prefecture. As is common in Japan, it is a third-sector operation, meaning that it is jointly owned by non-governmental and non-profit groups who wish to see the company continue to offer a service. It was established in 2002, following two major crashes that put its predecessor out of business.

Tsuruga, Obama, and Fukuchiyama

TRAVELING BY TRAIN SOUTHWEST from Hokuriku to the adjoining Chugoku region presents the kind of problems beloved of fanatics who pore over timetables and ponder the permutations. The system demands you take the main line inland to Kyoto and then back to the Sea of Japan. I was determined to continue along the coast, however, whatever the inconvenience. Eventually I came up with a train route to Tottori via a couple of stopovers.

The first leg of my journey was the short stretch to Tsuruga, which is a modest but appealing town of 66,000. A little loop bus runs round the main sights, and I got the impression of somewhere living on its past but looking to the future. The past was about connecting by ship with Vladivostok, the future was about connecting by Shinkansen to Kyoto. The latter is evident in the huge concrete pillars near the station, which stand like Titans waiting expectantly for high-speed tracks to be laid across their massive shoulders.

First stop for the loop bus is Kehi Shrine, the town's main Shinto site. As I got off, I noticed something odd, and turning round found myself face-to-face with a large brown owl perched on a coffee sign. For a moment we stared at each other, then it flapped its large wings and flew off to the shrine grove. I had never been that close to a wild owl, and without thinking I followed in the same direction, as if it were an animal messenger sent to guide me.

At the entrance to the shrine a small humpback bridge signified the transition to a sacred realm, a feeling enhanced by passing through the portal-like frame of Japan's third-largest wooden *torii*. Within the compound is an ever-flowing spring, the water of which is said to ensure a long life. Put all that together with the owl, and it is no wonder that the *Harry Potter* boom of recent years has led to a dramatic upturn in shrine visits among the young.

New Age wizardry, driven by bestselling anime and manga, holds Shinto's ancient shrines to be "power spots" charged with energy and home to glamorous young *miko* (shrine attendants). Shrine authorities have reacted with ambivalence, for "magick" speaks to the universal rather than to ancestral concerns. On the other hand, shrines are more than happy to welcome the increase in custom.

By this stage of my journey I had come to consider Basho an unseen travel companion, and it was comforting to find a statue of him in the grounds. The poet had come here intent on seeing the full moon, and when he arrived a day ahead of time the sky was promisingly clear. Alas, the following evening it clouded over.

> The autumn moon—
> ah, the Hokuriku climate
> so variable

Of the five haiku Basho wrote at Tsuruga, only the above made the final cut for *The Narrow Road to the Deep North*. Kehi Shrine, however, has chosen to immortalize another, which references the shrine. For over a thousand years Shinto and Buddhism were fused in religious expression, and the shrine was once part of a Buddhist complex. According to tradition, the monk Ippen, founder of the Ji sect, laboriously carried white sand from a beach to cover over the shrine's muddy access, and the practice was continued by his successors. Basho uses this to fashion an image of spiritual radiance.

> The moon so pure—
> shining on silver sand
> laid by monks

Next stop that the little loop bus took me to was a history museum. For long centuries the town had been little more than a fishing village, but with the opening of a modern port in 1899 foreign ships arrived. Shortly afterwards Tsuruga shot to prominence, for its port offered access to Vladivostok and the Trans-Siberian Railway (opened in 1904). Tokyo to Warsaw now took just fifteen days.

In its publicity material Tsuruga dubs itself, rather grandly, as Port of Humanity, a title based on two incidents twenty years apart. The first, in 1920, took place in the aftermath of the Russian Revolution, when up to two hundred thousand Poles were stranded in Siberia. They included some one thousand orphans, whom the Red Cross dispatched to Tsuruga, from where they passed to Japan's Pacific ports to be eventually repatriated.

Twenty years later, a vice-consul in Lithuania defied orders and issued transit visas to Jews, mainly Polish, fleeing Hitler's Europe. "The Japanese Schindler," Chiune Sugihara, is thought to have saved some five thousand lives in all (including descendants). The first group arrived in Tsuruga in September 1940, the last in June 1941. Like the orphans before them, they were moved on via Japan's Pacific ports to destinations overseas.

My final stop was at Kehi Matsubara, one of Japan's "top three beautiful pine groves." How do you measure the beauty of a pine grove? By the beauty of the beach next to it, in this case. Indeed, if you blank out the oil storage tanks at one end, the scene is certainly attractive, for the blue lapping water ripples onto white sand, which slopes up to a line of neatly roped off pine trees. A few arboreal rebels had managed to sneak past the rope and onto the beach, and seeing that they had been tagged, I feared for their future. Nature, it seemed, should be as orderly as humans.

Save for a few anglers the beach was deserted, and half a dozen seagulls had taken advantage to play some kind of tag game. The fresh air, the scent of pine, the lulling motion of the waves—how good it was to be in a place where even the birds felt free to frolic. I took off my shoes and walked barefoot over the soft sand, happy to be part of the cosmic play. Now I felt truly off the beaten tracks.

ON EITHER SIDE OF a single track, thick greenery scraped and scratched the little train headed for Obama. The mixed woodland gave way occasionally to unmanned stations serving small hamlets untouched by modern ways. Beyond them lay the inevitable mountains, on the lower slopes of which were the graves of all-seeing ancestors. At Mihama, meaning Beautiful Beach, a low-lying band of mist created a panorama of floating hills.

"Welcome to Hokuriku beauty," said the banners at Obama Station. Once upon a time this sleepy backwater had been a thriving port town under direct control of the imperial family, an important source of seafood for the capital in Kyoto. Now it had seemingly settled for an easy life. Tsuruga had made an effort in tourist terms, but Obama did not seem bothered.

In Japanese, Obama means Small Beach, but with the election of a namesake to US President, the town of thirty thousand had happily embraced the publicity it brought. The normally reserved citizens had got behind a "Go Obama!" campaign, and there were souvenirs which included confectionery bearing his face. Now all that remained was a cardboard cutout in my hotel lobby, alongside which guests could pose.

Historically the town's claim to fame is as starting point for the Saba Kaido (Mackerel Trail). It was a trading route that flourished in Edo times, leading directly over the mountains to Kyoto and finishing close to the former imperial palace. Since the marker for the endpoint is close to my apartment in Kyoto, I was eager to see the starting point. It lies in front of the small Mackerel Trail Museum, in which the most interesting exhibit, unrelated to mackerel, was a video of the town's festivals.

Like Tsuruga, Obama stands on Wakasa Bay. Such was the port's prestige that in 1408 Japan's first elephant arrived here, no doubt just as startled as the natives who welcomed it. Though seafood was plentiful, mackerel was king, and the fish were quickly salted to be dispatched to Kyoto. Runners were employed who could manage the eighty kilometers in a single day. This was no mean feat, as the course crosses three mountains eight hundred meters high. Mackerel was not the only item to be transported in this way, for the bay is rich in marine life, and the choicest products, like the elephant, were earmarked for the capital. Still today, pickled fish is a specialty of Obama, especially tilefish (*guji*), flounder (*karei*), and pufferfish (*fugu*).

The museum receptionist told me foreign visitors were often in quest of enlightenment at the Zen temple of Bukkoku. Japanese visitors on the other hand headed for Sanchomachi, part of the old castle town (the castle no longer exists). "Romantic Obama" was the pitch, and according to the brochure, the area was once Obama's red-light district, packed with inns, brothels, and tea houses. It sounded exciting, but sadly it wasn't.

Wandering back, I stumbled on the grave of an eight-hundred-year-old nun who was said to be related to mermaids. I also came across a large building that housed a historical noh stage. The door was open, the whole place deserted, so I took advantage of the quiet for a peaceful nap. A noh nap.

AFTERWARDS I FOUND JUST what I was hoping for—an arty cafe in a converted old house. There were no other customers, so I queried the owner about Romantic Obama. "Yes," she said, "we often have customers who ask about that." On the menu was a mackerel set meal boasting two generous pieces of fish on either side of grilled daikon, along with the usual suspects. It was more than I could eat, and I sat back replete, thinking of those runners who covered eighty kilometers in a single day.

The cafe was contained in a wooden-frame house, and the conversion had gutted the inside to leave a large open interior with exposed beams. The walls had been plastered and painted black in stylish fashion, adorned by a few simple decorations and a display of handmade pottery. I asked how long the conversion had taken.

"My son did it in a month," the owner told me.

"Really? If it was that simple, I guess others could do it. In the brochure it says there are shops and crafts, but I didn't see any."

"Yes, the town did nothing to help. But now my son is on the council. He's pushing them to hire a foreigner to promote the town. But it is difficult. People here are conservative. They don't like change."

I wondered what the town's namesake would have thought of that. Conservatism is part of Japan's DNA, a legacy of Confucian values, which tend towards support of the status quo. There was even a law during the Edo period forbidding any changes at all. Maybe they had a point. After all, change can sometimes mean Obama leading to Trump.

AS FUKUCHIYAMA CAME INTO view, its castle appeared, perched atop a hillock like a cardboard model in a children's pop-up book. At twenty-five kilometers from the coast, this was as far inland I had been since Hokkaido, yet bizarrely there was a poster at the station welcoming visitors to "Kyoto by the sea." The woman at the information office explained that it was part of a campaign to lure tourists away from Kyoto City. The prefecture had been divided up into parts, and Fukuchiyama was allotted to the part by the sea. But what if tourists turned up with bucket and spade, looking for a beach? "*So desu ne* [I see]," was all the response I got.

With a population of eighty thousand, Fukuchiyama is relatively small, but in 2020 it made a splash when its most famous son, Akechi Mitsuhide (1528–82), was the lead character in NHK's popular annual drama series. There is one thing every Japanese knows about Mitsuhide: he overthrew his superior, Japan's great unifier, Oda Nobunaga. But why? It is one of the most intriguing puzzles of Japanese history.

Nobunaga was the Putin of his time, a ruthless despot who sought to bring the country under his control. He dispatched Mitsuhide with an army to subdue Shikoku, but the general did a U-turn, headed back to Kyoto, and besieged the outmanned Nobunaga in a temple. The warmonger did the honorable thing and committed seppuku.

Mitsuhide assumed power, but only for a matter of days. Hearing the news, another general, Toyotomi Hideyoshi, rushed back to Kyoto and defeated his rival in battle. The defeated Mitsuhide fled for Fukuchiyama but was ambushed on the way and killed.

So why did a trusted general suddenly turn round and betray his commander? One theory claims it was personal ambition. Another suggests a grudge. And a third says that he acted at the behest of the imperial court. NHK's year-long drama favored the third. He was loyal to a higher authority.

Reconnecting after we split ways in Hokkaido, Hirota-san and I had arranged to meet at the station to visit Mitsuhide's castle, just a fifteen-minute walk away. Unfortunately it was closed for repairs, so we walked all the way round it. The castle must rank among the most compact in Japan, for it took no time at all. Mitsuhide had a personal interest in castle construction, and he influenced the design securely sited atop a small hill.

Historically Mitsuhide gets a good press, though you might think that someone who betrayed his superior would be vilified. I asked Hirota-san for his take. "I think he loved his wife," he replied gnomically, then continued, "Fukuchiyama citizens may like him because he was clever and helped stop their houses from flooding. He knew about engineering."

The more one studies Japanese history, the more one encounters acts of betrayal. Surprise attacks are common. For many people, including Lafcadio Hearn, Japan's greatest statesman is Tokugawa Ieyasu, founder of the Tokugawa shogunate, yet he broke promises and used deceit in the siege of Osaka Castle. Power mattered to him more than the code of the samurai. Forget the myth of dedicated service; Japanese history teaches might is right.

WITH HIROTA-SAN AT THE wheel of a rented car, we set off for Choan-ji, a Zen temple known for its hydrangeas. I was curious how Hirota-san felt about Zen, for it is based on an altogether different concept from his type of Buddhism. Zen is *jiriki* (relying on oneself); Jodo Shinshu, or Pure Land Buddhism, is *tariki* (depending on another). I once spoke with a Zen monk who told me his sect looked down on the Pure Land notion that salvation comes from surrender to the deity, Amida Nyorai. Zen requires effort and self-sacrifice; Pure Land simply requires submission.

"Does Pure Land have any bad feelings towards Zen?" I asked Hirota-san.

"Not at all," he said. "There are Zen followers who pray to Amida. The Obaku sect, for instance."

"That's like having your cake and eating it."

"What do you mean?"

"I mean if practicing Zen doesn't bring salvation, then calling on Amida will. It's like backing two different horses to win."

There was a pause as Hirota-san thought about this. Then he said, "Don't forget the saying of Shinran, 'Even a good person can get into the Pure Land. How much easier for a bad person.'"

The first time I came across the saying, I thought it was a misprint. How could it be easier for bad people to enter the Pure Land! Hirota-san put me on the right track, however, by explaining that good people think their virtue will save them, whereas bad people, aware of their failings, are more likely to throw themselves wholeheartedly on Amida's mercy.

Choan-ji was crammed with hydrangea bushes, which in spring comprise a vision of heaven—of the Pure Land indeed. The temple is nestled against the foot of a mountain, the upper slopes of which were covered in mist, and a stream cascaded down the hillside to course through the precincts. The sound of water was everywhere. Even the dry landscape dripped with moisture.

Behind the main building was a place for cold-water austerities, and it pleased me to think that the fresh clear water that enables the hydrangeas to bloom prompted awakening in humans too. As if to prove Hirota-san's point, a noticeboard in the Zen temple bore a verse by the Pure Land poet Wariko Kai, using water as a metaphor for faith.

Passing by rocks
and tree roots too
rippling
just rippling along
the ever-flowing brook

With Hirota-san at the wheel, we next headed for a Moto Ise Shrine and I was surprised to find that Hirota-san had no idea what it was. It was indicative of his sect's distance from Shinto and Japanese mythology. According to the *Nihon Shoki*, the story goes something like this: Around two thousand years ago, Emperor Suinin ordered one of his daughters to find a permanent home for the family ancestor Amaterasu, the Sun Goddess. The deity was represented by a bronze mirror, which Princess Yamato took with her on a journey that lasted twenty years. It was only when she got to Ise that she heard Amaterasu tell her that "This is a secluded and pleasant land. This is where I wish to dwell." To this day Ise remains the seat of Amaterasu and Japan's premier shrine.

On her journey Princess Yamato made several stops and erected shrines now known as Moto Ise (Original Ise). We had arrived at one of them, a ruined shrine set deep in the woods. Soaring cedars stretched heavenwards, bathed in the soothing sounds of a mountain stream, while the moss-covered rocks and crumbling woodwork spoke to long centuries of devoted pilgrimage. For me, the scene before us represented everything that is most attractive about the nature-worshipping aspect of Shinto.

It is possible to see in the layout of shrines like this, located in woodland, the setting for a symbolic enactment of procreation. Viewed from above, the approach and clearing resemble the shape of a womb. The Japanese word for the approach—*sando*—is a homonym for the birth canal, and the vaginal entrance through the *torii* leads to a holy sanctum where "fertilization" takes place in the meeting of the vertical (descent of the spirit) with the horizontal (arrival of the worshipper). Like other shamanic cultures, Shinto cherishes the life force.

Here at Moto Ise, the shrine looks an integral part of nature and there is a sense of timelessness, of reaching back to mankind's earliest impulses. Joseph Campbell saw awe as the essence of Shinto, and here one feels close to the source, close to the origin of it all. I found it inspiring. Hirota-san too was touched, yet we were viewing the scene through differing lens. Like Hearn, I saw in Shinto the ultimate expression of Japaneseness. Hirota-san, unfamiliar with the mythology, saw the scene in terms of Western Romanticism. Paradoxically, the Westerner was looking East, and the Easterner was looking West.

On Track ||||||||||||||||||||||||||||||||||||||||||||||||||

There is a small Tsuruga Railway Museum, housed in a re-creation of the former port station. The town has a special place in history because of its maritime link with Vladivostok, and it was the first municipality on the Sea of Japan to have a railway. The station was built in 1882 and the connection to Tokyo completed in 1889. This enabled Asia–Europe train travel in 1912, starting from Shinbashi in Tokyo and giving access to the Trans-Siberian Railway. In 1957, it became the first railway in Japan to be fully electrified. Five years later the Hokuriku Tunnel opened, at the time the longest in Japan.

These days Tsuruga Station is served by two lines, the Hokuriku Main Line and the single-track Obama Line. From Tsuruga to Obama, trains take sixty-six minutes. From there the slow train to Fukuchiyama takes an hour and forty minutes, with a change at Higashi-Maizuru.

Chugoku

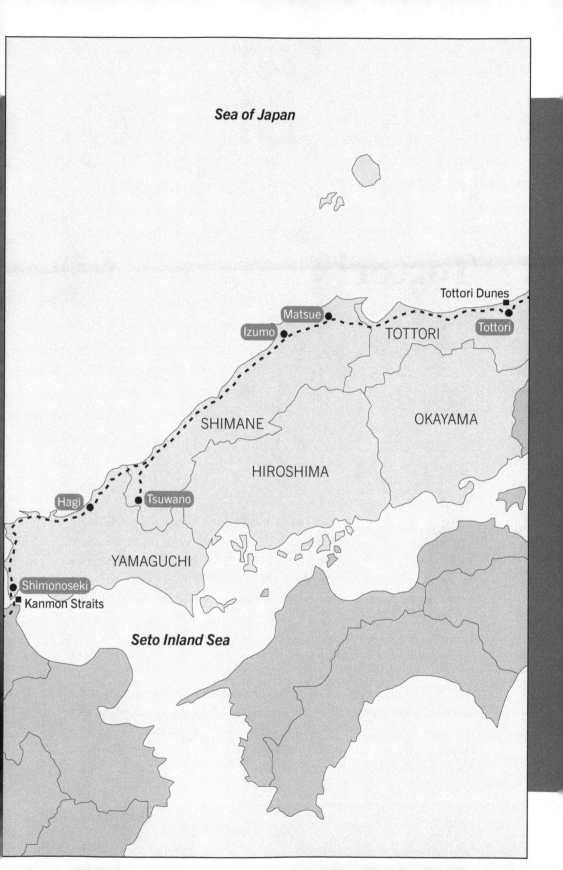

Tottori

FROM FUKUCHIYAMA THE TRAIN winds toward the coast on its way to Tottori, passing through Kinosaki, a charming hot spring resort set around a willow-lined stream. Lili and I once spent a weekend there enjoying the preserved architecture and basking in the sense of history (over one thousand years of public soaking). Crab is the big attraction when in season, and for carnivores there is "black beef" (from black cattle raised in Tajima). Dinner in your room, meals to die for, and futons laid out for your ease. Hot water soaks and chilled sake with the one you love. Is there greater bliss in this world?

From Kinosaki the railway winds its improbable way around bays and inlets, as if laid out by a drunkard having fun. A friend compares the scenery to Big Sur in California, and if you allow for a difference in scale, it is certainly attractive enough. When the train pulled into the small town of Kasumi, a few fishermen were sitting around the dock, their work done and the wharf swilled clean. They were enjoying a seafood breakfast—or was it lunch? Time operates here in a different dimension.

Tottori in the public imagination means one thing: sand dunes. It was not long before the first of them loomed into view, heralding a most unusual feature which extends for 16 kilometers along the coast with a width of up to 2.4 kilometers. Like a mirage, it seems out of place, conjuring up images of the Middle East. Publicity photos inevitably include a few imported camels to further the *Lawrence of Arabia* connection, though for anyone familiar with Kobo Abe's *Woman in the Dunes* images come to mind of kidnap and slavery in the unforgiving expanse.

All across Japan, communities compete to attract a larger share of the tourism market, and Tottori had come up with an innovative idea to offer subsidized taxi tours, with ten preplanned courses lasting three hours at a giveaway price of one thousand yen. Compare that with the two thousand yen it costs me for a twenty-minute ride to Kyoto Station, and you can see it is a bargain not to be missed. The good taxpayers of Tottori—long may they flourish—were more or less gifting visitors a three-hour taxi ride.

As it turned out, my visit to Tottori was very much a tale of two taxis. The first driver was not entirely suited to the job, more interested in cigarette breaks than imparting information. Seeing that he had a foreigner, he stuck obstinately to broken English, though I tried insisting on Japanese. Since his English was monosyllabic, I got little more than "Good" or "Not good" in response to my questions. Even at one thousand yen the tour felt overpriced.

Things were very different the next day. The driver was friendly, chatty, and willing to veer from the set course. She even volunteered to give me an extra forty minutes. She told me she had worked on an assembly line for eleven years before taking up taxi driving, so I asked what had prompted the change? The work had affected her eyesight, she told me. Wait a minute: failing eyesight and now driving my taxi! She laughed; it was only her reading vision that was impaired. At least that is what her optician said.

Japan can be rigid when it comes to second chances, so I wondered if changing jobs had been difficult. There was a special driving test but otherwise it was easy, she claimed. Because the pay was low, there was little competition. I had often heard Kyoto taxi drivers make similar complaints, many of whom were retired or burnt-out salarymen, often deprived of sleep from working through the night. How about in her case? She said she only had to work a daytime shift with weekends off because she was married with two children. She considered herself lucky. As for holidays, she could have national holidays off, without pay. How about summer vacation? She laughed dismissively. No such thing, she said, as if it was a fantasy. Sure, it was tough work, but she enjoyed it because she could meet all kinds of people. Such as foreigners like me.

Born and bred in Tottori, she was keen to promote her hometown and her enthusiasm was infectious. The biggest change in her lifetime, she said, was the increase in cars. The train stations used to be the busiest place in town; now the busiest parts were car parks for big department stores. Postwar Japan had been transformed from privation to consumer heaven.

First stop on the taxi tour was Tottori's number-one attraction, a giant horseback sand dune. It rises fifty meters high, and from the top there are views along the coast. A nearby ridge is covered with sand ripples created by the wind, a fine example of nature's artistry. By contrast, human artistry was on display at The Sand Museum in the form of some astonishing sculpted tableaux. Winter sees nature and humans combine their skills, when the dunes are covered in a blanket of snow augmented by thirty thousand lanterns.

For those who want to get into the spirit of things, there are camel rides. The spectacle reminded me of donkey rides on British beaches, except here there was a good deal further to fall. Nearby was an aquarium, and I made a brief tour pausing only to count twenty-five different varieties in a tank of local fish. Attached to the aquarium, with no sense of irony, was a section for seafood, featuring the town's most famous produce—crab. The season begins on November 1 with a *hatsu seri* (first auction), when the choicest catch is displayed and sold for an exorbitant price. Firms compete for the publicity it brings. The previous year the prize crab had raised a staggering thirty thousand dollars. At that price you would need hypersensitive taste buds to savor each and every mouthful!

In one of the restaurants, I was told it was too late for oysters (summer season) and too early for crab (winter season). So I tried another local delicacy—*tofu chikuwa* (tofu mixed with fish paste). It was firm and tasty. Then came a generous sashimi set of sea bream, horse mackerel, skipjack tuna, scallop, and salmon. It was so fresh you could positively taste the sea.

If crab is king of Tottori's sea produce, pears rank top of its land produce. The Pear Museum opened my eyes—and tastebuds—to an unfamiliar world. Who knew there are some three thousand varieties worldwide? Growing up in the north of England, I thought all pears were pear shaped, but when I arrived in Japan I found they could be round and deliciously juicy. Here in the Pear Museum I learnt there are pear connoisseurs who appreciate the distinctive flavors as if they are wines. Sweetness, acidity, crispness, and juiciness are the criteria, producing such evaluations as, "A crisp little pear with a hint of mellowness."

My visit coincided with peak season for pear harvesting, for the different varieties mature in a rolling succession between late August and October. This being Japan, appearance is all-important, and the pears were set out in perfectly ripened rows. The largest cost five dollars each and were big enough for a whole family to feast on. There were hybrids too, cultivated to make them last longer and taste better. Pride of place went to the Nijisseiki, or Twentieth Century Pear, celebrated in a lavish brochure as, "Round and crisp like an apple, juicy and sweet like a pear."

The next visit on my taxi tour was Hakuto Shrine, notable for enshrining a white rabbit. Not Alice's white rabbit, of course. In fact, not a rabbit at all but a hare, as the Japanese language makes no distinction between the two. The Hare of Inaba is its name, and it appears in Japan's oldest book, the *Kojiki.*

"Do you know the story?" my guide asked.

"More or less," I said. "There was a hare living on the Oki Islands that came to the mainland, where it was skinned and tortured by some bullies, but rescued by a younger man, who is now known as the kami Okuninushi."

"Oh, you know very well," she said. In fact, the story is famous in Japan, but she had made a point of learning details to explain to her customers.

"The hare wanted to get to the mainland," she continued, "so it challenged some sharks to see which animal had more followers."

"On the Oki Islands, right?"

"Yes. The cunning hare persuaded the shark leader to line up its followers all the way to the mainland so that they could be counted, then used them as stepping stones to hop its way across the sea."

The rest of the story reads like a tale of animal rights. When the sharks realized they had been duped, they seized the hare and tore off its fur in revenge. At this point the sons of the Izumo king passed by on their way to court a princess, and when they saw the poor hare pleading for help, they told it to wash in the sea and let the breeze dry off the water afterward, knowing full well the salty water and wind would bring more pain. The youngest of the brothers called Onamuchi (a.k.a. Okuninushi) took pity on the hare and after the others left told it to use fresh water, then wrap itself in healing medicinal leaves. Like all good folk tales, there was a reward for the hero when the hare revealed itself as a deity and granted to Onamuchi the right to marry the princess.

Hakuto Shrine is sited next to the very beach where the hare is said to have arrived, and the nearby Mitarashi Pond is where it supposedly purified itself. One way of decoding the story is to see it as marking the arrival of an immigrant clan from Korea. Since animals sense the unseen better than humans, they are regarded in Shinto as mediators between this world and the other. Here, unusually, the animal is the main kami of the shrine. The coloring may have played a part in this, for Inaba hares turn white in winter, and white is a signifier of purity. It is an attribute widely shared among the religion's sacred animals—white foxes, white snakes, white horses, white deer, white doves.

Purity underwrites the story in another way, as washing in fresh water suggests *misogi*, a Shinto practice involving ritual immersion in cold water. The purpose is to refresh and renew the human spirit, "polluted" through being in a material world. The striving for purity has left a mark on modern-day Japan, with its emphasis on cleanliness, reflected in the tendency for white cars, politicians who wear white gloves, and the readiness to wear white masks.

Next to the steps leading to the worship hall is a statue of a youthful-looking Onamuchi together with the hare, and at the shrine office white stones are on sale for tossing onto the lintel of the *torii* for good luck. I watched my taxi driver throw a coin into the offertory box, ring the bell, and do the standard two bows, two claps, and one final bow. Afterwards I asked if she had prayed, and she told me she was making a wish for the health of her family. I wondered to what she had made the wish—kami, the white hare, God, Onamuchi? All of them, she said, everything in fact. The universe in general. Wonderful, I thought. The nameless mystery that has neither shape nor substance.

IN *THE ROADS TO SATA* Alan Booth witnesses a car accident in a remote rural area and reports it to the local police. Instead of rushing to the scene, they ask for his ID and question his reasons for walking. For all his protestations, they were more interested in the strange foreigner than in a routine car accident. Something similar happened to me in Tottori.

I had popped out from my station hotel to a convenience store, and when I got back I could not find my iPhone. Panic! I checked in my laundry bag. Nothing. In the room. Nothing. In my bag. Nothing. So I rushed back to the convenience store where they told me to try Lost Property at the railway station. Nothing there either.

I retraced my steps to the hotel and asked the women at the reception desk. Again, nothing. Then I remembered that on my laptop was a Find My iPhone application. When I opened it, there was a flashing light just outside the hotel, so I searched the pavement there. Nothing. I went back to my room, grabbed the computer, and took it down to show the receptionists. The flashing light had changed from one side of the crossroads to the other. Aha! Someone was outside walking around with my iPhone!

The receptionists advised me to try the nearby *koban* (police box), so I rushed off in the hope the police might help stop the thief. Usually there are one or two police in a *koban*, but this one had five or six, being near the main station. Imagine their surprise when a wild-looking redhead burst in asking if they could help apprehend a nearby person.

"First things first," one of the police said, "please sit down and fill in a form." I explained there was a possible thief walking around just minutes away, and I could show them on my computer if they let me use their WiFi. "No WiFi," they said. This was a surprise, and my reaction initiated a lengthy conversation about Apple computers, foreigners, and Find My iPhone technology. Following this, one of the police asked to look at my laptop, another rang head office to explain they had a gaijin, while a third went over the details of the form I had filled in.

Despite my insistence that urgency was needed, the police insisted on checking my ID cards and proof of residence. Though I told them my name was John Dougill, the official ID said Dougill John Edward, which caused confusion about name order, first names, and middle names.

The upshot was that I was addressed as Eduardo-san. By this time my concern was no longer stopping the thief, but getting free of police

bureaucracy. After some pointless further questions, a female police officer came in from the back office and said, "Eduardo-san, you can go now."
This was unexpected.

"Can someone come with me?" I ventured. "It's just round the corner."

"No," said the female police officer, "we have registered the loss. If
you get more information, please ring this number." She ignored the fact I
could not ring without my iPhone.

Back at the hotel I reported to the receptionists and went up to my
room, and that is where this account should best be closed, for, dear reader,
I have a small confession. Buried beneath a shirt on my bed lay my iPhone.
The Find My iPhone application had been working correctly, but I had not
realized it was unable to flash inside the icon for the hotel, only next to it in
the adjoining street.

Reluctant though I was, I felt duty bound to report the find to the
police, but to save face I told them I had found it in the bushes outside the
hotel. "Good," said the female officer, "we can close the case as solved."
And so I went to bed satisfied not only at being reunited with my iPhone,
but also knowing that I had helped police statistics for the year.

On Track ||||||||||||||||||||||||||||||||||||||||||||||||||||

Several tourist trains stop at Tottori, one of which is the super-luxurious
(and super-expensive) Twilight Express Mizukaze. It runs two-day tours
between Osaka and Shimonoseki with deluxe private rooms, local delicacies, and outings to the dunes and Tottori Folk Crafts Museum.

More affordable is the Ametuchi (pronounced Ametsuchi), which
runs from Tottori to Izumo. On board are drinks, food, and fortune telling.
The train's deep blue exterior references the sea, and the silver along
the bottom represents a sword, as the region is famous for iron making.

Manga fans head for the Conan Train, decorated with figures from
the long-running *Great Detective Conan* (renamed in English as *Case
Closed*). Created by a local man, Gosho Aoyama, the series features a
high school detective and has sold over two hundred million copies
worldwide, with more than nine hundred anime episodes. The author's
hometown of Hokuei, through which the train runs, has a museum dedicated to him.

Fans of *yokai* (Japanese monsters) flock to the JR Sakai Line, a single-track branch line just eighteen kilometers long. Starting at Yonago, the "*Yokai* Train" ends at the port town of Sakaiminato, hometown of Shigeru Mizuki, who revived interest in folklore through his influential manga and anime, notably *GeGeGe no Kitaro*.

Matsue

THERE ARE ANY NUMBER of "best-kept secrets" in Japan, and mine is Matsue. Off the beaten track and on the dark side, the castle town is charming, unspoiled, and has some of the best sunsets in the country. Situated on the edge of Lake Shinji, it is filled with so many waterways that it has been dubbed the "Venice of central Japan." It is the prefectural capital of Shimane, an area steeped in myth and mystery. Lovers of folklore are invariably entranced, as was Japanophile Lafcadio Hearn, who reveled in the region.

The writer arrived in 1890 when the country was all the vogue, riding a wave of Japonisme in Europe and America. Over the years his bestselling books have led many notable figures to visit Japan, including Charlie Chaplin and Albert Einstein. His admirers range from the poet Edward Thomas, the potter Bernard Leech, and the politician Jawaharlal Nehru, to such novelists as E. M. Forster, Malcolm Cowley, and Henry Miller. No other writer on Japan can claim a similar impact.

Hearn lived in Matsue for just fourteen months, but the town imprinted itself on his consciousness. He spent another twelve years in Japan, but it was always Matsue that remained closest to his heart. It was here that he wrote his most appealing book, *Glimpses of Unfamiliar Japan*, filled with the joys of discovery.

> It then appears that everything Japanese is delicate, exquisite, admirable—even a pair of common wooden chopsticks in a paper bag with a little drawing upon it. . . . Curiosities and dainty objects bewilder you by their very multitude: on either side of you, wherever you turn your eyes, are countless wonderful things as yet incomprehensible.

By birth and upbringing, Hearn was a cosmopolitan. The son of a Greek islander and Anglo-Irish soldier, he spent the first two years of his life in Greece and was subsequently raised by a great aunt in Dublin. At thirteen he was sent to a Catholic boarding school in the north of England. Three years later, in a playground accident, he lost the sight of one eye (the other was myopic). Not long afterwards his great aunt ran out of money, and he had to leave school. After a spell of penury in London, he was sent to the United States where, in testimony to his talent, he worked his way up from sleeping on a print room floor to be one of the country's top journalists.

When Hearn got a commission to write about Japan, he embarked by boat for Yokohama. It shaped the rest of his life. Such was his fascination with the country that he took a job teaching in a remote provincial area with only a handful of Westerners. It was in the days before railways, when the usual mode of long-distance travel was by boat. From Yokohama he traveled to Okayama in the Inland Sea, and then by rickshaw deep into the interior, before emerging at the Sea of Japan. Within half a year he had married and was established in a former samurai house. It seemed the wanderer had settled, but fearful of Matsue's bitter winters affecting his fragile health, he moved to a warmer climate in Kumamoto.

For Hearniasts (Hearn enthusiasts), the house where he lived is revered ground. One of the wings has been removed, but the rest remains much as it was in his lifetime. Here Hearn enjoyed being lord of his domain, donning a kimono and following Japanese custom. He was particularly fond

of the garden, and the description he wrote in *Glimpses* shows how readily
he had absorbed Japanese values. "Its artistic purpose is to copy faithfully
the attractions of a veritable landscape," he wrote, "and to convey the real
impression that a real landscape communicates."

> It is paved with blue pebbles, and its centre is occupied by a pondlet,
> —a miniature lake fringed with rare plants, and containing a tiny
> island, mountains and dwarf peach-trees and pines and azaleas, some
> of which are perhaps more than a century old, though scarcely more
> than a foot high. Nevertheless, this work, seen as it was intended to
> be seen, does not appear to the eye in miniature at all. From a certain
> angle of the guest-room looking out upon it, the appearance is that of
> a real lake shore with a real island beyond it, a stone's throw away.

It was my third visit to the house, and much to my surprise the receptionist claimed to remember me. There was no one else around, and he said
there had been a drop-off in visitors, particularly from Korea. Why would
Koreans come here? Were they fans of Hearn? "Not at all," he laughed.
"A LCC [low-cost carrier] provides a cheap connection here, and they like
posing in kimono in an old house."

Such was Hearn's affection for Matsue that when he naturalized he
called himself Koizumi Yakumo, the name by which he is known to Japanese. Koizumi was his wife's family name, and he chose Yakumo meaning
"many clouds" in reference to the region's skies, which tend to be overcast.
It was not the first time he had changed his name, for in resentment of
his father and all he stood for he dropped his first name of Patrick for his
middle name, Lafcadio (adapted from the Greek island of Lefkada, where
he was born).

THE STREET ON WHICH Hearn lived, with its castle moat and traditional
housing, is officially one of "Japan's Top 100 Street Scenes." Impressive as
that might (or might not) be, the street with its row of pine trees and passing boats is certainly picturesque. And almost opposite Hearn's house is a
slope leading up to a well-preserved and attractive castle, one of only twelve
to have survived intact from Edo times.

Next to Hearn's residence, conveniently, is the Hearn Museum. It is the premier site for studies about him, with books, manuscripts, and a richly illustrated overview of his far-reaching life. He had moved from Lefkada to Dublin, from England to Cincinnati, from New Orleans to Martinique, before he ended up in Japan—literally ended up, for his grave is in Tokyo's Zoshigaya Cemetery.

Walking round the museum's display, I found much in Hearn's life that resonated with my own. A foreign mother—check. Abandonment at a young age—check. A stern father—check. Boarding school—check. A traumatic accident in teenage years—check. A Christian upbringing jettisoned for paganism—check. A restless love of travel—check. A short-lived marriage to an exotic female—check. Late-thirties arrival in Japan—check. Honeymoon period on the Sea of Japan—check. Decision to stay and write about Japan—check. Linguistic reliance on a Japanese female—check. Shinto as key to the culture—check. It added up to a lot of checks, but for all that there was one glaring difference: Hearn was a genius.

The word "genius" is too easily thrown around, but there is absolutely no doubt in the case of Hearn. The achievements in a relatively short life (he died at fifty-four) are simply astonishing. He excelled in every field with which he engaged. Journalist, novelist, translator of French, travel writer, author of a Creole cookbook, religious interpreter, critic, literary lecturer, essayist, letter writer, reteller of folklore—in every single field he has won admiration. And all that without higher education, with limited eyesight, and despite a globe-trotting lifestyle. Genius indeed!

His legacy includes twenty books of non-fiction, two novels, 1,089 news articles, and 1,584 letters. In addition, there are at least seven biographies of him, several reminiscences, four fictional accounts, three collections of academic papers, and a travelogue by someone who followed his footsteps through at least six different countries.

The easiest way to understand Hearn is as a late Romantic in revolt against industrialization. He was thrilled by the traditional culture of Matsue, and wanted it to stay untouched by Western values. Earlier he had reacted to Martinique in much the same way (his stay there coincided with that of Gaugin). He wrote of how travel to exotic parts was akin to the intensity of falling in love, which for Romantics was the greatest of all human experience.

There was one other factor in Hearn's love of Matsue. In a letter of 1890, he wrote, "How marvellously does this world resemble ancient Greece,– not only in its legends and the more joyous phases of its faith, but in all its graces of art and its senses of beauty." At the time ancient Greece was much in vogue with intellectuals, who championed it as a highpoint of civilization, and Hearn's esteem for Japan was such that he saw in it a modern equivalent.

There was a personal element too, for his affection was underwritten by sentimental attachment to the Greek mother he had lost at the age of four. His rosy-tinted Romanticism led him to see in Japan the same traits that he attributed to ancient Greece: the cultivation of beauty, closeness to nature, civility in everyday life, and a religion based on ancestor worship and anthropomorphic gods.

The result was a fantasy land in which everything and everybody is "elf-ish," "charming," "magical," "delightful," "enchanting," and "fabulous," in short, "a fairyland." The depictions delighted admirers of Japonisme, but for critics such as Arthur Waley and Donald Keene the gushing prose masks reality by creating a country that is weird and wonderful.

These were topics I was anxious to discuss with the great-grandson of Hearn, Bon Koizumi, who teaches locally and whose wife runs the Hearn Museum. I knew them from previous occasions, and over dinner we considered Hearn's role as a forerunner of globalism and the immigrant societies of modern times. He had what would now be called a fluid identity, for his Greek and Irish parentage was overlaid by an English public-school education and a career as an American writer before he naturalized as a Japanese.

Although Hearn is known in the West for his explication of Japanese culture, in Japan he is known for his ghost stories. The writer had a particular interest in the macabre and was an admirer of Edgar Allan Poe. As a child he claimed to have actually seen ghosts, which may be why his retelling of Japanese horror stories has such power. Although the word "ghost" occurs more than one thousand times in his writing, there is more than just a love of the macabre behind his use of the term. He thought for instance that Shinto shrines were "ghost houses," and he considered human beings to comprise a multitude of "ghostly" traces from the past (he believed each human cell contains ancestral memory).

If you say Koizumi Yakumo to a Japanese, they will most likely respond with *Kwaidan,* Hearn's retelling of supernatural stories. It remains popular even now, after more than a century has passed. Four of Hearn's stories feature in the stunning film *Kwaidan,* directed by Masaki Kobayashi in 1964. A visual masterpiece, it is made in a style that might be called "Japanese gothic," with elements from noh and kabuki. Even by today's standards it has some breathtaking scenes, and the Rotten Tomatoes website aptly says that it "operates less as a frightening example of horror and more as a meditative tribute to Japanese folklore."

In the decades around World War II, Hearn's reputation suffered a sharp decline, for he was seen as a supporter of the enemy and an apologist for State Shinto. There are disturbing elements in his writing, it is true. He was an ardent follower of Herbert Spencer, the man who coined "survival of the fittest," which prompted Hearn to claim that Japan's "race-soul" justified its colonization of neighbors. He glorified ants for their self-sacrifice and went so far as to tell his students they should be ready to lay down their lives for the emperor. He even flirted with eugenics, popular at the time he was writing.

As memory of World War II grows dimmer, there has been an upturn in Hearn's popularity. The Irish in particular have championed him as one of their own, despite his alienation from his father's culture. Within Japan the revival has been led by nationalists such as Tokyo University professor Sukehiro Hirakawa, who sees Hearn as having a special understanding of Japanese culture. On the other hand, there is greater awareness of his being an exoticist, prone to "othering" the Japanese. There is an underlying feeling in Hearn's books that Japan is different, and for Roger Pulver he is the founder of the genre of *nihonjinron,* which promotes the dangerous notion that Japan is unique and superior. A genius for sure, but a flawed one.

THE OU PILGRIMAGE COMPRISES six rural shrines near Matsue. The most popular is Yaegaki Shrine, at the entrance to which a noticeboard proclaims, Hearn was here. The shrine is dedicated to the kami Susanoo no Mikoto and his bride, Inadahime, which is why it is popular as an *enmusubi* shrine for those seeking a "love connection." Also enshrined is their son, which provides a fertility focus, and dotted around the precincts are a number of phallic representations.

As noted previously, promotion of the life force is a vital part of shamanic religions, which is why in Bhutan you can find phalluses painted
on the outside of houses for protection (the vigor of the phallus wards off
pestilence and evil demons). It is also why stone and wooden phallic sym-
bols are venerated here at Yaegaki. Somehow they have survived into the
present, despite the widespread removal of fertility objects as shameful in
Meiji times.

At one of the subshrines stands a large wooden phallus, and in a vaginal opening at the base of a nearby tree are placed a number of smaller
phalluses. There are several "*enmusubi* trees" too, whose split trunks sym-
bolize the union of lovers. And in the street outside the shrine is a shop
that sells phallus-shaped sweets on which to suck. It is a reminder that the
buttoned-down image of modern-day Japan conceals a Dionysian past,
which occasionally bursts into view particularly when alcohol is involved.

Yaegaki Shrine is part of a Hearn trail around Matsue, which connects
sixteen sites associated with its one-time resident. Most are not of much
interest except to Hearn enthusiasts, but there is one with wider appeal—a
prestigious Zen temple called Gessho. Hearn loved it; so did I.

The prime attraction is the atmospheric cemetery, which hosts imposing tombs, quirky statues, and vigorous vegetation. Here lie the feudal lords
of Edo times, drawn from the Matsudaira family. So enchanting is the spirit
of place that the forty-year-old Hearn said he wanted to be buried here.

Other items of interest include a monument thanking tea whisks for
their service; a rock with the giant handprint of a legendary sumo wrestler;
a tearoom used by feudal lords; a "spirit house" with memorial tablets; and
in June every year a riot of hydrangea in bloom. Pride of place is held by a
giant statue of a five-meter-long turtle (or tortoise), the head of which is
nearly two meters from the ground. This is the Cosmic Turtle that carries
the world on its back, an image that occurs across cultures in Hindu, Chinese, and Native American mythology. Local lore holds that the turtle sips
water at night from the temple pond before roaming around town. If you
like this kind of thing, then Hearn and Matsue are definitely for you. If not,
well, you might be better off in Fukuoka.

On Track ||||||||||||||||||||||||||||||||||||||||||||||||||

The modest town of two hundred thousand is served by two stations, roughly two kilometers from each other. One is the JR station on the San'in Line, along which limited express trains take roughly thirty minutes to Izumo and ninety minutes to Tottori.

The other station is Matsue Shinjiko Onsen Station, which is the terminus for the Ichibata Line to Izumo. Run by the private Ichibata Railway, it is located in a hot springs district (inside the station is a hot spring footbath). The track, laid out in 1912, skirts the north side of Lake Shinji, offering fine views of the mountain range.

Those seeking something more adventurous might try the JR Kisuki Line, which begins at Shinji Station, on the shore of the lake, and heads south through the remote Okuizumo area. Trains climb to more than seven hundred meters above sea level into the mountains of Okayama, which are on the Pacific side of Japan.

Izumo

MY FAVORITE PLACES ARE those enriched by myth and unspoiled by the ravages of modern life. The west of England, for instance, with its Arthurian tales and Glastonbury mystique. In Japan the time-honored pathways of Kumano have similar appeal, but they pale in comparison to the allure of Izumo. It is the setting for almost a third of Japan's mythology in the *Kojiki* and was the ancient capital of a kingdom that rivaled the Yamato in the Nara basin.

Izumo Taisha (Izumo Grand Shrine) is an imposing structure. But more than that, it is an institution, a symbol, a reminder of a once-glorious past. It has claims to be the oldest of all Shinto shrines, dating back to a time even before the imperial line "descended from heaven." It is Japan's foremost shrine for *enmusubi* (love connections), in addition to which it has the biggest inner sanctuary in the country and the largest *shimenawa* rope in the world. And as if that were not enough, experts think the shrine may once have been the tallest building on earth.

In terms of prestige, Izumo ranks second only to Ise Shrine. It stands on the darker side of Japan and is associated, fittingly, with the unruly storm god Susanoo no Mikoto. The kami is a complex character, a youthful rebel who became a culture hero and today haunts the imagination of manga and anime creators. Brother of the sun goddess Amaterasu, he held an exalted position until he blew it by some unforgivable behavior.

Impetuous and temperamental, Susanoo was distraught by the death of his mother, such that he upset the heavenly harmony with his grief and howling. When Amaterasu outwitted him in a contest to create other kami, he went on a rampage, excreting in the sacred rice fields and throwing a flayed horse among the women in the weaving room. One of them was so startled she stabbed her private parts with a needle.

For his sins Susanoo was exiled from heaven and he descended to earth at Izumo, where an eight-headed serpent called Yamata no Orochi was terrifying the locals. The chieftain had eight daughters, seven of whom had already been devoured by the monster, and Susanoo vowed to save the eighth. Cunningly, he put out eight buckets of sake for each of the serpent's heads, and when it was befuddled, he attacked and killed it.

Susanoo was rewarded for his victory by winning the hand of the remaining princess, Kushinada-hime. In addition, he found a sword called Kusanagi no Tsurugi (Grass-cutting Sword) in the tail of the serpent, which was such a rare item that he presented it to Amaterasu, who forgave him for his previous bad behavior. Later she handed the sword to her grandson when he descended to earth. It continues to play a very real part in Japanese affairs, for it is one of the three imperial regalia used in ascension rites. (It was featured in 2019, though shrouded and unseen, when the present emperor was inaugurated.)

There are many ways of interpreting myth—culturally, literally, historically, psychologically, spiritually. It is often taken as the basis for religious ritual, but my own instinct is to see it as history dressed up as fantasy. In this case Susanoo may represent immigrants from Silla (a Korean kingdom), who arrived on the Shimane coast near Izumo and defeated a many-headed coalition of chieftains. There are even shrines that claim to be the landing spot.

By contrast, the Yamato clan are thought to have arrived in Kyushu from Baekje, a different Korean kingdom. The two groups were related but rivals, hence the imaginative brother-sister pairing with origins in "heaven." Excavation of imperial graves would no doubt reveal the truth, but it is strictly forbidden to disturb the emperor's ancestral spirits. (Many suspect that the real reason is fear of unearthing Korean origins.)

At some point the Yamato Kingdom achieved hegemony over Izumo. Accounts compiled later tell of Izumo ceding temporal power in return for spiritual dominion. In this regard, Naoki Matsumoto of Waseda University posed an interesting question: "When did we become Japanese?" He pointed out that Yamato rulers integrated into their mythology the gods of those they subdued, similar to ancient Rome. In this case Yamato may have absorbed Izumo myths by making Susanoo a younger (and subordinate) brother of Amaterasu. Looking at the available evidence, Matsumoto believes the ceding of Izumo to Yamato took place in AD 380, which is the answer he gives to his initial question. So there we have it: Japan began in 380, and Izumo was key.

IZUMO LITERALLY MEANS "OUT of the clouds," and the area in which it lies is known as San'in. The character for *san* means mountain, and *in*, the second character, stands for yin (as in yin and yang). The area is thus all about the shadowy side of things—darkness, death, the moon, the subterranean, and the subconscious. By contrast, San'yo on the sunny Pacific side has yang written into its name.

Izumo Taisha is the grandest of shrines, set in open land and backed by foothills. There are a succession of *torii* before the visitor comes to the final approach, and the path leads first down a gentle gradient, then through a corridor of pine trees to the magnificent worship hall.

When I visited, there were swirling clouds over the tree-lined approach, and mist was strung out in patches along the hills. Ghostly shapes formed in the vapors, and as at Avalon the veil between this world and the other was stretched thin. Small wonder that, by tradition, the entrance to the underworld is located in this region.

The sheer size of the building commands respect, and at twenty-four meters it is the tallest shrine in Japan. The *shimenawa* weighs five tons and is a staggering thirteen meters in length. The custom is to throw a coin upwards, and if it lodges in the strands of the rope, it is a token of good luck. Mine stuck on the first throw, which put me in good spirits.

You soon get a sense that things are different here. Worshippers clap four times instead of the usual two (twice for oneself, twice for one's partner, according to tradition). The massive wooden buildings are rebuilt every sixty years based on the cycle of Chinese astrology (twelve animal signs for each of the five elements). Renewal is a vital part of Shinto thinking, which seeks to counter decay by reaffirming the life force. It is why the New Year is celebrated with such enthusiasm, a nationwide kickstart to the year ahead.

The first Westerner to write of the shrine was Lafcadio Hearn, who was lucky enough to have a letter of introduction to the head priest, eighty-first in a lineage that stretched back to the murky past. He was given a private tour and was so taken with what he saw that he declared Izumo to be the holiest shrine in Japan.

> I cannot suppress some slight exultation at the thought that I have been allowed to see what no other foreigner has been privileged to see,—the interior of Japan's most ancient shrine, and those sacred utensils and quaint rites of primitive worship so well worthy the study of the anthropologist and the evolutionist.
>
> But to have seen Kitzuki [the local name for Izumo Taisha] as I saw it is also to have seen something much more than a single wonderful temple. To see Kitzuki is to see the living centre of Shinto, and to feel the life-pulse of the ancient faith, throbbing as mightily in this nineteenth century as ever in that unknown past whereof the *Kojiki* itself, though written in a tongue no longer spoken, is but a modern record.

One contemporary event that would have delighted Hearn concerns a recent discovery. Ever since ancient times there have been claims of a huge worship hall converted from the palace of a former ruler. Annals from 950 describe it as being forty-eight meters high, which is three meters higher than the world's largest wooden building, the Great Buddha Hall at Todai-ji in Nara. Imagine the excitement, then, when in April 2000 the remains were found of three huge wooden pillars bound together to make one massive support. Could it be proof that the ancient records were true?

At the nearby Shimane Museum, there are architectural models of how the building might have looked. The museum also houses Japan's largest collection of excavated bronze swords and bronze bells. And for those looking for some local food, there is a restaurant offering Izumo soba, which uses wholemeal buckwheat, making it tougher and chewier than the usual noodles.

Izumo's most famous citizen, Izumo no Okuni, is the inspiration for the popular manga series *Kunisaki Izumo no Jijo* (Izumo Kunisaki's Circumstances). Okuni was a *miko* (shrine maiden) who danced for the kami at Izumo, before moving to Kyoto around 1600 and performing in a pop-up theater on the dry riverbed there. She drew attention by donning male clothing and mimicking a drunken samurai, a "crazy" style of theater that started a new trend called kabuki. Later she returned to Izumo, and her grave is not far from the shrine. Local manga artist Aya Hirakawa drew on the legend to create the contemporary story of a girlish boy still at school, who performs secretly as a female impersonator in kabuki.

One aspect of the shrine that had changed since my last visit was the proliferation of rabbits. Rabbit statues, to be precise. As we have seen, the Japanese term refers to both rabbits and hares, and the main deity worshipped here is Okuninushi (a.k.a. Onamuchi), hero of the White Hare of Inaba. From previous visits I could only recall a single rabbit statue, next to a giant sculpture of Okuninushi. Now, like real rabbits, the statues had multiplied, and a whole section of the grounds had been set aside for celebration of the sanctified creature. Like the animals at Nativity, they had taken on a life of their own.

There are *enmusubi* shrines all across Japan dedicated to finding a good match, but Izumo Taisha is the grandest and oldest of them all. "The Sacred Home of Good Connections," proudly declares the shrine. The status derives from the love match of Okuninushi with Princess Suseri, whose ancestor was Susanoo, the storm god.

In recent years the shrine's claim to promote love connections was given a huge boost by an imperial princess who met her husband on a visit to the shrine. Her partner? None other than the son of the head priest. I can't help thinking how much this would have pleased that great Japanophile Lafcadio Hearn, for 1,620 years after the pact between Yamato and Izumo, nuptial vows were exchanged between a descendant of the sun goddess and a descendant of the storm god.

HOW MANY KAMI DOES Shinto have? The standard answer is *"yaoyorozu,"* often translated as eight million but more like a myriad. The thought of them all gathering in one place might seem absurd, but every autumn at Izumo that is exactly what happens.

Until the nineteenth century, Japan used a lunar calendar, and throughout the country the tenth month was known as Kannazuki, or the Month with No Gods, except in Izumo where it was known as Kamiarizuki, Month with the Gods. The reason is that all the kami of Japan gather at Izumo at this time—all except Ebisu, that is, because he is deaf and does not hear the invitation.

The get-together is still held annually, and I once had the good fortune to attend. It was quite something, for the whole multitude of kami passed within feet of me. The arrival takes place on Inasa Beach, a twenty-minute walk from the main shrine. As darkness descends, priests light bonfires to guide the kami, who arrive from the sea. A tent is set up, with a simple altar on which sits Ryuja-san, a sea-serpent that serves as intermediary. As the kami descend into purified tree branches, a priest marks the moment with a cascading wail, and their presence is signified by rustling branches.

The welcoming rituals last about thirty minutes, and on the wide-open beach much of the chanting is absorbed by the lapping waves. By now there are hundreds if not thousands of onlookers crammed around the tent. All of a sudden, priests push through the crowd and spectators are asked to observe silence as the kami are borne on branches to the Grand Shrine. White sheets are held up to protect the kami from the "polluting" gaze of spectators, and the priests wear white masks to avoid breathing on them.

When the kami arrive at the main shrine, there is a welcome ceremony in the worship hall consisting of *kagura* dance, after which they are taken to a row of small shrines described as their "dormitory." I asked one of the priests what the kami were doing there, and he said they needed to rest because they had a busy schedule. Ahead of them was a week of rituals and discussions, after which they would go to pay respects at eight other shrines in the area. On the twenty-sixth day after their arrival, there would be a final leave-taking ritual.

The morning after the welcome ceremony, I noticed a line of people queueing before a small tent. Inside was Ryuja-san, the serpent spirit. Worshippers filed past, prayed, and at the exit were served sake and a few grains of rice—Shinto's equivalent of wine and wafer. The snake has been so demonized in the West that it seems counter-intuitive to see it treated as a focus of devotion, yet because of its skin-shedding ability it has long been cherished as a symbol of regeneration in shamanic cultures. Still today there is a custom in Japan of keeping snakeskin in a wallet to generate new growth.

But where were all the kami? An earnest young priest told me they were attending a conference some ten minutes' walk away. What about, I wondered? Deciding important matters for the coming year, he said, such as the granting of love matches and the grain yields for different regions. The "conference hall" turned out to be a shrine on the road to the sea, and to my surprise there was almost no one there except for a solitary priest. He too was dispensing sake and rice grain.

The doors of the main room stood open, though since kami are invisible there was naturally nothing to see. I mentioned this to the priest, who told me they were not there at all, but secreted behind the closed doors of the inner sanctuary. For eight million or so it seemed awfully cramped.

So much in Shinto makes sense to me that I sought to find meaning in this too. Then my historical instincts kicked in, and it struck me that the gathering here each year was the legacy of the power enjoyed by Izumo in ancient times. Could it, in fact, be an annual enactment of spiritual dominion granted to the kingdom in that pact with Yamato in AD 380? After all, in Japan tradition rules.

Even now, Izumo remains in an odd kind of way an alternative to the primacy of Ise, and I came away with the feeling of hidden depths in the spirit of place. When the ancients thought of death, they created an underworld called Yomi, and the entrance to it lies between rocks in rural Shimane. This is the yin side of Japan, rewarding for those who take the time to appreciate it. I could have chosen a different route along the more popular Pacific coast, but Izumo made me doubly glad that "I took the one less traveled by."

On Track ||||||||||||||||||||||||||||||||||||||||||||||||||

The small town of Izumo (population 170,000) is on the JR San'in Line, which runs parallel to the coast. The station is several kilometers from

Izumo Shrine, which can be reached by bus or taxi. The Former Taisha Station, dating from 1924, used to service the shrine but was closed in 1990 and is now a museum. It was built in the Imperial Crown Style, at a time when public policy favored Japanese rather than Western architecture.

Trains on the Ichibata Line from Matsue take longer than JR but offer more attractive views, and the station at Izumo Taisha, built eighty years ago, has stained-glass windows. The enterprising Ichibata Dentetsu Company (nicknamed Bataden) has some innovative ideas, such as a railcar pub, decorative exteriors, and hands-on train driving experience. It also has an excellent English-language website with tourist information and special deals.

Tsuwano

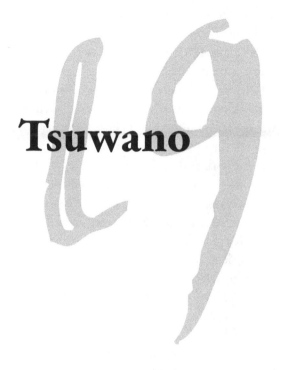

TSUWANO IS A CASTLE town that has lost its castle, a "little Kyoto" with the emphasis on little. The total population is just 7,500. Squeezed between steep mountains, it is compact yet intriguing. At first sight you would say there is nothing much worth seeing, yet for those who linger there is plenty. It may be off the beaten track, but it is another quiet secret on the yin side of Japan.

There are basically two main streets, one of which has the majority of shops. I came on the recommendation of a friend, but such was the underwhelming first impression that I thought I had got off at the wrong station. But then I met Akemi, a volunteer guide who was young, enthusiastic, and a graduate of Manchester University. Born and raised in Tsuwano, she had returned with the aim of helping make it healthy, organic, and environmentally conscious. A woman with a mission. I took to her immediately.

It may have been me, but nature here looked uninhibited and unbound. The hills around the town were greener, the slopes steeper and more thickly wooded. No doubt the stars were brighter too. Under Akemi's guidance, the little town came to life. Three small hills had been commandeered by the feudal lord, she explained, one for his castle, one for his retainers, and one to keep out the demons of ill fortune.

We headed first for the ruined castle, from where there was an overview of the town. The castle had been demolished in 1878 in the campaign against feudalism, but some of the walls remained. There was a choice, Akemi said, between a hundred-minute walk along a footpath with historical features, or a chairlift. I knew which was the right thing to do. I chose the other.

From the hill we looked down on a narrow stretch of red-tiled town houses. Akemi had done her homework and rattled off the vital statistics. The town was half a kilometer wide and two and a half long. The red roof tiles were different from the usual black tiles because they were baked at a high temperature, which made them stronger and less likely to crack in cold places with deep snow. Tsuwano, for instance.

"The town is known as 'the little Kyoto of San'in,'" Akemi explained, "because it's in a river basin with harsh winters, like Kyoto. We have *machiya* (merchant houses) too, like Kyoto. There is an Inari shrine with *torii* tunnel, like Kyoto's Fushimi Shrine. And we have Yasaka Shrine with a Gion Festival, like Kyoto. Especially we have Sagiodori (Heron dance), which was brought here from Kyoto in the sixteenth century.

"We try to keep a traditional atmosphere in the town. So far no Starbucks or anything like that. And restaurants use organic vegetables. We want to attract people from big cities like Hiroshima and Yamaguchi to come and enjoy fresh air and healthy food."

"How about foreigners?" I asked. "Do many come here?"

As the town's international representative, she knew all about it. "Before Covid there were 660,000 visitors. Just 600 were foreigners. That is one percent. Maybe you are the first since the lockdown," she laughed. "That's why I am glad to see you. Mostly we have American marines from nearby Hiroshima."

Back in the main street, we walked through the samurai district. The domain had once been significant enough to have one of the country's best Edo-period schools, and within its pounded-earth walls were long rooms where kendo and other martial arts were practiced. Teachers sat on tatami along one side, and there was a raised area for the feudal lord.

The school was not limited to training in fighting skills, for there were Chinese and Dutch studies too, important means of knowledge for a country in self-imposed isolation. Neighboring Hagi had produced politicians, but Tsuwano produced academics. The town also boasted a famous novelist—Mori Ogai (1862–1922). The son of a low-ranking samurai who practiced medicine, he only lived here to the age of eleven, but always prided himself on being "a son of Tsuwano." (The Ogai Memorial Hall stands next to his family home.)

Along the side of the street ran free-flowing water filled with enormous carp kitted out in white, grey, and orange. In Tsuwano water was abundant, Akemi said, though much of it was diverted underground for use in case of fire. The carp, she added, could outlive humans, even though the stream in which they lived was frozen in winter with deep snow piled high above it. Natural cryonics, perhaps.

The street was divided into two by a barrier gate, marking off the merchant district from that of the samurai. The houses of the samurai were within their own walled precincts, whereas the merchant houses faced directly onto the street and had guardrails to prevent scuffing. I had never seen such a clear boundary before between Edo-period districts, and not surprisingly the well-preserved street is a popular location for films and television programs.

Next up was a sake brewery, where Akemi had a friend who was the eleventh of his family to run the business. I supposed he must be the oldest son, but no, he said, his elder brother had not been interested. During the conversation it became clear that Akemi's family also ran a sake business. Rivals? "No, we cooperate," she said with a nervous laugh. I sensed the cooperation extended beyond business.

"Actually, there are three sake breweries in Tsuwano," said Akemi, "but we all work together because we want to make Tsuwano sake something special. This year is difficult because of Covid. Usually we make money from events like festivals, weddings, office parties, but of course the number is down. But we are not worried. We will succeed," she said defiantly.

After all the walking it was time for something to eat, and Akemi showed me an English-language flyer she had prepared that featured nineteen different outlets. The town was clearly making an effort. I asked for something typically Tsuwano, and Akemi took me to a shop that catered for tourists. Typical, I thought. Tourists want the local food, and the locals want pasta and hamburgers.

For the first course, I tried Tsuwano potato soup, consisting of *taro* in a light *dashi* broth with slivers of sea bream and *yuzu* citrus peel. Delicate taste, solid substance. Afterwards we enjoyed a green tea set with Tsuwano's most famous product, *genjimaki*, a rolled cake with *anko* (sweet red bean paste).

Over the meal Akemi told me of two other aspects of the town. One concerned Hidden Christians, who were descendants of sixteenth-century converts. Christianity was strictly banned in Edo times because of a fear of colonization, and the Meiji reformists at first continued the policy. Yet despite the risk of torture and death, many families handed down their faith in secret.

In 1868, when thousands of Hidden Christians were uncovered in Urakami, a district of Nagasaki, they were dispersed to different domains for "re-education." Here in Tsuwano their reception was among the worst: they were starved, tortured, and made to stand naked in the bitter cold of winter. Of the roughly 150 sent to the domain, 37 perished. Tragically it was just before Christianity was tolerated in 1873. Now there is a campaign to canonize the 37 who died and make Tsuwano a "sacred place of martyrdom."

A happier note is struck by the *kagura* plays, which enact scenes from Shinto's mythological past. The costumed dramas with musical accompaniment can be truly spectacular, and Iwami *kagura* (Iwami being the historical name of the area) has a reputation for being the best in the country. Unlike noh with its wooden masks, the Tsuwano tradition is for masks made of Japanese paper (*washi*), which makes them sturdy but light. It means actors can perform speedier actions, including acrobatics.

For those lucky enough to time their visit right, there are occasional performances in Tsuwano, but the real deal are the autumnal all-night sessions in village houses. For that you need to plan ahead. Iwami troupes occasionally perform in Kyoto, and the stage effects would not disgrace top Broadway productions. The slaying by Susanoo of the eight-headed monster Yamata no Orochi is their showpiece, for the serpent writhes and wriggles in such an improbable manner that it takes on a life of its own. The rapt audiences reminded me of village plays in Bali, at which mesmerized children sit open-eyed, soaking in the larger-than-life mythical stories of their ancestors.

That afternoon when I took my leave, I found myself the only person waiting on the station platform. Tsuwano had proved a delight to visit, free of crowds and full of interest. In its promotion of health and history, the town is making an effort to counter depopulation and attract young people like Akemi. In the end it turned out I had got off the train at the right station after all.

Thanks, Akemi!

On Track ||||||||||||||||||||||||||||||||||||||||||||||||||

Tsuwano Station opened in 1918 on the Yamaguchi Line and is served by the Super Oki limited express. The train runs for over five hours between Yamaguchi and Tottori, making it one of Japan's longest distances for a limited express (380 kilometers). The express takes its name from the Oki Islands.

For railway enthusiasts, there is a very special way to arrive—the once-a-week steam locomotive from Shin-Yamaguchi Station. Advanced reservations are necessary, and the train only operates on weekends from March to November. The journey takes just over two hours, with preserved carriages from different periods and staff in matching uniforms. At the back is an observation car with armchairs facing outward. The train attracts crowds of onlookers who see it off, as well as photographers who jostle for the best positions.

Hagi

JAPANESE TRAINS ARE SAFE, clean, and punctual. They pull up exactly at clearly marked lines on the platform. The conductors are polite and helpful, and at journey's end race through carriages to check for litter left behind. Nothing goes wrong, save for the horrifying shock of suiciders who throw themselves in front of passing trains.

So what happened at Hagi was unexpected. It was early evening and the sun had just gone down, but something felt very wrong. For one thing there were no lights at the station. "Is this Hagi?" I asked the driver. "Yes," he said. So I got off. There were three others, who headed straight for the footbridge to the other side of the station. By the time I heaved my luggage across, they had disappeared.

The station was unmanned. Not only unmanned, but curiously inactive. There was no one around, no taxis waiting, and no helpful notices. In front of the station was a small area for cars, but there were no cars. It was a no-taxi station and as far as I could tell a no-person town. This was more than odd since everything I had read suggested Hagi was an attractive castle town with tourist appeal.

Round the corner came a man walking a huge German Shepherd with bright flashing lights. For a moment I thought I had passed into some kind of alternative universe; this was not the cozy predictable Japan to which I was used.

"Excuse me, is this Hagi?"

"Are you looking for Hagi?"

"Yes. Where is it?"

"Here. This is Hagi."

"But there's nothing here."

"Yes. That's right."

"I don't understand. I thought Hagi was a town."

"Yes, it is."

"But I don't see a town."

"It's over there." He pointed along an empty road.

"Can I walk there?"

"Maybe."

"How many minutes."

"Maybe thirty."

"I have a hotel booking. Royal Intelligent Hotel. Do you know it?"

"Yes. It is next to the station."

"But isn't this the station?"

"This is Hagi Station. The hotel is at Higashi Hagi Station."

"Really? How can I get there?"

"You can catch a train."

"When is the next train?"

"There isn't a train. The last one has left."

"So what can I do?"

"You can catch a taxi."

"But there is no taxi."

"You want a taxi?"

"Yes, please."

"I see. Just a minute please. I will telephone my sister." He wrestled with his dog and moved off to one side. After a brief conversation he told me, "My sister will come soon. Please wait here. Okay?" And with that he disappeared with his illuminated dog.

Did my dog-loving savior have a taxi-driving sister? It seemed unlikely. When she turned up shortly afterward, I discovered she had nothing to do with taxi driving, but simply lived nearby. It was a random act of kindness that often typifies encounters in Japan.

The Royal Intelligent Hotel turned out to be high tech and post-human. Instead of a receptionist, there was a touchscreen. It was reminiscent of love hotels, where guests choose from a picture panel of exotic bedrooms. No such excitement at the Intelligent Hotel, however, where the blunt instructions led to a nondescript room with more directions, mainly about the all-important matter of bathing. The communal baths were on the top floor, together with a roof *rotenburo* (outdoor bath), so I changed into a *yukata* and took a pair of towels as instructed.

The outdoor bath had a fence around waist high, and as the surrounding buildings were only slightly lower, the modesty level was finely judged. There is something very liberating about standing nonchalantly naked under a bright starry sky, steam rising off a well-soaked body, with a whole town laid out before you. Hagi had been full of surprises so far, but I was definitely beginning to warm to it.

THE FOLLOWING MORNING I headed into the station next door to the hotel. Higashi Hagi (East Hagi) looked more like a proper station, and when I told the information office of my experience, they laughed knowingly and said I was not the first to make such a mistake. I suggested it would make sense to switch names and call this station Hagi and the other one Nishi Hagi (West Hagi). "*So desu ne,*" they said in a way that signified "We heard what you said, but we're not going to do anything."

On the ground floor of the hotel was a rental-bike shop with intelligent bicycles, so I rented one and set off to sample the delights of the town. And delightful it indeed is, once you get into the historical preservation district. The town brochure describes it as an "unroofed museum," the chief exhibits being white plastered walls sheltering samurai houses.

I let my intelligent bicycle take charge, happy to cruise at random down photogenic backstreets. Old gateways, craft shops, and cafes added to the charm. Here and there were the well-preserved houses of rich merchants with their own courtyards. Of particular note was the former residence of Hagi's most famous son, Yoshida Shoin (1830–59), which stood in a compound with a small shrine and a *juku* school. His achievement? Helping kickstart Japan's industrial revolution by motivating youngsters to study Western technology.

As a young man, Yoshida tried to board one of Commodore Perry's ships, knowing the probable punishment was death. He turned himself in, was imprisoned, then confined in his house to a tiny three-and-a-half-tatami room. Later, in his small school he taught foreign affairs, an unusual topic in an isolationist country. It did not last long, for he was implicated in an assassination plot and executed. He was just twenty-nine.

Following Yoshida's residence, I headed for the sprawling grounds of the former castle. Typically, the huge stone walls were impressively solid and sturdy, yet aesthetic too. Located on a delta, it was built in 1604 with three lines of defense. The keep was demolished in 1874 and only a section remains, now part of a park with five hundred cherry trees and a moat of greenish water. Turtles were paddling around for the sheer fun of it, occasionally taking time out to sun themselves on nearby rocks. This is how to live, they said. No life of toil for us.

On the way back I noticed a patch of water and headed down an alleyway to investigate. All of a sudden there opened up an unexpected scene, for laid out before me was the sea bordered by a sandy pine beach. A lone fisherman stood perfectly positioned in the foreground, with land curving elegantly behind him into the distance. It was such a beautiful scene I could scarcely believe I had it to myself. It used to be said that Fukuoka was Japan's best kept secret. Forget that; try Hagi. No crowds, no litter, no concrete, no tetrapods. Just a lone fisherman.

My intelligent bike steered me next past a climbing kiln and a huge, empty parking area. Pottery is Hagi's most famous product and schoolchildren are regularly bussed in for instruction in how it is produced. I was scheduled to visit a potter the following day, so I passed on in pursuit of another "famous Hagi product"—ice cream flavored with summer oranges. It was as refreshing as it sounds.

THE MEIRINKAN IS A magnificent long building, which constitutes the largest wooden schoolhouse in Japan. It is a glowing example of just how attractive the country's architecture used to be, and a slap in the face to every banal apartment block in contemporary Japan. Inside are a tourist information center, a World Heritage visitor center, a restaurant, and a museum explaining Hagi's role in modernization. Stars of the show are the Choshu Five, a name suggestive of a gang of outlaws. In a sense that is not far wrong, because they broke the law by escaping abroad. It was 1863, when awareness of the need to modernize had grown so acute that the authorities in Hagi arranged for five young samurai to be dispatched abroad to learn from the source. Their destination? The world's leading power—Great Britain.

A Japanese film, the *Choshu Five* (2006), contains a memorable scene in which the young samurai argue about whether to adopt a Western appearance. One of them acts unilaterally by cutting off his topknot, symbolically severing his ties to feudalism and prompting the others to follow suit. The subsequent change of clothing heralds a change of thinking.

In London, the Choshu Five were able to audit natural science and analytical chemistry at University College London. Two of them only stayed a year, but the experience proved invaluable. The group went on to become respectively the first prime minister of Japan, the first foreign minister, a construction minister, a mint master, and a founding figure of Japan's railways. Not bad for five young lawbreakers!

Meanwhile Hagi was playing a key role in the world's fastest-ever industrialization. Trial-and-error innovations constituted the first steps in building Western-style ships. For its role in the process of modernization, Hagi is included in a World Heritage site called, inelegantly, "Japan's Meiji Industrial Revolution: Iron and Steel, Shipbuilding and Coal Mining."

Here a hobby horse of mine rears its wooden head. There are twenty-three component parts to the World Heritage site, covering eight separate areas scattered between north Honshu and south Kyushu. That might be considered odd enough, but even odder is that each component gets to call itself a World Heritage site. The result is that a disused reverberatory furnace has equivalence with Mt. Fuji. How absurd is that!

By this stage my stomach craved something other than culture, and in the restaurant a special Hagi set meal was on offer. It consisted of an attractive basketful of seven little dishes, served with soup, rice, and a mini seafood salad. Highlights were pumpkin-flavored tofu topped with *azuki* bean paste; marinated fried fish in a *nanbanzuke* sauce; and *okara,* which translates unappetizingly as "tofu dregs" or "soy pulp." All in all, like my cycling tour of Hagi, it was more than satisfying.

"THE FIRST TIME I took an interest was in Paris, when my *cafe au lait* was served in a handmade mug. I thought, that's artistic, that's attractive. It made the coffee taste special."

Masanori was talking, a forty-eight-year-old potter with an unusual life story. Unlike the hereditary lineages, whose families have been potters for centuries, he was a vocational potter who had to struggle to survive. After university he took a job as a documentary cameraman, but there was a yearning for something different. One day he woke up and knew with absolute certainty he was going to be a potter. He was twenty-seven, an age at which in Japan's unforgiving career structure a person's fate is often sealed. But for Masanori there was not the slightest doubt.

"Pottery raises the human spirit. It is not just something for use, not just an object. It is organic, with its own character, and feel, and history. Once I sensed that, I couldn't forget it."

The light in his eyes showed that he still resonated with a youthful passion. It had moved him to drop his job and get apprenticed to Saka Kourai-zaemon, a twelfth-generation potter whose family were descended from a Korean immigrant in the early seventeenth century. As in Zen and the tea ceremony, lineages matter.

The hereditary principle in Japan means more than just blood and DNA; it means being steeped from birth in the family business. It remains an important element in Shinto, but you can see it most clearly in kabuki, where child heirs appear on stage not long after they have learnt to walk. The principle is so rooted in the art and religious world that it survived the imposition of democracy after World War II and continues to be widely accepted today. The emperor system is the supreme example.

As an outsider Masanori had to start from scratch, meaning a low salary and menial jobs like packing or preparing clay. When his master died after just four years, he survived on low wages by working for a pottery company, all the while aiming to be independent—tough when Hagi alone has over one hundred potters competing for a limited market.

"How did you go about setting up on your own?" I asked.

"At first I rented a climbing kiln, which I worked on in my spare time, but there was a problem with firing it so I decided to make my own. It took a long time to find suitable land, and luckily there was an old house nearby in bad condition which we renovated."

"It looks good," I said, looking around at the renovated walls and neatly arranged shelves.

"Thank you. It took a lot of time."

"How about the pottery?"

"Well, I decided something crazy. I decided to make a traditional kiln. It is very difficult and took two years. That's why no one does that anymore. People called me a crazy potter!"

Many modern kilns are automatically fired, using electricity. The traditional kiln, fired by wood, is not only less controllable, but needs more time and money to set up. By some estimates there are only around fifty in Japan. Though Masanori was told his idea was impractical, it simply made him more determined. Fortunately there was one person who supported him, emotionally and practically—Izumi, his devoted wife.

To make his kiln, Masanori needed a suitable piece of land, which was no easy task because of safety standards. It took a while, but eventually he found somewhere. Then the hard work began. First he cut down trees and cleared the vegetation. A professional was hired to level the ground, and a professional carpenter built the roof. The climbing kiln was built with the help of a specialist team from Kyushu, possibly the last of their type, and Masanori constructed the chimney and extended the roof on his own.

There had been several setbacks, but finally the big day arrived when the kiln was fired for the first time. It was a success. It lasted twenty-eight hours, during which he had no sleep because of the constant need to add wood (roughly every fifteen minutes). The result was the production of one thousand pieces. At the age of forty-seven Masanori's dream had come true. It must have been a great feeling: "Yes," he said with a big smile. "It took a long time."

Contrary to the popular image, shaping clay at the wheel is but a fraction of a potter's work. It takes three minutes to shape a vessel; it takes months to prepare for a firing. Apart from the mixing of clay and preparation for the glaze, the traditional kiln necessitates masses and masses of wood. Where did it all come from?

"Old houses and wood from timber merchants," he told me.

"Why were you so determined to have a traditional kiln?"

"Because the pottery is true," Masanori said. "It has more character, more color and texture. Modern kilns are too controlled, so pieces look similar."

"What do you think makes Hagi pottery different from other styles?"

"It is soft textured, plain, because it is fired at a lower temperature. The earth here makes it a reddish orange. It was made for the tea ceremony, for special occasions."

"And the glaze?"

"Transparent, white. To show the color of the clay. The white is from burnt rice straw. Sometimes it has a purple tint. Heat, amount of oxygen, position in the kiln, all can change the color."

"All your pottery looks very traditional. Was that your intention?"

"Yes, it's strange. I am from outside, but I try to keep Hagi tradition. But potters from Hagi, especially young ones, they want something new. For example, they sometimes add painting."

Masanori and Izumi now run their own business, called Makino Hagi-yaki Studio, which emphasizes the product's rootedness in Hagi. Masanori digs part of the clay himself, and the wood is sourced locally. He may not have been born here, but the pottery is Hagi through and through. "We believe that there exists an ethereal beauty in the traditional and simple Hagi pottery," states their website.

Izumi offers me some green tea in one of her husband's cups and tells me that because of the soft texture the liquid seeps into the cracks of the glaze. With the passage of time, it affects the color, and tea masters appreciate the *nanabake* (seven levels of change) acquired over long years of use. In this way the consumer shares in the creation. "When you drink, you too are adding to the color," Izumi tells me, and the tea took on an extra tang.

The hours with Masanori and his wife had been edifying and transformed my view of pottery. As I looked at the cup I was drinking from, I thought of all the dedication and personal investment that had gone into it. "Follow your bliss," said Joseph Campbell. It felt a privilege to meet someone who so thoroughly had.

On Track ||||||||||||||||||||||||||||||||||||||||||||||||||||||

Both Hagi and Higashi Hagi Stations were built in 1925 on the San'in Main Line. Daily passenger numbers in 2009 were just sixty-four for the former and 278 for the latter, indicative of which is the town's main station. From Hagi to Shimonoseki, the coastal route takes over three hours with two changes.

Hagi is the birthplace of Masaru Inoue, "father of the Japanese railways." Son of a samurai, as part of the Choshu Five he stowed away with four friends on a ship bound for London, where he studied engineering and mining before returning in the tumultuous year of 1868. Three years later he was appointed Director of the Railway Board, and he was instrumental in setting up a national network. After retirement he established the country's first locomotive manufacturing company and was made President of the Railway Board. His statue stands outside Tokyo Station.

Shimonoseki

THERE ARE QUICKER WAYS to Shimonoseki than the local train, but within minutes I knew I had made the right choice. Along the right ranged blue sea, golden sand, brown-grey rocks, and sun-kissed pine trees. Sometimes our little train would rattle past villages with houses so tightly packed they might have belonged to the same family. Successive generations had somehow eked out a living here. How different from the big-city slickers of contemporary Japan!

It was as picturesque a ride as I could recall so far, with idyllic scenes opening up one after another—undulating ridges, undisturbed inlets, seagulls perched on rocks. Occasionally an angler could be seen casting a line, and I sensed something primeval in the scene, as if metamorphosed from a ghostly hunter-gatherer in Yayoi times.

At Nagatoshi we changed to a two-carriage train running on a single track. It was the most local of all the local trains I had taken so far. There were just eight passengers, and such was the rattle it was impossible to hear anything else. For a while the train ran inland, with woodland to either side, then emerged into an open expanse with wind turbines. On a newly cut field of rice, twenty or more egrets were eagerly scavenging for food.

Suddenly the train screeched to a halt, and the driver got up and ran from his seat to the back of the second carriage. The passengers stood up in concern to see what was going on. The driver opened the carriage door, jumped down onto the tracks, and started running back the way we had come. Was he all right? Was he having a breakdown?

Some fifty meters from the train he stopped and peered into the woods. "It might be a wild boar," said one of the passengers. "Or a vandal," added another. When the driver came back, he announced there had been a deer. Having reported the incident, he said over the speaker, "Sorry to keep you waiting," gave a blast on the whistle, and added, "Don't forget to put your phones on silent mode and wear a mask." And with that we were back to our rattling progress once more.

For the rest of the journey the train wound its way around the sides of hills or simply plunged straight through them. In *Dogs and Demons,* Alex Kerr put together a frightening dystopia of Japan as a concrete junkie, unable to stop needlessly covering the whole country. One statistic I would be curious about is the distance of all the tunnels in Japan laid end to end. Just how far could you travel without ever seeing daylight, I wonder? To Korea, for sure. To Hawaii? There are so many on train trips like this that I fancy you could even tunnel your way to the moon.

THE NARROW KANMON STRAITS separate Kyushu from Honshu, and fast-flowing currents surge between them as the tide changes. Nowadays you can cross by train, road, ferry, and even on foot—not by walking on water, but underneath it. The pedestrian tunnel is less than a kilometer in length, the sole feature being a white line marking the official divide between prefectures. Take a small step, and you can have one foot in Honshu's Yamaguchi and one in Kyushu's Fukuoka at the same time.

The unusual geography goes along with some unusual history. Three great clashes have taken place here, the most famous being in 1185, when the Genji clan overcame the Heike. The second clash, in 1612, is the most celebrated duel in Japanese history, when Miyamoto Musashi, author of *The Five Rings,* defeated top swordsman Sasaki Kojiro.

The third of the clashes, known as the Shimonoseki Bombardment (1863–64), saw the upstart Choshu clan take on the might of the Great Powers. The domain wanted to challenge the shogunate policy of appease-ment, so fired on foreign ships passing through the straits. In retaliation British, American, French, and Dutch warships let loose their cannons on the city.

Nowadays, Shimonoseki, like other coastal towns, is a resort as well as fishing port, marketing itself as "the hometown of blowfish." The word for blowfish (also known as pufferfish) is *fugu* in standard Japanese, but locals here call it *fuku*. It seemed appropriate. It was raining heavily when I arrived, and though I had chosen a hotel within walking distance, I had not reckoned on having to heave my luggage up steps in the downpour. By the time I checked in, I was soaked. It was my first *fuku* moment.

The second came when I was on my way to explore the harbor area. I had stopped to check my map, when there was a screech of brakes and I found myself face to face with a middle-aged cyclist glaring at me. His hairstyle was that of gangsters in a Beat Takeshi movie, and his expression made it clear I was not about to have a good day. Looking down, I saw that I was inadvertently in the cycle lane and quickly gave way. Nonetheless, his behavior was unlike anything I had come across in Kyoto, where people apologize even when they are in the right. It felt like *fuku* number two.

The next *fuku* moment had to do with whales. Dead ones. I had taken a side street and found myself in an alleyway full of restaurants, all advertis-ing whale meat. There was even a large chart detailing the parts from which the meat was taken. Later I noticed there was whale meat in the fish mar-ket, and whale meat in the sushi bar too. Up until a couple of years earlier, Japan had been officially killing whales for "research purposes" only, but the research had enabled a whole food industry to continue. It was more than just a personal *fuku*; it was a *fuku* to the world at large and to the Inter-national Whaling Commission in particular.

DOWN AT THE SEASIDE, promenaders were promenading in such great number that I thought there must be a special event. But it was simply a sunny Sunday. People watching was the name of the game, and all around there were families, friends, youngsters, oldsters, goths, and unleashed children running amok. There were even one or two overweight Westerners.

I wandered into a souvenir shop and marveled at the ingenious merchandise. Cute little blowfish, cuddly huge blowfish, blowfish in all shapes and sizes. Blow-up blowfish were the best. The downstairs restaurant offered meals at rip-off rates, but upstairs there was conveyor belt sushi at a more reasonable price. I took a seat, whereupon the man in the next seat added another *fuku* by deliberately turning his back on me.

In Kanazawa I was once treated to a blowfish meal by a company chairman, who impressed on me how special (i.e., expensive) it was. The fish was beautifully presented, with transparent thin slices arranged in circular fashion on a large plate. There were long explanations about the fish being poisonous, and how a famous kabuki actor had died from eating it. The skill, it was said, is to cut as close to the toxic area as possible so as to give the tongue a slight buzz. It was a great build up, but our chef must have been incompetent, because there was no buzz and little taste. But then again, no one died.

How would "the hometown of blowfish" measure up? The sushi came garnished with dried chilies, a sure way of adding spice. One of the staff prompted me to use *ponzu*, a delicious citrus-based soy sauce, and I added a generous amount to good effect. The result was soft, tender, and doused with the distinctive taste of *ponzu*.

Next I tried pufferfish sperm, which looked creamy but did not taste creamy. At this point the friendly couple next to me got up and left with a polite exchange of courtesies. I took the opportunity to count their pile of plates. The woman had managed six like me, but the man had piled up an impressive eleven, including a portion of whale meat.

Back on the promenade I followed the flow of people past funfair amenities, cheap souvenirs, and ice cream parlors. There were posters for boat trips, advertisements for an aquarium, and warnings about deceptive tides.

The sea air, the crowds of people, the smell of fish, the rough manners and the gaudy goods—there was something familiar about it all. Then I realized what it was: Grimsby! The working-class port in Britain where I had grown up. Substitute sushi with fish and chips, replace the straits with an estuary, and it could almost be the same crowds milling about on a day out by the sea. The same salty fisherfolk too.

FOR LOVERS OF JAPANESE literature, the Kanmon Straits mean above all the tragic climax of *The Tale of the Heike*. The fourteenth-century epic is Japan's great equivalent of *The Iliad* and charts the rise and fall of the Heike clan, underwritten by Buddhist notions of karma and transience. It is history raised to the level of art.

The story centers on the Genpei War (1180–85), fought between two rival clans, the Heike (based in Kyoto) and the Genji (based in Kamakura). As the war turns in favor of the latter, the Heike are pushed further and further away from Kyoto, retreating along the Inland Sea until their boats are encircled at Dan-no-ura in the Kanmon Straits. Rather than be captured, the mother of the child-emperor Antoku, just eight years old, jumps with him into the sea. He is drowned, but she is hauled out of the water by her hair.

Such is the power of the epic that it has spawned countless retellings—in noh and kabuki, television and film, manga and anime. Akama Shrine serves as focal point, for it deifies the child-emperor at the place where he died. With its imperial connections, the shrine is kept in pristine condition; bright red doors and golden chrysanthemums are highlighted by the clean white walls. Alan Booth found it garish, but on the day I visited, it positively sparkled in the sunshine. In the adjacent cemetery are graves for fourteen Heike warriors, commemorated in an inscribed verse.

The waning moon—
from the bottom of the sea
the Heike harp

In a corner of the shrine precincts is a statue of an earless man, and I stood behind a young mother as she explained to her child its significance. It is Japan's most famous ghost story, retold by Lafcadio Hearn in *Kwaidan*. But for Hearn, it is said, it might well have been forgotten, and I listened as the mother told her son the story.

A blind *biwa* musician named Hoichi used to come to the temple-shrine complex to rest and sleep. He was skilled at reciting *The Tale of the Heike*, and one night was bewitched into giving a performance for the Dragon King, who lived at the bottom of the sea. To protect him from this happening again, the temple priest wrote onto Hoichi's body the words of the sacred Heart Sutra. However, he omitted to cover the ears, so when the bewitching spirit returned, only Hoichi's ears were visible. To prove he had tried to fulfil his task, the spirit cut off the minstrel's ears to present them to the Dragon King. Hence the earless statue in front of us, which the young child, having listened to his mother, was now regarding with awed fascination.

What dreams would assail him that night, I wondered?

NEAR SHIMONOSEKI STATION IS an eye-catching gate at the entrance to a shopping arcade with Korean restaurants, food shops, and boutiques. The "Little Busan" has a despondent feel, so to get away from the traffic fumes I took a side road that zigzagged its way up a hill. It was steep enough that the door on one lane overlooked the roof on that below. Towards the top the houses were little more than shacks, and the lane narrowed to such an extent that it was impassable for cars.

By Western standards the area would be designated a slum, yet there was no litter of any kind, no sign of vandalism, alcoholism, or alienation— not even graffiti. When my father visited Japan at the age of seventy-five, the main impression he took away was how cleanliness was so ingrained in the culture that even the homeless set their shoes tidily outside their cardboard-box shelters. How do the Japanese maintain such civilized standards? It is a question that Westerners have been asking ever since the first missionaries arrived in the sixteenth century. However, there is one section of the population that might have a different take on the subject.

The sorry story of Koreans in Japan is laid out in the bestselling *Pachinko* (published in 2017 and adapted into a TV series in 2022). The generational saga traces developments after the annexation of Korea in 1910, when thousands of jobless Koreans moved to Japan, desperate for work. Subject to discrimination and exploited as cheap labor, they had to endure harsh conditions. Many of the families stayed on after the war, and it is estimated there are currently some 850,000 Koreans living in Japan. Most have permanent residency but retain Korean nationality (either by attachment to South or North Korea). Even today they are subject to hate speech by Japanese nationalists, and to escape discrimination some of the younger generation take on Japanese identity. One of my students was a case in point, passing as pure Japanese to her fellow students but confessing to me a distressing childhood in a Korean neighborhood.

In Kyoto there used to be a similar Korean area near the station that after long negotiation had been cleared for modern housing. I wondered what the official policy was here, so asked at the station's information office.

"There is an interesting district over there," I said, pointing to the clearly visible hill opposite.

"Is it some kind of special area?"

"It is a residential area," came the response.

"But it is different from other areas. There are no roads at the top."

The two women looked at each other.

"It is a housing area."

"I see. Is it connected with that Korean gate?"

"There are Korean shops. We call it Little Busan."

"So is that hill where Japanese Koreans live?'

There was a pause. The women looked at each other again.

"Mm, it's difficult."

"What's difficult?"

"It's difficult. We can't explain. I'm sorry."

Avoiding sensitive subjects is a way of preserving harmony, and some topics are considered taboo. This applies for instance to *burakumin*, outcasts who in the past were despised for doing "dirty" work such as slaughtering animals, working with leather, and preparing funerals. Officially they no longer exist, and discrimination has diminished to the extent that the founder of Uniqlo, Tadashi Yanai, has been able to be open about his family connections. When Lili was young she was told not to visit the area where I live because of its association with *burakumin*. Now she visits regularly, though it is not a *burakumin* but a gaijin she comes to see. Also an outsider, but much more respectable.

LITTLE FERRIES SHUTTLE IN a triangle between Shimonoseki, the island of Ganryu, and Mojiko in Kyushu. Distances are short, and minutes after departing we were pulling up at a small island. It was the site of Japan's most famous sword fight.

There are various versions of the duel, but the official account runs as follows. The cunning Miyamoto Musashi and top swordsman Sasaki Kojiro had arranged a showdown on Ganryu Island. The encounter was set for eight in the morning but Musashi deliberately arrived late, with only a shaved oar for a weapon. The enraged Sasaki drew his long sword, threw away the sheaf, and swung at Musashi's head, slicing the knot of his headband. Ensuring the sun was behind him, Musashi attacked and killed the momentarily dazzled Sasaki, then jumped back in his boat to escape his opponent's vengeful students.

There is little to see on the island, save for a striking sculpture. It shows the two swordsmen, one with upright sword gripped between two hands, the other with oar raised kendo-style. Such is the artistry that it encapsulates the whole event in this one frozen moment, and the dynamic tension between the two figures recalls the celebrated painting by Sotatsu of *The Wind and Thunder Gods*.

Next stop was Kyushu, or at least the little part of it that is Moji Harbor. I had come on a whim with no idea what to expect, so the "retro town" was a surprise. Ranged round the small harbor were large Western buildings from Meiji times. Some housed shops, others were administrative offices. The biggest was for Lloyd's Insurance. Curiously, the various food outlets all offered curry.

The five-story Kanmon Strait Historical Museum offers a panoramic view of the waterway, extending over to Shimonoseki. The amenity was plush in a way that suggested money had flowed as free as the straits, and there was ample space for comfortable sofas and a programmed grand piano. The main feature was an eight-minute film projected onto a huge three-story screen, showing in close-up how pufferfish swarm and swoop en masse. The first part focused on marine life, but then the film segued into boats, ships, and tankers as if they were a natural extension of dolphins. The number of vessels in the narrow waters was alarming, yet the film concluded with an upbeat vision of even more and bigger ships after the planned dredging of the straits. Japan Inc. was clearly in control of the script and no doubt had funded the plush sofas and programmed piano too. I came away with the feeling that for all the historical awareness, there was little environmental awareness. It struck me the same could be said of Japan as a whole.

Shimonoseki had proved unusual in a number of ways, one of which was the number of unmasked people. I had seen at least six! They stood out because elsewhere the number had been a firm zero. Perhaps it said something about the town. Whaling, Japanese Koreans, salty fisherfolk, medieval sea battles, sword fights, bombarding foreign ships—it seemed to me, with its surging currents and vibrant history, that the place was quirky, colorful, and upfront. It had attitude. A *fuku* attitude.

On Track ||||||||||||||||||||||||||||||||||||||||||||||||||

The port town of 268,000 is the westernmost city in Honshu, and its railway line first opened in 1901. In Natsume Soseki's novel *Sanshiro*, set in 1907, the eponym travels by train from Kyushu to Tokyo via Shimonoseki. At the time the express to the capital took 29 hours. Ferries transported trains across the straits until 1942, when a tunnel was opened. This was joined in 1975 by a Shinkansen tunnel, initiating high-speed service from Osaka to Kyushu.

Shimonoseki Station is the meeting point of the San'in Line along the Sea of Japan coast and the San'yo Line along the Pacific Coast. From Shimonoseki to Hakata in Kyushu, regular trains take almost ninety minutes, whereas the Shinkansen will whizz you there in twenty-six.

In 1999 the Shimonoseki Station Massacre took place, when a former architect with mental problems drove a car into the building and ran amok, killing five and injuring several others. He was arrested, and in 2012 executed. In 2006 the same portion of the station was again destroyed, this time by arson. A seventy-six-year-old man who had gone there to keep warm was ejected and set fire to it out of resentment. He was sentenced to ten years in prison.

The Misuzu Shiosai Train for tourists does a daily round trip from Shimonoseki along the picturesque coast to Senzaki (in Nagato). It has an Art Deco exterior with triangular and octagonal windows, a 1920s-style interior, and a carriage with sofas facing outward.

Kyushu

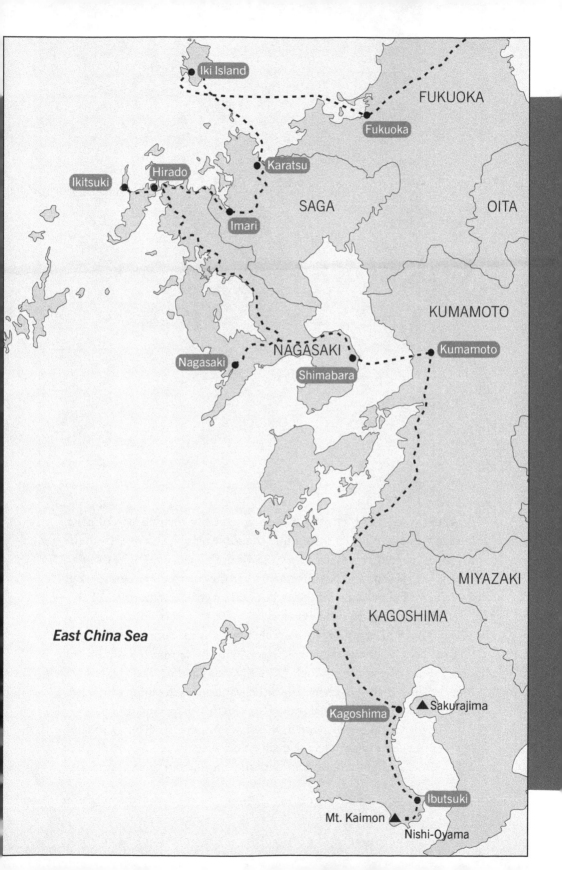

Iki Island

FUKUOKA

Fukuoka

Karatsu

Hirado

Ikitsuki

SAGA

OITA

Imari

KUMAMOTO

NAGASAKI

Kumamoto

Nagasaki

Shimabara

East China Sea

MIYAZAKI

KAGOSHIMA

Kagoshima

▲Sakurajima

Ibutsuki

Mt. Kaimon ▲

Nishi-Oyama

Fukuoka

CONFUSINGLY, FAST TRAINS NEVER stop at anywhere called Fukuoka. Instead they arrive at Hakata Station, the name of which derives from the town's prime feature—Hakata Bay. The reason? There used to be two separate towns, Hakata and Fukuoka, and when they merged, they jostled over the naming. Fukuoka got the town, but Hakata got the station.

Geographically Kyushu is remote, closer to the continent than to Tokyo. The third largest of Japan's main islands, it has been dubbed "Land of Fire" because of the many volcanoes. With its southern location, the island speaks of warmth through its mild winters and natural hot springs. Like the climate, the people are said to be warm and welcoming too. When the gods descended to earth, it was to Kyushu that they came.

The island was once known as Saikaido (Western Sea Route), making it a southern equivalent of Hokkaido (Northern Sea Route). Both have a central area of volcanic mountains, and the surrounding pastureland enables production of beef and milk. Both also have an independent past, being remote from the capital, and both have a distinctive character owing to the climate; Hokkaido is partly subarctic, Kyushu is partly subtropical. Historically, however, there is a major difference. Hokkaido was on the outside until the Meiji Restoration, whereas Kyushu was a vital element in the formation of premodern Japan.

And yet for all the positives, those coming by train may not get the best of first impressions. My journey from Shimonoseki, for instance, which took just over an hour, passed through one of Japan's most industrial areas. Lafcadio Hearn would have been horrified, for the pursuit of beauty lies buried beneath the pursuit of wealth. Petrol stations, convenience stores, and soulless apartment blocks are the chief features, while the hills that once provided a spiritual link with nature are obscured by intrusive high rises and sprawling shopping malls. Poor Alan Booth had to walk through it all, pausing only long enough to note that a scummy river he passed contained rotting cardboard boxes.

The city of Fukuoka provides an antidote, for the bright lights, vibrant architecture, and pleasant amenities speak of optimism about the future. This is Kyushu's unofficial capital, home to over a third of the island's population, and there is a buzz about the place. After Hagi and Shimonoseki, the station felt like a whirlpool of swirling humanity, while outside a queue of fifty taxis or more were doing brisk business in ferrying away customers, replacements for whom continued to stream out of subway exits.

The city used to be called Japan's best kept secret, but it is no secret anymore. A sprawling city of just under 1.5 million, similar in size to Kyoto, its reputation as a fun place to visit derives in large measure from the *yatai* stalls, where you can share convivial company in the manner of the Netflix hit *Midnight Diner*.

Hirota-san had flown down to join me for the weekend, and together we set off in search of the local delicacies. Fukuoka might just offer the widest choice in Japan, for there are over nine thousand restaurants. Statistically, that works out to more than four restaurants per thousand people. Or to put it more graphically, if you ate out at a different restaurant every single day, you could keep going for twenty-five years.

The coastal location means seafood is prominent, and a poster offering a Fukuoka fish set soon caught my attention. It comprised three kinds of sashimi, which according to our waiter represented the three basic fish colors. Skipjack tuna (or bonito) represented red; sea bream was silver; and amberjack stood for blue. Alongside were small dishes, attractively presented in a box and garnished with *wakame* seaweed. They were only bite-size servings, but each packed a distinct taste. There was steamed potato with sesame, mushroom with *komatsuna* (a type of brassica), and a chunk of pumpkin with half a chestnut. My one reservation was the brassica stalk, not at all tasty and, like its cousin *mizuna,* prone to sticking in the throat. It is said to be healthy, that is if it does not throttle you.

For his part, Hirota-san was keen to try Hakata ramen, which is a pork-based broth with thin noodles and a creamy milk broth. "The ramen has a rich flavor," he pronounced. "It suits black fungus rather than bamboo." Black fungus? I looked up the Japanese word (*kikurage*) on my iPhone. "Cloud ear mushroom," it said unhelpfully, though at least it sounded poetic.

"The noodles can be soft, hard, or super hard," Hirota-san went on, and mentioned that he had once tried the super hard only to find that it was not that hard. "Maybe it was Kyoto version," he said. "Kyoto people are rather gentle." Then he added almost as an afterthought, "Eighty percent of people in Fukuoka prefer hard noodle. It may reflect their character."

In the pause that followed I imagined the characters in *Tampopo* trying with difficulty to slurp super-hard noodles. We had ordered *shochu*, a distilled spirit for which Kyushu is famous, and Hirota-san was talking about *The Sea and Poison* by Shusaku Endo. The short story is based on real Japanese officers in World War II who ate human flesh, but what was its relevance?

"The story takes place in Fukuoka," he said.

"So?" I asked.

"So the people may have their own ideas," he said. "They have their own strong character. Their own dialect too. Maybe because of mountain terrain and being distant from Honshu. They were able to overthrow military power of Tokugawa. And Kyushu women are very fiery, they say. Also the *shochu*."

It was a cue to order another glass of the spirit. It can be made from different ingredients, and the typical Fukuoka variety is distilled from rice or barley. We were drinking the latter, mine on the rocks, Hirota-san's watered down.

"By the way, do you know *Cooking Papa*?"

"The manga? I know it's about a salaryman who is good at cooking."

"Yes. It is a long-running manga. It has recipes as well as story. The author is from Fukuoka. I had a chance once to take a bath with his son in Tokyo. He was so proud of Fukuoka and the high-energy Kunchi festival. Do you know that festival?"

"I saw it on video once."

"It shows strong adverse spirit."

"Adverse?"

"Yes, like enemy."

"You mean adversarial?"

"Yes. Kyushu people are strong and adversarial, so they are not easy to bend to central power."

THE INFORMATION CENTER AT Hakata Station has a fine array of tourist brochures featuring temples, shrines, and the city's castle. But I had seen enough of the like, and wondered if there was something different, something unique to the town. Out came a leaflet on the Mongol invasions in the thirteenth century. Perfect! After all, until World War II no other town in Japan had suffered invasion, and Fukuoka in the form of Hakata Bay was invaded by the Mongols twice, once in 1274 and the second time in 1281.

For the Japanese, the invasions mark as glorious a victory as that over the Spanish Armada in 1588 for the English. In both cases an island country was attacked by the continent's most powerful force and secured an unlikely victory, leading to an upsurge in national pride. And in both countries the victory was aided by the weather, fueling the notion that the nations were divinely blessed.

In Japan's case, the invasion was initiated by the formidable Kublai Khan, who demanded the country become a vassal state. When this was refused, he put together a large force, which overwhelmed the outnumbered Japanese and burnt down Hakata. The samurai were skilled in single combat, but the attackers used hand-thrown bombs and huddled together in a tight-knit group. Just when it seemed all was lost for the Japanese, a timely storm destroyed some two hundred Mongol ships and the invaders fled home.

For their next attempt, the Mongols amassed a much larger force, estimated at 1,500 ships and some 70,000 soldiers. This time the Japanese were better prepared and prevented the Mongol army from taking control of the mainland. Instead the invaders set up base on an offshore island. Fighting was more or less at a stalemate when a typhoon intervened. In the chaos that followed, hundreds of ships collided or sank, and over half the invasion force perished. For the victorious Japanese it was proof that the gods were on their side, thanks to what they dubbed *kamikaze* (divine wind).

There remain some physical reminders of the events even now, centuries later, such as decaying defensive walls and lookout spots. Hakozaki Shrine, razed in the first invasion and rebuilt by the time of the second, still acts as a locus for thanksgiving and bears a slogan on its tower gate: *Teki-koku Kofuku* (Submission of Enemy Countries). This is Shinto in its guise of national rather than natural religion.

To get a feel of the past, Hirota-san and I headed for Higashi Park, which was the site of fighting in the first invasion. It hosts a Mongolian Invasion Museum in which are shields worn by the two sides, as well as armor made of hardened animal skin.

"It is said the Mongolians were very cruel," said Hirota-san. "I saw a program with Marco Polo."

"Marco Polo?" I said in surprise. "What did he have to do with the invasion?"

"They said he was involved in the negotiations."

"Really? That must be fiction, surely."

"Maybe. It was an NHK drama. Marco Polo brought a Japanese to meet Kublai Khan's son. And there is a historical manga, *Angolmois: Record of Mongol Invasion.* It was very popular, so it became anime on television."

In the middle of the park stood a bronze statue of Emperor Kameyama in an exaggeratedly tall *eboshi*, the black-lacquered hat worn by aristocrats. "He was retired, but he kept power," said Hirota-san, who then added, "The length of the hat shows masculinity." A signboard noted that in a prayer at the time of the invasion the retired emperor had offered his own life in return for peace.

To my surprise the park hosted a much larger statue, of the Buddhist leader Nichiren. Bigger than the emperor; what was that about? His belief in the supremacy of the Lotus Sutra had led him to denigrate "false prophets" who thought differently, and he ascribed to them all the ills of the country. He predicted Japan would be invaded, so when the Mongols appeared it seemed to validate his teaching. For Nichiren, you could say the *kamikaze* was doubly divine—not just heaven sent, but testimony to the truth of his teaching.

HIROTA-SAN HAD BUSINESS AT one of the temples, so I took the opportunity to visit an old friend from university days who had an apartment with a panoramic view over Hakata Bay. "You see that," he said, pointing to an island near the shore, "that is where the Mongols set up camp during the second invasion." It looked frighteningly close for an enemy base.

These days Nokonoshima is marketed as a nature reserve for flowers, cosmos being its chief jewel. It is relatively small, with a population of just seven hundred and a circumference of twelve kilometers. The following day Hirota-san and I took the ten-minute ferry there, and from the small port headed for some Mongol graves marked on our map. There was little to see, but the peaceful setting and pleasant weather prompted rumination about the dead.

The Mongol army included soldiers from diverse vassal states such as Korea and parts of China, but whatever the origin of the unknown soldiers who had died here, they were certainly hundreds if not thousands of miles from home. In all probability it would have been a miserable end, and all at the whim of a power-hungry individual. It was over seven hundred years ago, but it brings to mind a certain contemporary war.

Apart from its Mongol past, Nokonoshima has literary associations in which death also looms large. The author Kazuo Dan (1912–76) was so taken with the island that he retired there after a star-studded career. He had begun writing while attending high school in Fukuoka, and went on to be an award-winning poet and novelist who traveled extensively in both hemispheres. There is even a street named after him in Portugal, where he lived for a year. Here on Nokonoshima stands a stone monument that bears a poem he wrote after the death of his first wife, Ritsuko.

The leaves of the wax tree
completely crimson—

would she were beneath them
yet she is no more
leaving grief and misery

Back at the port again, Hirota-san and I hired bicycles and set off for
the north of the island. There we found another of Kazuo Dan's poems,
inscribed on a rock overlooking the peninsula where his book *Ritsuko: Love
and Death* is set. The poem was written in 1975, just four days before his own
death, and it uses nature to describe his hopes for a posthumous reunion.

Whistling wind
all the long nights—
yet spring flowers await

Around thirteen hundred years ago coast guards were posted on Cape
Yara, at the northern end of Nokonoshima. It must have been a lonely occupation, staring out to sea, but a poem from that time suggests they played
an important role. The verse comes from the eighth-century collection
of poems *Manyoshu,* and though it was composed by a court official, it is
couched in the voice of a fisherman's wife whose husband has not returned.
The verse plays with the boat's name Kamo, which is a clan name as well as
meaning duck (i.e., waterfowl). As a result the poem can be read in different
ways, and the deliberate ambiguity is one of the reasons Japanese poetry is
so intriguing, as is evident in these two translations.

When an offshore bird
called Kamo returns
in the distant sea—
guards of Cape Yara,
please tell me immediately

You offshore birds,
when the Kamo returns
in the distant sea—
let the Yara guards know
as soon as possible

Cycling back to the port, Hirota-san and I enjoyed lungfuls of fresh air and eyefuls of verdant nature. The little island brought to mind the Old Japan that Hearn so loved: a traditional way of life sustained by shrine and temple, poetry inscribed on rock, history written into the land. The spirit of place was enriched by the very real sense of the past that lingered in the air, and the result was quite delightful. Somehow the island had escaped the predations of modern life. No unwanted concrete, no ugly factories, no fast food. Just cosmos and communion with something greater than self.

On Track ||||||||||||||||||||||||||||||||||||||||||||||||||

As the main station for Fukuoka, Hakata is the regional hub for main lines and the Shinkansen, resulting in a total of fourteen platforms and over 120,000 visitors a day. The station was rebuilt in 2011, and the multistory complex contains department stores, a subway station, and three underground shopping malls. A roof garden at the top of Amu Plaza offers 360-degree views of the city.

JR Kyushu prides itself on sightseeing trains, which it calls "Design and Story Trains." Among their number (eleven in all) are Aso Boy, with on-board mascot and panoramic viewing of the Aso caldera; an A-Train for jazz enthusiasts; and a luxury train called Aru Ressha running to Yufuin hot spring resort. Cream of the crop though is Seven Stars, a superluxury train with sleeping cars and deluxe suites as well as lounge and dining car with gourmet cuisine. Modeled on the Orient Express, it showcases the island's assets by stopping at scenic spots, hot springs, and places of mythic resonance. Trips are either for two or four days, and the prices are steep.

Iki Island

JAPAN IS BLESSED WITH an abundance of attractive small islands, and for anyone traveling along the coast it is hard not to feel drawn by their siren call. In Honshu, Sado had lured me; in Kyushu, it was Iki. The jetfoil from Hakata takes just over an hour, and as is the way with islands there is a sense of entering a different realm. According to mythology, Iki is the fifth of the original eight islands created by the primal deities, Izanagi and Izanami. Palm trees and a Shinto *torii* greet visitors, and a welcome poster announces that this is "the island of kami."

A Canadian friend called Chad happened to be living on the island. He and his family had moved to Iki as part of a remote island exchange scheme, the idea being that outsiders and island dwellers strengthen mutual understanding by getting to experience each other's lives.

From Chad I got a quick lowdown on the island. A mild climate with few typhoons, interesting history, and plenty of folklore. Among the twenty-seven thousand population, there were seven Westerners teaching or studying, six Filipinas working in a *futon* factory, and a Chinese family running a Chinese restaurant. On a monocultural island foreigners are of special note.

As with other islands, the population was in serious decline. Thirty years ago there had been a healthy fifty thousand; now the elementary school that Chad's children attended had an average of seven children per class. At some point its viability would end, and though there was awareness of depopulation, there were few easy solutions. Stormy seas lay ahead, and aspiring youth were already abandoning ship.

Iki measures seventeen kilometers by fifteen, and as we drove to my hotel Chad pointed out the two types of villages, for farmers or fisherfolk. Apart from rice, the main crops are asparagus and, surprisingly, tobacco. Another island specialty is cattle, and Iki beef is said to have just the right proportion of fat due to seaborne breezes enriching the grass with minerals.

A longer-standing tradition is the production of *shochu*, which, like brandy, is in the range of twenty-five to thirty-seven percent alcohol content. Iki *shochu* dates back to the sixteenth century and is distilled from rice and wheat, the sweetness of one complemented by the aroma of the other. Later, at Chad's urging, I tried a glass. Smooth but sharp at the same time, it slid down the throat with a fiery warmth—fitting for a fiery region.

Climate change was already apparent in that fishermen were finding it difficult to catch tuna, for the fish were moving north as the sea warmed up. Overfishing had reduced the stock too, and locals blamed the Chinese, who were encroaching ever closer. Friction between them was growing more intense.

Geographically Iki is hilly but low lying. The highest of the hills is just 212 meters, yet from the top on a clear day you can see the island of Tsushima, close to the Korean peninsula. The Mongol invaders of the thirteenth century had left their mark on Iki too, for an advance guard had stayed for a month, pillaging and plundering as they waited for the rest of the fleet. A "thousand-man grave" testifies to the bloody events of the time.

RURAL JAPAN LIKES TO promote communal cohesion through loud public announcements, which regulate the working day, notably a break at noon for lunch. Some of the messages make good sense, such as warnings about heavy rain, but some can be annoying, such as the one to wake you up at seven a.m. Still, there is much to be said for an early start, and my hotel provided the opportunity to linger over a generous breakfast. There were no fewer than twelve different dishes, the centerpiece of which was grilled horse mackerel for which Iki is famous. Other items included burdock, pickles, and jellyfish in vinegar, and Iki tofu, too, which is harder and chewier than the soft, creamy Kyoto version. No doubt Hirota-san would say it matches the character of the people.

My plan was to do a loop of the island by bus, stopping off at Iki's showpiece museum. Things got off to an inauspicious start, for the driver was having a bad day. Either that, or he did not like foreigners. Or perhaps it was just me he disliked. Whichever, when the other passengers got off, he asked tersely where I was going.

"Gonoura," I said, whereupon he abruptly told me to get off.

"But this bus goes to Gonoura," I protested. "Yes, but it takes a long time," he snapped back.

"I know," I said, "it takes an hour and a half."

"You want a different bus," he insisted.

"No, I want to see the island," I said, whereupon he stomped off back to the driver's wheel and the rest of the journey passed in a sulky silence.

Iki is associated with demons, and all over the island there are places named after them—Demon's Rock, Demon's Harbor, even Demon's Footprint. They could have added Demon Busdriver. (In fact, though they look like monsters, the demons are not necessarily evil, and legend even has it that they helped the islanders overcome the Mongols by guarding bridges and other valiant deeds.)

At Gonoura there was a change of driver, and the new man proved polite and friendly, just the opposite to the first. Again I was the only passenger left after others had got off, and we struck up a conversation. Fishermen who went to work at night lost all sense of time, he told me, and recently one had been seen banging on a shop door at four a.m. demanding a haircut. I gathered it was the talk of the island.

Around two thousand years ago, Iki played a vital role in the maritime extension of the Silk Road to Nara. At the time Japan was made up of independent kingdoms, much like Saxon England, and the Kingdom of Iki (Ikikoku) was one of the most important. It had strategic importance as a stopover on the busy route between Hakata and Korea. The capital was located inland on a fertile plain, and traders reached it by river after mooring their boats at the coast and transferring their goods onto smaller vessels.

Today the site of the former capital is overlooked by the Ikikoku Museum, which stands on a small hill. Inside is a model showing life at the time. High-ranking officials at the riverside are welcoming a foreign delegation, while laborers are engaged in such activities as planting rice, weaving, making earthenware, and roofing huts with straw. The inhabitants enjoyed a varied diet, as seen by food-related activities: picking fruit, drying abalone, hunting wild boar, sorting shellfish, growing gourd, grilling fish, and making *mochi* (rice cakes). There are shamanic rites too, including ritual dance round a sacred pillar, divination by burning the shoulder blade of a deer, and burial in large jars.

From the top of the museum is an overview of the open plain, dotted with reconstructions of buildings based on archaeological digs. A palisade kept out wild animals, and a watchtower enabled early warning of incomers. Houses consisted of a single room, shielded within a sturdy frame over which woodwork was held in place by rope (no nails). A sunken floor helped keep the dwelling warm in winter, and food was stored in buildings raised off the ground to keep the produce dry and away from animals.

I was pondering the lifestyle when an elderly guide approached. He told me he was eighty-five and started reeling off information he had memorized. Once started, he was impossible to stop, but the combination of face mask, dentures, and Iki accent made him barely comprehensible. When I tried to clarify what he had said, he proved almost deaf as well. From what I could tell, the gist was that Iki was self-sufficient, whereas the island of Tsushima was not. As a result, historically Iki had had little concern with the outside world, whereas Tsushima had to play a delicate balancing game between superior powers in Japan and Korea.

Since my friendly guide was keen to converse, I asked about a brochure I had seen that said Iki was "the birthplace of Shintoism." It was a startling statement, and in all the years I had studied Shinto I had never come across the claim before. He had a set answer for that too, and though I found his explanation difficult to follow, I enjoyed the flame of enthusiasm in his eyes. When he finished, I could not resist one last question: "How do you manage to keep your vigor at the age of eighty-five?"

"Me?" he responded, and this time gave the most comprehensible of answers. "Iki shochu!"

THE NEXT DAY CHAD had devised a custom-made tour for me. First and foremost was the island's prime attraction, Monkey Rock. No prizes for guessing how it got its name. In fact the likeness was uncanny. Shaped by wind and salt water, the creature looks pensively towards the horizon, as if contemplating the future of monkeykind. It would make the perfect prop for *Planet of the Apes*. There is something too of King Kong in the formidable size, for it stands on a vertical piece of cliff that rises a massive twenty-five meters from the sea.

Nature's artwork here reminded me of a large shamanic rock overlooking Seoul, which resembles a monk casting a protective eye over the city. On the slopes around it worshippers pray directly to the rock face. Sacred rocks in Japan have long intrigued me, for they form the essence of ancient Shinto. Most of the major shrines in the country originated with worship of a numinous rock (*iwakura*), yet curiously there is almost nothing written about the subject. The standard book on Shinto, by Sokyo Ono, does not contain a single mention, which is puzzling. Over the years I have had to piece together my own understanding of the phenomenon.

For ancient humans rock stood for permanence in contrast to vegetation, which was perishable. Humans were impermanent of course, but on death their spirit was thought to live on forever. Rocks were therefore associated with the dead, and came to be seen as a vessel into which spirits could enter. In other words they were physical containers for what was intangible and invisible, which is why they were revered as "spirit bodies" (*goshintai*).

Sacred rocks are particularly prominent along the ancient migration route that leads from Korea to northern Kyushu, then along the fringes of the Inland Sea to the Yamato heartland in Nara. Since Korea had a formative influence on early religion in Japan, and since Korean shamanism derives from Siberia, it struck me that in prehistoric times Shinto-style shamanism would also have its origins there.

One day, while internet surfing, a picture popped up on my screen of an outcrop on the edge of Lake Baikal in Siberia. My heart immediately leapt up, and I knew with absolute certainty that I had to go there. It was located on the island of Olkhon in the middle of the lake, and contained a sacred cave venerated by the Buryat Mongols as the origin of shamanism. That summer I flew to Irkutsk and took a minivan to Olkhon, where I sat on a slope overlooking the sacred rock, for it was forbidden to enter the cave at its base. Prayer flags fluttered in the wind, and as I pondered the scene thoughts coursed through my mind. Could it be that within the dark mystery of the vaginal opening lay the origin of Japanese rock worship?

In shamanic thinking distinctive features are often an indication of special powers. The leading shaman at Lake Baikal, for instance, has six fingers, and trees struck by lightning are thought to have been picked out by the gods on high. Similarly rocks with striking shapes are attributed to divine creation. So I asked Chad if there was any evidence of rituals being conducted at the Monkey Rock. Disappointingly he did not know of any, and though he had been to meetings of Iki's official guides, there had been no mention of a religious connection. On the other hand, he had met my eighty-five-year-old guide there. "Unique," he agreed. Perhaps the old man too had a touch of the divine.

THERE ARE OVER A thousand shrines in Iki, testimony to the very real presence of kami in the island life. You get the feeling that here is the true soul of Shinto, rooted in folk belief rather than the top-down imperial Shinto set up by the Meiji government. Iki shrines speak to the ancient tradition of animism, and as we drove around the island the bond with nature was everywhere apparent.

Some of the shrines are very special. Take Kojima Shrine, for instance, which stands on a small island and is only accessible at low tide. It has one of those evocative *torii* that stand at the water's edge and whose pillars are submerged by the incoming tide. It symbolizes immersion in the life force, and reminds us of our cosmic connections. Or take Sai Shrine's large wooden phallus, which stands erect before the worship hall. Though demonized by Christianity, the male organ is here a powerful force for good, promoting fertility, conjugal harmony, easy childbirth, and protection from sexual disease.

The next stop on our tour brought a surprise: the grave of Basho's walking companion, Kawai Sora (1649–1710). I had not expected to come across him again after our parting in Hokuriku, but it seems Sora ended his life as a government official sent to check on places in and around Kyushu. He had taken leave of Basho at the small town of Yamanaka, near Kanazawa, due to ill health, and in his account the famous poet describes the circumstances.

> Sora was afflicted with terrible stomach pain and left for relatives in the province of Ise. He wrote a parting haiku.
>
> > Wherever I go
> > should I fall
> > a field of bush clover

Given Sora's condition, his poem is cleverly wrought for it combines the seasonal word "bush clover" (early autumn) with the comforting thought of collapsing onto a bed of bright, delicate flowers.

The next stop on our island tour provided a further example of Japan's cult of the cute. Ondake Shrine is filled to overflowing with small statues of cows and monkeys. According to the priest, they were donated in Meiji times and individualized so that each has distinctive features. He also let drop that according to local tradition, this was the earliest Shinto shrine in Japan. Aha, I thought! That would explain the brochure's claim that Shinto originated in Iki. And the location would also support the notion of Korean shamanism playing an influential role in early Shinto.

The last stop on Chad's busy schedule was Sumiyoshi Shrine, and as we pulled up the sun was just beginning to set. We could hear the sound of a drum, followed by the ethereal music of *gagaku*. A woman rushed up to us saying, "Quickly, quickly. It is just about to begin. Please follow me." Apparently she had recognized Chad, and we followed her into a small hall where some fifteen people were seated on benches. At the front was a small stage, along the side of which sat five musicians.

We had only just taken our seats when a priest appeared with a sacred *sakaki* branch, which he proceeded to offer to the kami in a slow and stately dance ritual. It was followed by a black-masked performer, who whirled and swirled in dramatic fashion as if flying, before submitting to the kami by prostrating himself full length before the altar. (Later we found out he was representing *yatagarasu*, the three-legged crow of Japanese mythology.)

Next came something astonishing—a priest juggling plates while performing acrobatics. Even the kami must have been startled by this one. Holding two plates on the flat of his hands, the priest walked with slow steps while moving the plates in circles. Steadily the circles became more complex, not only passing under the armpit but over the head. All of a sudden he did a backflip while keeping the plates horizontal in his open palms. Then, as if that was not enough, he went into high-energy mode, swirling like a Sufi but somehow keeping control of the plates. It was breathtaking, as if he was operating on a different plane of existence.

Other performances followed, but nothing that could match the eye-popping spectacle of the plates. Afterwards we learnt from a member of the audience that we had attended a trial run by the Iki promotion board for a shrine event aimed at tour groups. It was meant for Japanese, we were told, as it would surely be too strange for foreigners. No, no, we retorted, it was just what foreigners would want.

Next day I was booked on the ferry to Karatsu, and though I had only been on the island for three days, it felt like a week. *Iki iki* in Japanese means lively or vigorous, and I had seen plenty of evidence of that. It was exemplified by the near horizontal trees on the coast, battered and blasted by cold salty winds, yet clinging tenaciously to life. Then there was the old man at the museum, the priest's performance, the fiery shochu, the island demons, the erect phallus, and the many "power spots." Iki had something special for sure. Maybe that welcome poster on my arrival was right after all, for it really did feel like "the island of kami."

On Track ||||||||||||||||||||||||||||||||||||||||||||||||||

Access to Iki Island from Hakata/Fukuoka is by jetfoil (just over one hour) or car ferry (two hours and twenty minutes). The ferry goes to either Gonoura or Ashibe.

From Karatsu East Port there is also a car ferry, which takes one hour and forty minutes to Indoji Port. Alternatively, it is possible to fly from Nagasaki (thirty minutes).

Karatsu and Imari

INVIGORATING. REVITALIZING. LIFE ENHANCING. These were the words that came to mind as I stood alone on the top deck of the ferry from Iki to Karatsu. It was a clear, sunny day and I had the whole panorama to myself. The handful of other passengers, being regulars, had forgone the fine view for the dingy tatami room downstairs, where they stretched out to relax and sleep.

From my solitary vantage point, small islands were visible virtually the whole way to the mainland. It must have been a comfort in ancient times, when sea travel was so hazardous that those setting out never knew if they would return. The large embassies exchanged with Korea and China comprised two or three hundred people, all of whom required food and shelter. The strain on Iki had been so severe that the islanders petitioned a wish-fulfilling rock to hasten the departure of their unwanted guests.

As the ferry neared Karatsu, the town's pristine white castle glistened like a sparkling jewel amid the grey sea. The name derives from *kara,* meaning Korean or continental, and *tsu,* meaning harbor. In ancient times it had been an important trading port; in Meiji times it hosted coal barges; and more recently it has catered to cruise ships. Historically the highpoint was in the 1590s when 130 feudal lords gathered for Hideyoshi's invasion of Korea. Imagine all those autocrats, all-mighty within their domains, jostling for status and intriguing with one another!

I had given myself a day to see the small town, and a thirty-minute walk provided a pretty good idea of the layout. First port of call, so to speak, was the castle, one of those ferro-concrete reconstructions complete with elevator which purists love to disparage. Nonetheless one can still admire the design and see why it was nicknamed Dancing Crane. From the top there are spectacular 360-degree views, with water just about everywhere you look, from Karatsu Bay and the Genkai Sea to the broad Matsuura River and the castle's moat. Striking too is the grove of black pine, which stretches in an arc along the coastline. Planted in Edo times, it comprises "one of the three best pine beaches in Japan." That made two out of three that I could check off.

It turned out that I was not as shielded from overtourism as I might have wished, for three elementary school outings were simultaneously launching assaults on the castle, and I found myself surrounded by yellow caps, white shirts, blue shorts, and black rucksacks. They were masked, but social distancing was clearly an alien concept, and they happily invaded my private space. "Are you a gaijin?" one of them asked. I told her I was a human.

"Eh, can you speak Japanese?"

"Yes, I'm speaking Japanese now."

"My name is Emi, what's yours?"

"John."

"*Jam?*"

"No, it's John."

"His name is *Jam,*" she told her friends, to shrieks of delight.

"Where are you from?" another one asked.

"From Kyoto."

"Is that in another country?"

"No, it's in Japan."

"Will you be my friend?"

"Sure."

"And will you teach me English?"

"Okay," I said.

"Teacher, teacher," she burst out, running towards her schoolteacher, "that gaijin will teach me English."

Emboldened by the conversation so far, a young girl challenged me by pointing to the castle and asking, "What's that?"

"It's a castle," I answered.

"No, that's wrong" she shouted. "It's Karatsu Castle," and with that she and her friends ran off in great excitement. Their teacher turned to me and said in English, "I'm sorry," and hurried after them. The entertainment was over.

On the way back to my hotel, I took to the side streets and got pleasantly lost for a while. It is one of the great joys of Japan that you can wander down almost any small street and find something odd or quirky. A smart clothes shop called Covent Garden stood opposite an aging statue of Ebisu, deity of fisherfolk. There was too a Halloween display of pumpkins. Around the corner was a nineteenth-century villa open to the public, which had once belonged to the oldest son of the last Karatsu *daimyo*. Born in 1859, he was groomed to succeed his father, but with the abolition of the feudal system in 1871 he turned to business instead. It was a time of opportunity, and he took advantage by cofounding a bank, a railroad company, and the Karatsu Electric Company. Fiscal power replaced feudal power.

A nearby cafe offered a sardine set lunch, so I popped in for a healthy meal of grilled fish with what in Japan is known as "salad"—chopped cabbage. It came with that holy trinity of Japanese food: pickles, miso soup, and white rice. It turned out that the owner's daughter was studying at a college in Kyoto, five minutes from where I lived.

"Does she like Kyoto?" I asked.

"She says it is interesting, but she misses Karatsu's fresh fish and clean air."

"I'm not surprised," I said.

"The Kunchi festival is coming up in a couple of days. But it's too bad, this year it may not happen because of Covid," she said. "There is a museum near here. You should see it."

Kunchi refers to the lively festivals of north Kyushu. Karatsu, Nagasaki, and Hakata (Fukuoka) are the Big Three, with Karatsu in particular famed for its elaborate floats made of *papier-mâché*. At the museum, fourteen of them were lined up in a large hall, along with explanations, and I was quietly making notes when a middle-school excursion arrived armed with question-naires. Suddenly the hall was as busy as a beehive, with students rushing hither and thither to ferret out answers and get to the ice cream shop.

If the students had allowed themselves time to stop and stare, they would have seen how wondrous were the *papier-mâché* creations. From the depths of an artist's imagination were conjured up mythic monsters, auspi-cious animals, and historical heroes. My favorite was the head of a drunken demon, which had bitten into a samurai's helmet and been beheaded as a result.

At one end of the hall was a large screen showing previous festivals in which the floats, weighed down by people inside and on top, were hauled along by men inebriated by copious amounts of sacred sake (*miki*). Musical accompaniment was provided by drum, bell, and flute. Moving slowly at first, the teams suddenly surged forward, then broke into high-speed cor-nering that was positively life endangering. Were it not a tradition, it would surely be banned.

Karatsu claims to be the first place in Japan where rice was grown, which is a big deal in a country that sanctifies the grain. It means sake is a natural fit, and at one of the bars a tasting set of local brews was on offer. First step consisted of choosing a *choko* (cup) from a selection of the highly prized Karatsu ware. Next, several bottles of locally produced sake were lined up, with a brief description of the content, vintage, and taste. After selecting three, I was invited to savor them in the fashion of wine: first appreciating the fragrance, then letting the sake roll around the mouth. Appetizers included sashimi, smoked nuts, and a type of tofu. By the end of the third sake I had become so attached to my *choko* that I bought it. I bet they do good business that way.

FROM AN ARTS AND crafts point of view, north Kyushu means just one thing. Pottery. As well as Karatsu, the towns of Imari, Arita, and Nabeshima have their own traditions, deriving from the influx of Korean potters in the sixteenth century. The legacy is very much still evident.

From Karatsu the train to Imari takes fifty minutes along a rattling, rackety single track. There were few passengers and I had the view of morning mist all to myself. It spread low over the foothills like a fluffy duvet, and much as in an ink painting the rice fields dissolved into an indistinct wash. For a while we passed through a mixed forest, the trees of which crowded in on both sides, branches brushing gently against windowpanes. It came as a shock when a wide plain suddenly appeared in which a modern harvester, like a mechanized intruder, was plowing stubble back into the soil.

At one of the stations uniformed high school students piled onto the train, and one brave soul sat in the seat next to me. He asked in English where I was from, and when I said Kyoto, he switched to Japanese and told me his father was *tanshinfunin* (living apart for work). How did he feel about that, I wondered? Good, he said, because his father did not bother him anymore. As for school, he did not like learning English because it was, he declared with great emphasis, boring. The only good lesson had been when a gaijin gave the class a general knowledge quiz.

It was soon time for the student to get off, and I felt sorry to see him go. It is unusual on trains to talk with strangers, and he was clearly a loner alienated from his peers. Perhaps he had recognized something similar in me. It recalled a verse by the wandering poet Saigyo, Basho's favorite, who wrote of longing for someone with whom to share his mountain solitude.

Loneliness—
Would there were another
To bear it with me
Our huts side by side
In this wintry mountain home

Imari was to be my base for the next couple of days, so I was intrigued to see stalls being set up outside the station. There would be a food fair the next day, a woman told me, then added in a low voice that there would be a festival too, but she was not supposed to say because of Covid. The town prides itself on producing the country's first porcelain, and pottery displays were everywhere apparent. Large colorful Imari pots decorated either end of bridges, and two towering ceramic statues portraying kimono-clad women stood at the entrance to a shopping arcade.

The Sea Silk Route Museum sounded promising, and at the entrance a volunteer guide asked me to fill out a registration form. I wrote Kyoto as my place of residence. "Oh," he said, "I thought you were a gaijin." There was not much in the museum, but one of the exhibits consisted of straw bales. "They used that for packing pottery from Arita. It was put on ships here, which is why in Europe they call it Imari pottery. You see? Packing had to be very, very good, because boats went all around Japan. Many storms. And sometimes they went to Europe."

On the wall was a map of the world with a sailing route that ran south to Singapore, then on to India, round southern Africa, and up to Holland, which was Japan's sole European partner in Edo times. To get there ships took anything from six months to well over a year. There was much buffeting en route, and some ships never made it. They needed all the Good Hope they could get.

A poster next to the map told of the exhausting process that went into producing the frangible porcelain pots: shaping, drying, firing, overlay painting, glazing, firing, overpainting, and finishing. Apart from pottery, the main exhibit was a *kura* (storehouse). Merchandise was stored on the ground floor, and upstairs was a small dormitory where traders from surrounding areas could stay. Being of a certain age, I had some concerns.

"What did they do about going to the toilet?" I asked.

"It was the same place as now. Near the bottom of the stairs."

"But in Edo times it must have been just a hole."

"Yes. But the place was the same. Near the bottom of the stairs. I'll show you."

He opened the door on a shining new toilet, with jet, aroma, and bidet functions. Contemporary comfort in place of a cesspit; modern life had its blessings, for sure.

"One more thing," I said to the elderly volunteer, "what is the difference between Arita pottery and Imari?"

"Maybe there are some differences," my guide said.

"What are they?" I pressed him.

"Maybe an expert can tell you. But I can't. I can just show you the toilet."

THE NEXT MORNING I visited the main shrine and wandered down to the port. By good fortune my return coincided with the arrival of the festival procession, and by equally good fortune the lack of publicity meant there were few spectators, so I had an excellent view of the proceedings.

At the heart of Shinto's annual festivals are portable shrines that contain the kami. The heavy wooden *mikoshi* are usually borne on the hardened shoulders of men, but in this case the three kami arrived on the back of small vans. Men in *happi* festival jackets waited to unload them, then took up positions sitting along three sides of a square. At the front was a temporary altar. Participants were dressed in a colorful array of costumes: four priests in purple robes, *miko* dancers in red and white, child flautists in blue kimonos, and taiko drummers in all white, their sleeves tied back for action. But the undoubted star was a *chigo* (sacred child) in embroidered kimono and golden crown. (In former times, the *chigo* served as an unpolluted vessel into which the kami descended, a remnant of Shinto's shamanic roots.)

The rituals included purification, offerings, a formal prayer, sacred dance, and stunning taiko performance. Then the three *mikoshi* were loaded onto trucks again, each followed by a troupe of attendants. I tagged along behind one of them. The musicians played festival tunes, there was much shouting, and sake was passed around. This was religion as celebration, and all around were smiling happy faces.

Unexpectedly an argument broke out, and men were yelling at each other, even grabbing each other's jackets. It looked like a confrontation between rival groups, and tensions were running high. But then all of a sudden, it came to an abrupt end. It turned out to be a feigned quarrel, and everyone was laughing.

"What do you think of it?" said a man in English, thrusting a microphone at me. Behind him was a television camera man.

"Great," I said.

"Where are you from?" he asked.

"Kyoto," I said. "No, what is your country?"

"England," I said.

"So you came all the way from England to see this?"

"Yes, I said." It was the answer he and the viewers would want, and what I wanted was to get on with the fun.

THE NEXT DAY I was taken to visit the studio of one of Imari's leading potters, Sofu Mizokami. Though he was in his eighties, he retained a youthful enthusiasm, and he told me his family had been in the business since the early nineteenth century. His studio was testimony to a lifelong passion, crowded with collections acquired on his travels. One broken fragment that could have passed for garden rubble was worth three hundred thousand yen, he told me. How had he managed to acquire so many valuable pieces? "By only drinking water, not sake," he laughed.

"By the way, where are you from?" he asked.

"England."

"The British Museum has one of my pieces, called Sunrise." He showed me a picture in a catalogue. Orange-yellow against light blue, it was a true work of art.

"When I was a child, I wanted to be a painter. Now I do that with my pottery. I can get inspiration walking in the woods. Or by the sea. But it is difficult to sell these days."

"There must be a lot of competition," I said.

"Yes. In the Hizen area we have three hundred potters."

"How do you manage to sell anything?"

"You must build a clientele. I have a list of 1,400 people. You must cherish each one. Especially collectors. Actually tea masters are best." He paused for a moment. "But money is not important. It is love of the work. You must love it like life itself. Even if you make no money, you can die satisfied."

In the afternoon I was scheduled to visit the Secret Valley of Kilns at Nabeshima. The seductive name derives from 1662, when the local *daimyo* set up a center of excellence, secluded from the outside world. If he could have taken out a patent, he would have, for pottery was cherished at the time as a valuable commodity.

The valley has one narrow entrance, at which formerly stood a guardhouse. The potters were thus able to concentrate on high-quality pieces, and in two hundred years it is estimated they produced just five thousand items. The *daimyo* and his descendants either kept the porcelain for themselves or presented it to VIPs.

The valley lies only fifteen minutes' drive from Imari, and any sense of mystery was quickly dispelled by large souvenir shops and an enormous carpark for tourist coaches. On the other hand, the scenery was beautiful, the hills protective, and there was poetry too. Nabeshima porcelain is colored red, blue, green, or yellow, giving rise to an anonymous verse inscribed on one of the rocks.

> In makeup
> colored Nabeshima
> mountains and rivers

With its shops and tour groups, the modern valley has little sense of secrecy. There are even notices asking people not to peep into the houses where potters reside. Here and there are items of interest: a mosaic wall shaped like a sloping kiln and decorated with embedded pottery fragments; a walkway along a stream displaying blue and white porcelain; and graves for Korean potters, who in death faced towards the homeland for which they had yearned in life.

The next morning my iPhone registered a startlingly low eleven degrees Celsius, and it was hard to believe just two months previously I had been sweating in a Hokkaido heatwave. My original plan had been to head south in pace with the retreating warmth, so perhaps I was moving too slow. Perhaps by now I should have been in Okinawa.

By midday it had warmed up, and I was seated in a barber's shop. As he set about my wispy strands, the barber told me I was the first foreigner of the year. By foreign he meant Western, for he later let drop that he had had several Korean customers. "They come because of the history," he said. As is the way with neighboring countries, the history is controversial. Some Korean potters had come voluntarily, lured by patronage, but others had been forcibly abducted in Hideyoshi's madcap invasions. As a result there are competing narratives, or to put it figuratively, it is a can of worms which my barber was clearly unwilling to open. Fearful for my hair, neither was I.

On Track ||||||||||||||||||||||||||||||||||||||||||||||||||

Karatsu Station first opened in 1898 and is served by two lines, the Chikuhi Line from Fukuoka to the east, and the Karatsu Line running south. The latter was constructed to carry coal to Karatsu Port from the region's coal mines. From Karatsu, trains to Imari take just over fifty minutes.

The small Imari Station has little but its platforms. To travel west, passengers take the private Nishi-Kyushu Line, which runs parallel to the coast, past Hirado down to Sasebo. The route was a loss-maker for JR West, and in 1988 it was taken over by the third-sector Matsuura Railway. Its station in Imari is across the road from the JR station, but connected by an overhead passage.

Hirado

HIRADO IS A LITTLE gem. Like Karatsu, it is a small port overlooked by a castle, and in the past it had important continental connections. Tucked into Kyushu's northwest corner, it is mostly neglected by tourists because of its remoteness. You only need a leisurely day to "do" Hirado. You could for instance wander around the harbor, visit the touristy shopping street and walk up the castle hill to see the commanding view. But if you have any kind of feel for history, you will want to savor the past by lingering a while, for the small town of thirty-one thousand has some fascinating associations.

Two large buildings dominate Hirado. One is the reconstructed castle, the other a reconstructed Dutch trading post. Soon they will be joined by a reconstructed English trading post. The expensive reconstructions show how much Japanese value their past—and the tourism that goes with it.

Hirado took center stage in the early seventeenth century, when the

Dutch and the English set up "factories" (an old-fashioned term for trading post). The Dutch were first in 1609, and they stayed until forced to relocate in 1640. They were more adept at business than the English, who arrived in 1613 and barely lasted ten years.

A notice at the information office offered a half-day guided tour, which I joined along with a party of three middle-aged Japanese. We headed first to the nearby promontory on which the Dutch trading post stands. The guide pointed out the deep channel where ocean-going ships from Europe would anchor, before transferring their goods to small boats that ferried them to the stone steps where we stood.

Before us was an island with an attractive Benten shrine, a fine example for the Europeans of the sanctification of nature. The deity is the only female among the Seven Lucky Gods, and as muse of the arts she is closely associated with water and the subconscious. The Dutch traders would have seen her every single day, but only at a distance. "It was forbidden to tread on Benten's sacred soil," our guide told us. "Still today we citizens of Hirado keep that tradition."

"Please look over there," he continued, pointing at the castle. "The original belonged to the Matsuura clan, but in 1613 they themselves destroyed it. It is very unique, I think. The reason is because they fought against the Tokugawa at Sekigahara, so they were not trusted. They worried about that. So they wanted to show they were not a threat. It was very clever, because they could keep their power."

Next stop was the solid-looking Dutch warehouse, where some startling statistics were thrown at us. The building has eighteen wooden beams and massive square pillars half a meter wide. Altogether there are twenty-one thousand interlocking stone blocks. Yes, twenty-one thousand! The result was a huge Dutch-style building, finished off with a Japanese tiled roof.

The original warehouse took eight months to complete; the reconstruction took two years. The reason was a concern to be as authentic as possible, which meant timber had to be imported from Canada because Japan no longer has trees of sufficient thickness—pause for thought in a country that is sixty-seven percent forested.

"What happened to the original building?" asked one of the Japanese. "Ah, that is an interesting question," said the guide, looking at his watch.

We were behind schedule. "To make a long story short, the Dutch wrote the date of the building above the entrance, and when the Tokugawa heard of that, they demanded it be torn down."

Our guide then asked if we could guess why. As it happened, I knew the answer all too well, because in my book about Hidden Christians I had used the Dutch trading post as an example to illustrate how paranoid the Tokugawa were about stamping out Christianity. So after a decent pause, I piped up with, "They wrote 1639, which was the date according to the Christian calendar. Anything to do with Christianity was banned."

"*Sugoi*" (amazing), said one of the Japanese.

"He knows our history better than we do," said another. "We should study harder."

Inside the building was an overview of Dutch-Japanese trade, and among the items on display were two gorgeous boxes lacquered in black and decorated with flowers and birds in mother of pearl. Such goods sold well in Europe. There was too a beautiful model of the *Liefde*, the first Dutch ship to reach Japan in 1600. The two main masts were as high as the ship was long. What a giddy prospect to have to climb them in stormy seas!

With another look at his watch, the guide moved us on briskly to the documents housed in the small Hirado Museum, the most interesting of which was a seventeenth-century "Batavia letter" written on embroidered silk. The ban on all things Christian led in the 1630s to the expulsion of anyone who might be "infected," such as the wives, women, and children of Europeans. Those connected with Catholics were sent to Macao; those with Dutch or English connections went to Batavia (Jakarta), capital of the Dutch East Indies. From there they wrote touching letters to the family and friends they would never see again.

"And now," announced our guide, hurrying us along, "we have to walk a little uphill to a small park." He turned to me and said, "By the way, do you know Miura Anjin?" I certainly did, for it was the Japanese name of Will Adams, the English samurai who inspired James Clavell's famous novel *Shogun*. Before I could respond, however, the guide continued, "I will explain to you. Miura is a place name and Anjin means ship's pilot. The Ship's Pilot of Miura. Do you know him?" "Yes, I do" I answered, but he carried on nonetheless with, "It is Englishman like you. It is Will Adams. Are you okay?"

Adams (1564–1620) had a remarkable life, and his story has been often told, nowhere better than in the page-turning best seller by Giles Milton, *Samurai William*. An almost exact contemporary of Shakespeare, he learnt shipbuilding and other skills when young, and in 1588 probably fought against the Spanish Armada. When he was thirty-five, he took a job as navigator with a Dutch fleet of five ships looking to trade in the Far East. After a disastrous nineteen months, the only surviving ship, the *Liefde*, turned up off the Japanese coast with just twenty-three sick and dying men. Among them was Adams, who was imprisoned in Osaka Castle and interrogated by Tokugawa Ieyasu. The future shogun was impressed by the newcomer, and he asked Adams to use his shipbuilding skills on his behalf. In return, he rewarded the Englishman with the title of samurai.

Adams not only settled into Japanese life, but he went on to play a major role in Japanese history. Through his relationship with Ieyasu, he spread suspicion of Catholics while agitating in favor of fellow Protestants. He was instrumental in gaining permission for the trading posts at Hirado, and when the first English ship arrived in 1613 Adams went to meet it. It involved traveling by boat from his estate on the Izu Peninsula to Osaka, then overland on foot for thirty days to Hirado. Surprisingly, the meeting did not go well.

To the shock of the newcomers, Adams stayed in Japanese lodgings, ate Japanese food, wore a kimono, and carried two swords in samurai style. As a result Captain John Sarris reported that Adams had gone native and could not be trusted. For his part Adams found Sarris unsympathetic and the goods he had brought—broadcloth, cloves, and moldy wool—laughably unsuited for the quality-minded Japanese.

In Confucian societies people are ranked by seniority, and those who are older or more senior are respected as *senpai*. The founder or first to inaugurate a practice is not just a *senpai*, but a great *senpai*, a *daisenpai*. For an Englishman in Japan Will Adams is undoubtedly a *daisenpai*, so when our guide pointed at a large rock saying "The grave of Miura Anjin," a thrill of proximity ran through me.

We had arrived at a small park overlooking the port, where there was a group of memorial rocks for Will Adams, put up in 1954. Next to it was a rock inscribed in English, saying "In memory of William Adams and his wife Mary, married in 1589." The Englishness of the scene was completed by a noticeboard commemorating twenty other Englishmen known to have died in Hirado.

It struck me there was something odd about all this, and I wondered if it was a tourist stunt. Adams had a grave near where he lived at Anjinzuka in Yokosuka, so why should there be a grave in Hirado? Was it a case of divided bones (*bunkotsu*)? Our guide had an answer. Actually, two answers.

"There is a theory that he was on a trading trip to Ryukyu (Okinawa) when he caught malaria. So maybe he died and was brought here. But there is also another theory, that he had a mistress in Hirado. Maybe he came to see her. And if he died in Hirado, he would have been buried in the Christian graveyard here in this park. However, the Tokugawa wanted all Christian influence removed, so they ordered destruction of the graves. They were all mixed together.

"Now our English guest will find this interesting," continued the guide. "You see that stone there? Local legend says it once marked the grave of Adams. Of course it could be not true. But recently the area was excavated and bones were found. They were sent for DNA testing. The result was ninety percent positive that they were the bones of a Northern European. Around the time given for death, the only European reported as dying at Hirado was Adams. It means it is almost certain that the bones are his."

This was indeed interesting. But something still irked me. What was his English wife doing here? I knew she was buried in her hometown of Gillingham in Kent. What is more, Adams had taken a Japanese wife, called Oyuki, with whom he was buried at Yokosuka. Surely she should take precedence? I quizzed the guide about it. "Some English people wanted Mary to be together with her husband," he explained, "so they paid for a monument and brought pebbles from her grave to be buried here." Not so much a case of divided bones, but of divided stones.

I still had a host of questions, but our guide was in a hurry. Guided tours run on tight schedules, and guides are often anxious to finish as punctually as they start. So I wandered off to see the excavations of the English trading post and on the way found myself in what was signposted as "an English shopping street." There was a window display of Peter Rabbit, and a shop selling Burberry. There was too a Will Adams–themed cafe selling, of all things, *kasutera*, the name of which derives from Portuguese Castella cake. It was a shock; Adams would have hated the association with Southern Barbarians.

Around the corner was a restaurant advertising Hirado specialties. Apart from whale meat and beef, there was a range of seafood including flounder, slipper lobster, and *ara* (for which my dictionary gives the charming translation "honeycomb grouper"). For a moment I was tempted by ramen with flying fish broth, but in the end settled for the working man's dish of *ochazuke*, rice doused in green tea with slivers of sea bream. "Popular with sailors," said the menu. Adams would have liked that.

HIRADO HAS A SPECIAL relationship with Christianity. It was here that Francis Xavier had his first real success in the quixotic mission to convert Japan. He was only in the country from 1549 to 1552 but visited Hirado three times and gathered over one hundred converts. Japan's first church was built here, and still today fifteen percent of the population identify as Christian, the second highest proportion in the country. Fun fact: the highest, at twenty-five percent, is on the island of Kamigoto, off the Nagasaki coast.

The Jesuit mission won the support of several *daimyo* in Kyushu, who realized there were trade and military advantages in being allied with the powerful Portuguese. At its peak in the late sixteenth century the mission boasted four hundred thousand converts. Meanwhile, the colonizing powers of Spain and Portugal were edging ever closer, having taken over Mexico, Macao, and the Philippines. It prompted Hideyoshi to issue a ban on conversion, and under his successors ever stricter measures were taken, including imprisonment, torture and execution. The "final solution" was total eradication, and by the 1640s, following a ban on foreign travel, the authorities thought their grisly goal of zero Christians had been achieved. They were wrong.

Shusaku Endo's novel *Silence,* filmed by Martin Scorsese in 2016, illustrates how Hidden Christians went underground and worshipped in secret. As the persecution worsened, the communities were left with no Bible, no priests, and no churches, yet for seven generations they handed down their faith despite the constant risk of torture and death. Their existence was unknown until 1865, after which it was discovered that there were some eighty thousand in all.

Following the opening of Japan, most Hidden Christians joined the Catholic Church or abandoned their faith. Now it is thought there are only around one thousand left who practice in the way of their fore-fathers. There remains one substantial community, however, on the island of Ikitsuki, next to Hirado. I had gone there for research on my book and met with an engaging practitioner called Shigetsugu Kawakami, who was brought up to worship secretly in the manner of his ancestors. However, as an adult he decided it no longer made sense in an age of toleration, so he went public and became an "Open Hidden."

During my visit to the island, the director of the Ikitsuki Museum had been very helpful, and I wanted to thank him in person. So I took the bus across the bridge that links Hirado and Ikitsuki, but after getting off at the right stop could not remember the way. As I hesitated, a lone cyclist in racing gear appeared and offered to take me to the museum. He was a sprightly fellow, who said he was training for the triathlon. I asked his age, and thought I must have misheard when he told me. Eighty! I looked again. With his small muscular body and beaming smile he might have been in his thirties. Even his voice was loud and vigorous.

At the museum my elderly cyclist strode into the office and announced that he had brought them a *gaikokujin* (polite word for foreigner). The director was away, so I left a gift and went to review the museum exhibits. The first floor is given over to whale hunting, in which Ikitsuki was once engaged, and the second floor houses Hidden Christian exhibits. Bloody persecution links them both.

I was headed back to the bus stop when my energetic cyclist appeared again. "Stay here," he said, "I will take you in my car." Shortly afterwards we drove off at an alarmingly fast speed. At one point only a small fence stood between us and a sheer drop, but he swung the car round with all the confidence of someone who had done the route hundreds of times. For my part, I had all the anxiety of someone being driven at breakneck speed by an eighty-year-old.

The bridge from Ikitsuki to Hirado, built in 1991, is the longest contin-uous truss bridge in the world, according to Wikipedia. I wondered how it had affected island life. "Good and bad," said my driver. Some things were easier, like getting to hospital. But community feeling had suffered, especially the social life. Islanders now drove to shops and restaurants in Hirado. The local dialect was dying out too, he added, and when I asked for an example, he said they used to add *-bai* to nearly everything. *So desubai*, for instance.

As we drove into Hirado, I learnt that the eighty-year-old had lived in Ikitsuki all his life and worked as a fisherman, once on a large ship with a crew of sixty. He had been to Hokkaido too, to catch sardines. He also told me he swam in the sea from May, when the cold water must be close to torture, and he said he was a mountaineer too.

"Look," he said, pointing up a steep hillside. "You see something shining in the sunlight halfway up?"

I did.

"I put it there," he said proudly. I looked again. The slope was suicidally steep.

"When did you do that?"

"Oh, when I was young. Not yet seventy."

Back in Hirado we stopped at a convenience store where I forced some GoTo coupons (part of the tourism subsidy program) on him by way of thanks. When he went to pay for his beer, he cheerfully told the cashier that a *gaikokujin* had given him the vouchers, which they both found hilarious. The longevity of Japan's island folk is legendary. Sea air, fresh food, exercise, camaraderie, and self-reliance all play a part, and you could not have asked for a better advertisement for island living than my energetic cyclist. I came away invigorated by his company. People talk with approval of salt-of-the-earth characters, but salt-of-the-sea characters are undoubtedly part of what gives islands their special appeal.

On Track ||||||||||||||||||||||||||||||||||||||||||||||||||

Hirado's rail connection is listed under T for Tabira-Hiradoguchi. The reason is simple: Hirado is an island and trains do not run there. Instead, they stop on the mainland, at the small community of Tabira, from where taxis take visitors to the island over a road bridge built in 1977. (Tabira's sole attraction is an insect park.)

This is the most westerly station in Japan—a monument stands outside the station—so my journey would include three of Japan's geo-graphically extreme stations. The fourth is on the easternmost tip of Hok-kaido, at Higashi-Nemuro.

From Tabira-Hiradoguchi to Sasebo, the private Matsuura Line pro-vides a winding single track that takes eighty-six minutes and arrives at a harbor-side station. From Sasebo to Nagasaki, JR Kyushu's Seaside Liner takes just under two hours with attractive views of Omuro Bay.

Nagasaki

THE FIRST TIME I visited Nagasaki, I remember standing on the Glover Garden hill, admiring the panorama. The view was exhilarating. Down below were cranes, wharfs, and ocean-going ships. At the foot of the hill was a Catholic Church, and behind me was an English garden and house in colonial style. It was quite unlike any other Japanese city I had seen. Hong Kong came to mind.

Later I discovered how special the history is too. Nagasaki's foundation dates from the sixteenth century, when missionaries saw its potential as a harbor for Portuguese ships. The settlement that grew up around it became a magnet for converts, and before long Japan was host to a New Jerusalem. It was run by Jesuits, who owned the city. Yes, literally owned it, for in 1580 a converted *daimyo* called Omura Sumitada thought fit to give them jurisdiction. The missionaries took the opportunity to profit from the lucrative trade in silk from Macao.

日本最南端の駅

北緯
31
度
11
分

西大山駅

The result was a most unusual city. Churches dominated the skyline, and citizens indulged in meat, wine, and the wearing of crosses. The mission had ties to military bases in Manila and Macao, and when Hideyoshi realized the threat this represented in terms of colonization, he issued the most drastic of warnings. In 1586 a group of twenty-six Catholics (six foreigners and twenty Japanese) were rounded up and had their ears cut off before being paraded around Kyoto. They were then force marched to Nagasaki, where they were publicly crucified, a portent of the persecution that followed in Tokugawa times. Eventually the fear of colonization led to a national lockdown as the country sealed itself off from encroachment by powerful Christian countries.

IN THE EDO PERIOD, Dejima was a small artificial island that hosted Dutch traders, separated from Nagasaki by a narrow strip of water. Access was across a short, well-guarded bridge, and the occasional arrival of trading ships provided the only relief for the twenty or so men who lived there. During the period of seclusion, it was Japan's sole portal to the wider European world.

The handful of men on Dejima were under nominal control of the Dutch, though they were overseen by the Nagasaki governor. They were trusted because they were not Catholics and claimed to have no interest in religion (arriving ships were searched for Bibles). Moreover, they already had a proven record of trading at Hirado.

What was life like for them? How did they spend their time? What did they talk about? You might think it impossible to answer such questions, yet David Mitchell did just that in *The Thousand Autumns of Jacob de Zoet*, an extraordinary feat of imagination that spotlights the men's situation in 1799. The detail is astonishing, the language stunning. Those who have read it will understand why Mitchell said in an interview that before he finished it off, it very nearly finished him off.

Another English writer drawn to the subject was the poet Anthony Thwaite, whose "On Dejima: 1845" begins:

A turn around the yard, then back again:
A pint of gin, a game of dice, to bed

Knocked out, locked in. Twenty-two exiled men
Marooned like ghosts who do not know they're dead.

The "open prison" was not short of comforts. European beds and arm-chairs were set on tatami, and there was even a billiard room. Nor were the Europeans totally isolated, for Japanese cooks, carpenters, and clerks passed regularly over the small, guarded bridge. Interpreters and women from the pleasure quarters too. There were even romantic liaisons with "temporary wives."

Not all the men were in fact Dutch. African servants were picked up on the long voyage from Europe, and the occasional German specialist was employed, such as the medical doctor, Englebert Kaempfer, and the bota-nist, von Siebold. And here's a fun fact: during the Napoleonic wars when Holland was overrun, the only place in the world to fly a Dutch flag was the little outpost at Dejima.

Following the opening of Japan Dejima became obsolete, and in 1858 it was demolished, to be subsequently swallowed up by land reclamation. A century later, an ambitious plan was announced to recreate the island in its entirety. So far, ten of twenty-five buildings have been erected, and visitors now get to see such features as warehouses, offices, and the residence of the chief factor. Eventually the whole island will be recreated by diverting a river to surround it.

A visit to the site is rewarding for those like myself, curious about the oddity of life on such a small island. As well as copious notice boards, there are attendants to answer questions. How many ships a year came? Five to seven a year at first, but after 1715 a maximum of two. What kind of mer-chandise? Silver was the chief export, later copper. How about imports? Mainly silk, but also other goods such as spice from the East Indies. Did the Europeans ever get to cross the bridge? Rarely. Some years they were allowed to see Nagasaki's annual festival, and once a year the chief factor led a delegation to Tokyo to pay respects.

Cultural novelties flowed through Dejima. The Europeans were intro-duced to Japanese lacquer, pottery, and tea. In return the Japanese got cof-fee, chocolate, cabbage, tomatoes, beer, and photography. The country's first piano made its debut here. Exotic animals too. The first ostrich arrived in 1658, the first crocodile in 1780, and the first orangutan in 1792.

Dejima's most important contribution, however, was Dutch learning (*rangaku*). Studious samurai were allowed onto the island to take classes in Western science, particularly astronomy, physics, and anatomy. Military matters were taken up too, and the knowledge was spread around the country through regional schools. Once Japan opened, the Dutch learning helped the country transition from feudalism to industrialization. Dejima may have been small, but it played a big part in Japanese history. It is a big part too of what makes Nagasaki so special.

TWO OF THE CITY'S major attractions are located conveniently close to one another. Both are World Heritage sites, but with a very different focus. Oura Church is part of the UNESCO registered "Hidden Christian Sites in the Nagasaki Region." Glover Garden belongs to "Sites of Japan's Meiji Industrial Revolution." The former features persecution, villagers, and secret ceremonies. The latter features wharfs, machinery, and business meetings.

Japan has many notable churches, but none so famous as Oura Church. It was here in 1865 that a group of Hidden Christians revealed themselves for the first time. So runs the tourist literature, but there is just one small snag. The church is not the one where, in the words of Pope Pius, "the miracle of the Orient" took place. It was built afterwards.

In fact, the self-revelation of the Hidden Christians took place in a wooden church that no longer exists. Father Petitjean, who was in charge of it, was taken aback when he saw a group of some fifteen Japanese approach him. Only foreigners were allowed to practice Christianity, and Japanese could suffer severe punishment for showing interest. He described what happened next in a letter.

> As I opened the church door and approached the altar, the group followed me. A woman aged 40–50 came closer to me, placing her hand on her chest and said, "All of us here have the same heart as you." "Really?" I asked, "then where are you from?" "From Urakami," said she. "All of us in Urakami have the same heart as you." Then a question followed, "Where is the statue of Santa Maria?"

A statue of Father Petitjean stands in the grounds of the present church, and inside the building is the Madonna that the Hidden Christians so longed to see. There is too a small museum with Hidden Christian artifacts, the most striking of which are the Maria-Kannon statues, which appear Buddhist for the outside world but whose true purpose was Christian worship.

Around the corner and up the hill is Glover Garden, named after Thomas Glover (1838–1911). The Scottish entrepreneur arrived in Japan as a twenty-one-year-old, and within two years he had set up his own trading company. He sided with the anti-shogunate rebels in Kyushu, supplying guns and ships, and after they came to power, he was involved with setting up the first shipbuilding company, the first dry dock, the first modern coal mine, and the first beer brewery (now called Kirin).

None of this was of much concern to my Japanese companion, an old friend, whom I had invited to join me. Raised in a fishing village, she had trained as a nurse and had settled in Nagasaki after marrying. Like locals the world over, she did not normally visit the tourist sites. Though she took little interest in history, she had a keen appreciation for art and beauty, and while I reveled in the proximity to the past she was taken with the nearby craft shops.

The route up Glover Hill is relatively steep, but there's a surprisingly modern touch—an escalator. At the top, European grandeur is augmented by Japanese touches in an estate that boasts expansive views over the city's harbor and waterways. Even the nurse was impressed by the beauty of the scene. The well-furnished rooms of the house, with its hillside setting and prominent chimney, have a colonial feel reminiscent of the lordly manor of Glover's fellow Scot, Robert Louis Stevenson, set on a hillside in Samoa.

Dotted around the estate are relocated villas, making it something of an outdoor museum, and unexpectedly there is a statue of Puccini. What, we wondered, was he doing there? The connection stems from Glover's marriage to a geisha, which is said to have provided inspiration for Pierre Loti's novel *Madame Chrysanthème*. It was on the Frenchman's story that Puccini's *Madama Butterfly* was based.

Afterwards we stopped for a coffee and *kasutera* (castella). Nagasaki and sponge cake are virtually synonymous, and the cake is a standard souvenir for any visitor to take home. It was introduced in the sixteenth century by the Portuguese, hence the name, and typically the Japanese adapted it to their taste, adding a moist starch-syrup flavor (sugar was in short supply).

When I asked my friend about the best local food, she recommended *chanpon*, a kind of noodle soup that not only contains pork and lard but a broth of chicken and pork bones. Instead I stuck to my favorite standby of *ochazuke* (green tea on rice), with a side dish of dried flying fish to add a local touch. The fish was salty but tasty, though disconcertingly after crunching through the body all that was left was a pair of entreating eyes staring up from a decapitated head.

Over dinner our conversation focused on the nurse's job. Overworked and underpaid was the unsurprising conclusion. She worked in the acute ward, meaning heavy responsibilities rested on her narrow shoulders: suicide cases, dealing with depression, consoling those who were dying. I told her of my own experience in hospital, and the exceptional patience of nurses. "Yes, they are so polite and can endure very much," she agreed, then added, "We don't complain, but afterwards feel bad inside. It is the Japanese way, I think."

Covid had increased the workload, she told me, particularly when colleagues fell sick, but overall her hospital had not been badly affected. There had been few lockdowns too.

"Why do you think that is?" I asked.

"I think because Japanese are private people. Social distance is natural for us."

"And it's not usual to hug or kiss."

"And we talk quietly," she added.

"Yes. On the train here I noticed there were announcements not to talk."

"And Japanese are clean. We wash hands and take off shoes."

"True. And there is alcohol spray outside shops for customers to use."

"Yes, also I think we obey rules," the nurse said. "For example there was no punishment for breaking lockdown, but everyone followed the rules."

NAGASAKI'S TWO WORLD HERITAGE sites are overshadowed by one single event. In 1945 the city became the second target, after Hiroshima, to be decimated by an atomic bomb. The horrific consequences are set out in graphic detail at the Atomic Bomb Museum. It is an experience that few forget.

Shock, distress, empathy, horror—the museum evokes a mix of dark emotions. Numbers vary, but the official estimate is that 73,884 lives were abruptly ended and a similar number were badly injured or suffered radiation illness. The statistics are difficult to digest, but it is the images that linger in the mind. Skin torn off bodies; children struck blind; kimono patterns seared onto human flesh.

The Japanese experience is captured in a popular manga story, *Hadashi no Gen* (*Barefoot Gen*), made into a memorable anime in 1983. The story by Keiji Nakazawa, based on his experience as a seven-year-old, starts with family life in the war years and the hunger that plagued the populace. All of a sudden the bomb shatters normal life. Visions of hell are conjured up as bodies are stripped of skin and humans turned into ghouls. Members of Gen's family burn before his very eyes, and black rain spreads the radioactivity. Although Japan as usually portrayed as a victim, in Nakazawa's narrative blame is directed towards the Japanese government, which strives to continue a war that is already lost. It is a sensitive subject, as was apparent in 1990 when the mayor of Nagasaki was shot by an extreme right-winger for expressing similar views.

Barefoot Gen is set in Hiroshima, but a Nagasaki perspective is given by leukemia specialist Takashi Nagai, who witnessed the event from his hospital. Despite being exposed to radiation, he continued to work selflessly to help others. His book *The Bells of Nagasaki* is dedicated to the dozens of Christians gathered in the cathedral on the morning of August 9. Not a single one survived, and in his account can be sensed the magnitude of what occurred.

> Houses and trees and everything else collapsed. It was as though a huge, invisible fist had gone wild and smashed everything in the room. The bed, the chair, the bookcases, my steel helmet, my shoes, my clothes were thrown into the air, hurled around the room with a wild clattering noise, and all piled on top of me as I lay helpless on the floor. Then the blast of dirty dusty wind rushed in and filled my nostrils so that I could scarcely breathe. I kept my eyes open, looking always at the window. And as I looked, everything outside grew dark.

The lesson Nagasaki draws from the event is the need for peace, and city authorities continue to seek a worldwide ban on nuclear bombs. The Peace Park near the epicenter features a huge statue of a man, which British author Kazuo Ishiguro, born in Nagasaki, describes in his novel *A Pale View of Hills.*

The statue resembled some muscular Greek god, seated with both arms outstretched. With his right hand, he pointed to the sky from where the bomb had fallen; with his other arm—stretched out to his left—the figure was supposedly holding back the forces of evil.

"Whatever you do, don't mention the war," says John Cleese in the comedy series *Fawlty Towers.* He's referring of course to the Germans, but it could equally be the Japanese. Even the easygoing Lili and I have agreed to disagree. We are shaped after all by a very different upbringing. My view of the war was fashioned by a math teacher who was waterboarded and tortured as a POW, and the perspective was reinforced by images from David Lean's *Bridge over the River Kwai.* Lili has never seen Lean's masterpiece, and similarly before coming to Japan I had never seen *Barefoot Gen* or other influential films, such as *Burmese Harp* and *Grave of the Fireflies.*

Things have changed in the thirty years I have been in Japan, and there has been a noticeable shift towards resurgent nationalism under prime ministers Junichiro Koizumi and Shinzo Abe. It was exemplified by the popular 1990s manga *On War* by Yoshinori Kobayashi, which excused war atrocities and justified Japan's actions as liberating Asia from colonization. Such views have become more widespread in ruling circles, as evidenced by a powerful political group called Nippon Kaigi to which leading politicians belong.

A Japanese friend of mine did a comparative study of English and Japanese pages on Wikipedia. Pages in English spoke of Korean "comfort women" as a euphemism for Koreans forced into sexual slavery. In contrast, the Japanese version uses the term "prostitution," with the implication that it was a free choice. Such differences could be found throughout Wikipedia in other references to the war, so that instead of bringing people together, the global encyclopedia reinforces entrenched opinion.

As always, there are exceptions to the rule. Take the Oka Masaharu Museum for example, which is little known in Nagasaki, let alone the wider world. The name honors a Catholic priest who dedicated his life to revealing the truth about war issues, and the small museum is crammed full with documents, photos, and newspaper articles covering matters usually overlooked in Japan—comfort women, the Nanjing Massacre, the biological experiments of Unit 731, the Bataan March, and the Burma Death Railway.

The museum focuses too on a Nagasaki issue: Korean laborers forced to work in a coal mine on Gunkanjima (Hashima Island). Now a World Heritage site, the abandoned island is popular with visitors because the ruined concrete structures make it look like a battleship. It was used as a setting for the James Bond movie *Skyfall*, yet for the Korean miners who worked there it was "The island of Hell." When the site was registered with UNESCO, it was on the understanding that the Korean workers be featured, but on the guided boat tour I went on there was not a single mention. The silence contrasts with the Munch-like scream of the A-bomb Museum. Few cities have as much to offer as Nagasaki, or prompt so much ground for thought.

On Track ||||||||||||||||||||||||||||||||||||||||||||||||

Even in modern times Nagasaki has felt somewhat remote, as it is located in the west of Kyushu, far from the other centers of population. Moreover, the Shinkansen line running down the center of the island misses the city altogether. However, in 2022 the Nagasaki Shinkansen opened, but only as far as Takeo Onsen, where passengers transfer to a limited express for Hakata. The connection to Fukuoka has thus been reduced by half an hour, to just eighty minutes.

Not far from the Atomic Bomb Museum is a small Electric Train Museum, on the fourth floor of the Nagasaki Seiyokan. Here the claim is made that the Thomas Glover estate hosted Japan's first railway. In 1865 the Scotsman imported a steam engine called Iron Duke and laid out a four-hundred-meter track, open to the public. It took place seven years earlier than the Yokohama Line, acclaimed as Japan's first railway. (In fact, even Glover was outdone by Commodore Perry, who on his first visit in 1853 had impressed the Japanese by setting up a small circular railway with model steam engine. To show goodwill, he gifted it to the Japanese—an early example of train diplomacy and the importance with which the railway was taken in the West.)

Shimabara

THE RAIL LINE TO Shimabara transports passengers into a different world from that of big-city Nagasaki. Glimpses of the sea appear at unmanned stations where not a single person gets on or off. At Omikake the track runs so close to the lapping water that you could almost lean out and touch it. At another station carriages run parallel to roof tops, and I found myself eye to eye with an *onigawara* (demon roof tile)—a good omen, for the frightening face scares off evil spirits. Or maybe I was the evil spirit!

The small town of Shimabara has an unmanned station, yet the town boasts two major attractions. One is a castle, and the other a samurai district. In its heyday the district boasted 690 homes grouped together to house foot soldiers. The area is known as Teppomachi (Gun District) since the guards were armed with rifles as well as swords. (The first gun arrived in Japan with Portuguese merchants in 1543, following which Japanese smiths copied it and produced their own.)

The samurai houses are set on either side of a small stream, and three were open to the public. The multipurpose tatami rooms looked almost identical, save for the *tokonoma* alcove in one of them displaying seasonal items. The minimalism and harmony with nature were in keeping with the Zen the warriors practiced. When the sliding walls that divide house and garden were removed, a unified space was created merging interior with the outdoors.

One of the residences served as a museum, focused on the samurai heritage. The fee was just three hundred yen, but nonetheless when the eighty-year-old running the museum heard I was English, she insisted that I have a discount. The collection had an engagingly *ad hoc* feel, despite the chronological theme. The deeper you penetrated, the further it strayed from samurai matters, until finally there were simply beer cans and a gramophone from the 1950s.

As we walked round the exhibits, the old lady told me snippets about her life. Her father had died in the war, her daughter had married an Englishman, and when she visited London people had been kind to her, even though she did not speak the language.

"Did you see the stream that flows between the houses?" she asked. "It was the gift of Lord Matsudaira. Can you guess why?"

"For their daily life," I suggested. "They needed water to live."

"Yes, but he wanted them to be thankful," she said, "so he provided fresh spring water. It was a gift of life, as if he was a god."

At this point a Japanese man came in and started asking questions in a loud voice. He was eccentrically dressed, with unkempt hair and baggy trousers, and as I was hungry I took the opportunity to leave.

SHIMABARA CASTLE IS A concrete reconstruction from 1964, but you can still detect its one-time magnificence. The original five-story keep, sixteen watch towers, and thirty-one lookouts took seven years to build and involved several hundreds of people. The taxation to pay for it all was so severe that it led to a peasant uprising, the most famous and dramatic of them all.

The modern castle houses an interesting museum, and at the entrance I ran into the eccentric again. We greeted each other and entered the exhibition together. He took me for a tourist and assumed I knew nothing of

Japanese history. Had I heard of the Shimabara Rebellion, he asked? Yes, I told him, and mentioned that I had done some research on it for a book. Nonetheless he kindly explained to me that it was an uprising in 1636 of downtrodden peasants. I assured him I knew that, but he carried on regardless. The conversation developed into something of a contest between us.

"People think it was a Christian revolt, but actually the rioters were poor peasants. Just the leaders were Christian."

"Yes," I said. "The peasants were suffering from high tax and no food." Then to show him that I truly did know of the event, I added, "The leader, Amakusa Shiro, was just fifteen years old."

He was not convinced. "By the way, I think you don't know Hara Castle?"

I told him I had once visited it.

"It is where many people died," he said.

"Yes, I know," I replied, and to prove the point added, "thirty-six thousand people died, including women and children. They were massacred by the shogunate army. Every single one."

He remained stubbornly unconvinced. "Maybe you don't know why the rebels could take over Hara Castle?"

"It had been abandoned, because of the 'one castle, one domain' law introduced by the Tokugawa," I said, thinking that this would surely clinch the contest. But he refused to capitulate.

"They could hold out a long time. They even beat the *daimyo*'s army."

"Yes," I retorted, "but not the shogunate army." And sensing a hesitation, I followed up with, "They were surrounded and bombarded from the sea, including by the Dutch."

Thwarted, he turned back to an earlier subject. "What do you know about Amakusa Shiro?"

"He was the figurehead, a charismatic teenager and a Christian. He told the peasants that in the next life they would be rewarded for their terrible suffering."

"Yes, yes," he said dismissively. "But how could he become leader at such a young age, that is the point."

"He learned special skills from the missionaries in Nagasaki. How to preach, and how to answer questions about Christianity."

By this point we had reached an exhibit in a glass case. "Maybe you don't know what that is," he said, pointing at a straw jacket. I knew full well, for I had paid particular attention to it on an earlier visit. It was the dreaded "dancing jacket" which peasants who could not pay their taxes had to wear. It would be set alight, and the name derived from the way those burning to death jumped around in agony. The cruelty of the *daimyo* at the time reminded me of someone I knew.

"By the way," I said, "one of my university colleagues was a descendant of the Matsudaira *daimyo* who ruled Shimabara. He told me that when he was at school, he was bullied about the cruelty of his ancestor."

"Is that right?" said my challenger.

Silence followed. It was as if we had reached some kind of settlement.

FROM THE CENTER OF Shimabara to the ferry port is but a short train ride, and at the unmanned station I met up with the eccentric again. We got to chatting, and improbably he told me he was a salesman, though of what I never discovered. We compared impressions of Shimabara, talked of Kumamoto, and he told me that his hobby was traveling round historical sites. He was, he said proudly, an *otaku* (nerd). "By the way," he added, "where are you from?" Kyoto, I said, but he wanted to know my nationality. When I told him, he came out with a further surprise. His "second hobby" was London musicals.

Whenever he could, he liked to go to the West End, which he clearly knew far better than I. He had first gone some twenty years ago, and though he could not follow the language, it had ignited a passion. *Cats, Les Miserables, Phantom of the Opera, Miss Saigon*—he had seen everything I could think of. What was his favorite? *Beauty and the Beast*, he said without hesitation. I wondered if anything much had changed over the decades. "Yes, the price," he said. "Now it is too expensive. So I cannot go." The tables had turned, for when I first came to Japan it was considered so expensive that one hesitated to buy a coffee.

The ferry to Kumamoto was less than half full and he wanted to take a nap, so I headed for the deck and a view of the Ariake Sea. It is Kyushu's largest bay, with a narrow passage in the south connecting to the wider ocean. It was late afternoon and the little uninhabited islands lay at peace, framed by a hazy hilly background. Sun rays kissed the crests of waves, behind which ranged the steep slopes of the Unzen volcanic range. The 360-degree panorama of lake, hills, and mountains formed an enclosed little world of its own. At one point we sailed between rows and rows of cultivation nets. "For *nori* or for oysters?" I asked the only other person on deck, but he was not sure either.

Nearly all the passengers, like my eccentric companion, were below, either sleeping, drinking, or playing with smart phones. Why miss out on all the magnificence? There had been a spectacular sunset, writ large across the wide expanse of sky. The color, the sea, the mountains; one could hardly ask for more. But of course I was a tourist whereas they were commuters, dulled by familiarity to the wonders of the crossing. It was a reminder, if one needed it, of the great joy of travel—to see things afresh.

As the sun took refuge behind the western horizon, thoughts bubbled up about endings. Only two stops remained before my final destination, and with the end goal approaching I found myself taking stock. "The meaning of life is just to be alive," said Alan Watts, and from that perspective here on deck, enhanced by sea air and open skies, I felt fully alive and engaged. Call me a Romantic, but never had I been more aware of escape from the numbing reality of routine. It brought to mind the words of Leo Tolstoy, whose works had inspired me as a youth studying Russian literature. The great sage wrote that "The most difficult thing but an essential one—is to love Life." At the age of eighty-two he had left the comfort of his house in search of something more meaningful, and died, appropriately, at a railway station, where he embarked on the final journey we all must face.

On Track |||||||||||||||||||||||||||||||||||||||||||||||||||

From Nagasaki the line less traveled to Shimabara, which is the one I took, involves transferring from the JR line at Isahaya onto the private Shimabara Line. It runs around the Shimabara Peninsula, skirting the sea. From central Shimabara a ten-minute train ride takes one to the Kyusho Ferry terminal, from where boats cross to the other side of the Ariake Sea. A bus covers the final thirty minutes to Kumamoto town center.

Shimabara Railway, like many other private railway operations, is third sector, meaning it is funded by nonprofit groups such as local authorities. It also operates buses and ships. The company uses trains developed in the mid-1950s with pre-privatization colors of red and beige, making it popular with nostalgia enthusiasts.

Kumamoto

IN KUMAMOTO I ONCE again crossed tracks with Alan Booth on his long walk through Japan. We had parted ways at Shimonoseki, and while he strode doggedly down the middle of Kyushu I slow-trained the north-western coast. As Booth draws nearer his final destination, the descriptions in his book get shorter and shorter, reflecting his urge to reach journey's end. Beer, hot springs, and wild swimming had sustained him, he claims, though humor and intelligence clearly played a part too.

In Kumamoto, as he considered the sprawling earthworks of the castle, Booth wrote about the similarities between Japanese and European fortresses. Both have concentric defenses narrowing towards an inner structure, but with one big difference. Whereas European keeps have massive walls of impenetrable stone, Japanese castles at their core have a palace-like hall of wood and plaster. This suggests the delicacy at the heart of Japanese culture, symbolized by an emperor virtually unprotected in the imperial palace.

Kumamoto's castle is humongous—no other word quite captures the scale of the fortress. Built in 1607, it was one of the largest in the land, with an outer perimeter of thirteen kilometers in length. The castle Booth visited and the one I was viewing were different. Very different, in fact. In 2016 a terrifying earthquake laid waste to the fortifications, and the television images from that time—the collapsed rooms, damaged walls, and shattered structures—remain imprinted on the mind of those who saw them.

Japan is a land of disasters, and one sometimes forgets the fragility of existence in the archipelago. Floods, earthquakes, typhoons, eruptions, and tsunami issue constant reminders of the thin veneer between life and death, as if the gods want to warn against complacency. Even the most robust of human constructs, like the stone walls of Kumamoto Castle, can be casually tossed aside by terrifying powers of unknown origins. It fosters a placatory attitude towards the kami, and a stoic acceptance of adversity. As Donald Richie put it, *shikata ga nai* (it can't be helped) is Japan's national mantra.

AT THE FOOT OF the castle is an area of reconstructed eighteenth-century shops called Josaien. I had arranged to meet a volunteer guide there, and arrived early to have a look around. There was a southern feel to the abundance of fruit, which included watermelon and the world's largest citrus fruit, *banpeiyu*. Among the specialties was a dish with vermicelli and a hard-boiled egg atop seafood and pork. Plenty there for an omnivore. Also on offer was lotus root with mustard, favored by generations of *daimyo* (though not to my taste at all). Raw horsemeat is supposedly Kumamoto's finest delicacy, though anyone reading Alan Booth's account may well veer away from it.

> That evening I learned that raw horsemeat was a speciality of the area, so instead of eating dinner at my ryokan, I went to a little restaurant near Kumamoto station with my mind made up to try some. It was disappointingly stringy and, having come straight out of the refrigerator, was hard with bits of ice.

My guide was an energetic seventy-nine-year-old named Mr. Tai, an ex-schoolteacher who had taken up volunteer work to feel useful in his old age. He cut a dapper figure in his flat hat and yellow jacket, and true to his pedagogic past he had a thick folder of notes. He enjoyed trying out new vocabulary, one of which, atrial fibrillation, he particularly favored after he discovered that both his wife and I shared the affliction.

Our first stop was a viewing spot, where the scale of the reconstruction was all too apparent. "The earthquake caused fifty places to collapse, and a total of thirteen important cultural properties were destroyed," Mr. Tai rattled off in well-rehearsed manner. Laid out before us was a massive building site, in which stood excavators, mechanical diggers, and giant cranes. The work is scheduled to continue until 2037 because of budgeting constraints. It means that altogether there will be over twenty years of digging, dismantling, and rebuilding, all driven by the desire for authenticity.

Remarkably, while all this work is going on, a constant flow of visitors is maintained along a specially constructed walkway. Like my guide in Kanazawa, Mr. Tai had memorized important passages, and he delivered them in a monotone voice as we walked around the damaged castle. Some of the words tripped him up.

"John-san, do you know the last sieve of a castle in Japan?"

"Sieve? No, I don't think so."

"It was 1877. Maybe you know Saigo Takamori, the last samurai?"

"Ah, I see. The siege of the castle. When he was defeated."

"Yes. So we say Kumamoto is strong for its resilents," said Mr. Tai.

"You mean the people who live here?"

"No, resilence. Strong again after disaster."

"Ah, resilience. The people had a strong spirit."

"Yes, yes, that's right."

Another characteristic of Mr. Tai was the use of Japanese to help smooth along his English. It was such an endearing trait that after a while I wanted to join in too.

"*Ano, ne*, this is Honmaru, we call the main building. Its hill is forty meters above the land. You see the ginkgo tree, it was—*nan to iu*—special because burnt in a war, *kedo* it sprouted out again. Please see the joists—is it okay, 'joists'?"

He repeated the word, letting the word roll around his mouth as if savoring the taste.

"You see, John-san, joists prevent sinking the building, because it stands on ash from volcano. *To iu no wa*, the building may not be stable. So joists make stable. You understand? It was the thinking of Kato Kiyomasa, the *daimyo*. We think he was clever man, *naze desuka*, because he knew design. So he could put many secrets in the castle. *Tatoeba*, path to Honmaru building goes round many times, so attackers are easy to shoot by defenders. And under floor of Honmaru is passageway, we call it Passage of Darkness. It is special for Kumamoto, *to omou kedo*."

As is the way with Japanese castles, the walls alone commanded admiration for combining functionality with aesthetics. Here they were unusually big. Very big. Up to twenty meters high, yet built with a graceful upwards curve designed to thwart attackers. "Do you know three types of stone wall?" my guide asked, pulling out some helpful illustrations from his file of notes. The first, he explained, was a formal style, with neatly cut blocks fitted close together. The second a rough cut, in which the blocks do not fit so exactly. And the third a natural style, in which boulders and stones are piled up in *ad hoc* manner.

"Can you see bay windows?" asked Mr. Tai. "They have an opening for using spears and arrows or dropping stones on the enemy. I think in Europe you have like this, *kedo* they used boiling oil. In Japan we did not have that, just we used boiling water. Also there are covered gun holes. Actually you cannot see from outside, but if they smash with their rifle—you see, like this (he mimed smashing with a rifle butt)—they could make hole for shooting.

"Now I tell you about Kato family, which was disliked by Tokugawa because of fighting against them. They were moved to Tohoku in 1636. Kumamoto domain was 540,000 rice bushel. Very big *desu ne* . . . but in Tohoku was only 10,000. Can you imagine? And many bassals."

"Bassals?"

"Yes, bassals, followers."

"Ah, vassals."

"Yes, yes. And Kato-sama did design. You see turret is curve, *nan to iu, kana*?"

"Gable?"

"Yes, gable. . . . Other turrets, straight-line style."

"I see," I gasped breathlessly, as we climbed a set of steep steps.

"Ah," he said with delight, "it is atrial fibrillation." His joy at this was infectious, and we both burst out laughing.

"Yes," continued Mr. Tai, "maybe *daimyo* also had atrial fibrillation. *Naze desuka?* Because he built residence there at bottom of the castle. No need for him to walk up."

As we headed for the exit, we passed a cemetery for dead rocks. At least that is what it looked like, for the large boulders were neatly laid out and numbered like the Commonwealth graves of World War I. A signboard said it was a temporary resting ground, a purgatory as it were, for the rocks were in limbo until they could be slotted back into place in the fortifications.

We had reached the end of the tour, and like all good teachers Mr. Tai was concerned to make sure I had understood everything. "So now I told you two main points about the castle design: one is joists and one is curved gable. Are you okay?" I assured him I was. But there was one more bit of information he was eager to impart.

"Now I tell you interesting history," said Mr. Tai. "Hideyoshi was ruler. Okay? But, *zannen*, he died. Next his successor Hideyori but he was too young. Then Tokugawa Ieyasu took power. And he became shogun. But Kato-sama chose wrong side. But in Kumamoto he is great man. And he defied in Kato Jinja."

"He defied?"

"Yes, he defied. Became *kamisama*."

"A kami? So he was deified. He became a god."

"Yes, yes. It was great achievement. *Kore wa* way out. Now you will go to Suizenji Garden?"

Suizenji is Kumamoto's number two attraction, and I had visited it on a previous occasion. Built in the 1630s as a tea retreat, it centers around a spring of fresh water originating in Mt. Aso. Later a stroll garden was laid out to reproduce scenes from Tokaido, with a lake and Fuji-shaped hill. Originally there was a temple, now there is a shrine, but tea, water, and spirituality remain written into the fabric of the garden, as suggested in the following haiku.

Sacred straw rope
spring water wells up
at Suizen-ji

There is often more to haiku than meets the eye. In this case the haiku was written by novelist Natsume Soseki, who lived for four years in the city and whose residence is reassembled at Suizenji. The haiku he wrote here was sent for feedback to his mentor Masaoka Shiki. A noticeboard at the park says that the poem was in fact a New Year's greeting, as the straw rope (*shimenawa*) is a seasonal reference (it is used in New Year's decorations).

On this occasion, rather than Suizenji I wanted to visit the house of Lafcadio Hearn. Although Mr. Tai had done his duty, he asked to accompany me, for he knew little of the writer apart from the ghost stories of *Kwaidan*. And so our positions were reversed as I turned guide to my tour guide and told him about Hearn's multinational background and literary output.

The writer moved here from Matsue because of the milder climate, and the first house in which he lived is now preserved as a museum. It was relocated in 1961 to a site at the back of a department store, crammed in by utilitarian buildings. The museum attendant was happy to see me, as I was the first foreigner of the year, and he told me I was a harbinger of good luck. Hearn would have liked that traditional touch.

The writer did not take to Kumamoto at first, because of the extent of westernization. He himself wore a kimono and cultivated daily use of a *kamidana* (house altar for kami). At the same time he saw in the local populace the strength the country needed to resist colonization. In a letter of 1894 he wrote that "The future greatness of Japan will depend on the preservation of that Kyushu or Kumamoto spirit—the love of what is plain and good and simple and the hatred of useless luxury and extravagance in life."

CASTLE REPAIRS WERE NOT the only large-scale building going on in Kumamoto, for the whole station area was under construction too, in preparation for a new Shinkansen station. As at the castle there was a special route to allow access while building went on above and around. If the castle represented tradition, the Shinkansen embodied modernity, and with characteristic diligence Japan was securing both past and future.

The Toyoko Inn was unusually high, and the twenty-seven floors offered expansive views over the city. Nagasaki had been full of sailors, but here the clientele were construction workers, hungrily eating breakfast in thick waistbands from which hung work tools. The early morning temperature was just seven Celsius, but there was heathy food to sustain them: rice, seaweed, pickled plum, and cucumber, potato salad, noodles, slice of omelet, and miso soup full of cabbage and onion. Not bad for a free breakfast.

Next morning I took the Shinkansen to Kagoshima. I had wanted to avoid high-speed trains, yet JR Kyushu all but forced me to take their preferred transport. The luxury was not unwelcome, and I happily sank down into the padded seat with its laminated pull-down table rest. On the other hand it meant no "people watching" as on local trains, and I missed the quirkiness of decorative English. "Always do the right thing. Thank you," said a typically polite T-shirt. But what irked me most was that the speed of the train did not allow for the leisurely appreciation of the passing scenery.

As we hurtled through the landscape, I had an odd feeling of unease and could not at first fathom why. Then I hit on it. There were no hills, just a vast flatness. It was uncanny. But then after a brief stop, there they were again—forested hillsides. A shrouded ravine appeared between two steep slopes before darkness descended in a long, long tunnel. This was more like the Japan I was used to, though at more than twice the speed.

Between tunnels there opened up mist-enveloped scenes of delicate beauty. The "show and withhold" effect of the tunnels reminded me of the traditional "conceal and reveal" technique used in stroll gardens. We were hurtling along at a terrifying speed, and it was all happening way too fast. Hillsides passed in a blur, and villages were gone before they could be taken in.

At Shin-Minamata there was an attractive cluster of wooden houses alongside white apartment blocks, devoid of soul. And then came an annoying series of tunnels, abruptly cutting off connection with the world outside. At Izumi a golden Buddha overlooked concrete and factory roofs, followed by vegetation dripping in the misty moistness. At Sendai the elevated tracks afforded views across low-lying house roofs, then all too soon there loomed high rises and commercial enterprises, which spoke of conurbation and the end of the line.

Welcome back to civilization, they said. Welcome back to city ways. Welcome to Kagoshima.

On Track |||||||||||||||||||||||||||||||||||||||||||||||||||||||||

With its 740,000 inhabitants, Kumamoto Station is an important regional hub, servicing an average of 14,500 passengers daily. The new station is stylish as well as substantial, typified by the elegant sweep of the modern roofing. The completion of the Kyushu Shinkansen in 2011 meant that central parts of Kyushu became much more accessible, and from Kumamoto the journey to Hakata now takes just thirty-two minutes.

In 2016 the section from Kumamoto to Kagoshima was completely shut down after the powerful earthquake which destroyed the castle. A train was derailed, and there was extensive damage to sound-insulation walls and numerous cracks in the supporting structure.

The station concourse features Kumamon, the city's popular black bear mascot. (The name derives from *kuma* meaning bear, and *kumamoto-mon* meaning Kumamoto people.) Kumamon was created to increase tourism, and such has been the success that his fame has even spread overseas. Kumamon trains with decorative exteriors are run by Orange Hisatsu, a private railway that connects Yatsushiro in Kumamoto Prefecture with Sendai in Kagoshima Prefecture.

Kagoshima

IT WAS EARLY MORNING when I pulled back the curtains, and at first I thought I was seeing things. In front of me was a giant Ferris wheel apparently rising out of the railway station. Japan's stations often look like gigantic shopping malls. This looked more like an entertainment complex.

For Japanese, Kagoshima brings to mind three S's—Satsuma, Saigo Takamori, and Sakurajima. Satsuma was the feudal domain, and Saigo Takamori ("the last samurai") was one of its leading members. Together they were crucial to the overthrow of the Tokugawa shogunate in 1868 and the restoration of imperial authority.

Sakurajima is a volcano that covers the city in occasional coatings of ash. "Blink, don't wipe," is the advice for eyes. On the plus side, the geothermal activity makes Kagoshima the number one prefecture for hot springs. There are 270 separate sources, all of which boast minerals with healing properties.

In 1914 Sakurajima erupted with terrifying force. The eruption lasted a month, spewing out more than three billion tons of lava and burying 687 houses. So powerful was the eruption that the once volcanic island became joined to a neighboring peninsula. Today it is a prime tourist destination, and at the visitor center is a volcanic footbath and live stream of how close you are to being Pompeiied, so to speak. Elsewhere there are observatories, pottery made from ash, even paintings created with ash. There's a hot spring complex too. Particularly memorable is a half-buried *torii* gateway. Once it stood three meters high; now only the top beam is visible. The rest of it, like the nearby village, lies buried in ash.

FOR CHRISTIANS, KAGOSHIMA MEANS Francis Xavier, leader of Japan's first mission in 1549. The quay where he landed can still be seen today. If ever there was a man who walked the walk it was Xavier, and though I side with Lafcadio Hearn in wishing missionaries would stay at home, it is hard not to admire the Jesuit. Born to the aristocracy in a castle in Navarre, he gave up a life of ease for one of penury. He slept rough, went without, and insisted on walking even when offered horse or carriage. In practicing frugality, he believed he was following the example of Christ.

While researching the history of Christianity in Japan, I came across a Japanese convert of Xavier called Yajiro (or Angero). It strikes me he would make a great subject for a film, for all the ingredients are there—drama, mystery, culture clash, strong lead characters, and all based on a true story. Here follows the scenario that I am willing to offer any Hollywood mogul who happens to read this.

Kagoshima, 1540s. A man is running through the streets, looking anxiously behind him. He is dressed as a low-ranking samurai and has blood on his hands. It is Yajiro. He reaches a house and tells the two men there to pack and follow him. One looks like a servant, the other may be a younger brother. In the darkness, narrowly evading the guards looking for them, the three men make their way to the harbor and secretly board a large ship.

The scene changes to Macao. We see a bustling street with European and Chinese traders. Nine months have passed and the three Japanese have settled to a new life. Yajiro can already communicate in Portuguese and has taken an interest in Christianity. He is puzzled by the notion of an almighty

Creator and asks questions of a Portuguese captain, who advises him to seek out a priest in Malacca with all the answers—a Jesuit called Francis Xavier.

Malacca. The three Japanese are in search of Xavier, and manage to track him down to a church where he is conducting a wedding. Yajiro gets to question him and takes notes of the answers. This is the first Japanese Xavier has met and he is impressed, so he commissions a report about the country from a Portuguese captain.

Goa. Yajiro and companions have traveled to the Portuguese enclave on Xavier's advice, and after receiving instruction the three men are baptized as Japan's first-ever converts. It is a historic moment. The sun goddess has been replaced by the son of God, the feudal lord by the Lord Almighty, polytheism by monotheism.

In the next scene we see a Chinese junk tossed around by stormy seas. Apart from the Chinese crew, on board are Xavier, the three Japanese, two European Jesuits, and an Indian servant. The ship is barely seaworthy, and the captain is rough-mannered; he may even be a pirate. After a turbulent night at sea the sun rises on a new day and the boat is seen sailing up a wide estuary. At the prow, the three Japanese call out to each other excitedly as they see Sakurajima in the distance. After travels in strange lands, here it is at last—their beloved hometown.

The final scene takes place on the wharf at Kagoshima, where the boat lands. As the passengers alight and get their affairs in order, curious onlookers gather to see the exotic mix. The Japanese are dressed strangely, wearing crosses and speaking Portuguese. Yajiro explains to the crowd that they have come to spread a new religion, and people presume it is a new form of Buddhism. Then word arrives that the *daimyo* wishes to see the arrivals. It seems whatever crime Yajiro had committed has now been forgiven.

The film ends with a caption saying that the mission eventuated in over four hundred thousand converts, but no one knows what became of Yajiro in later life. It is possible he became a businessman, perhaps even a pirate. On the outskirts of Kagoshima is a road sign saying in English, "Presumed grave of Yajiro," though there is little to see save a few stones piled on top of each other. Ironically, Japan's first Christian did not even end up with a cross.

BAKUMATSU **IS A TERM** for the turbulent end of the Edo period, roughly 1853–67. It was a vibrant time when foreign powers were pressing in, the old order was collapsing, and the streets of Kyoto echoed with the sound of clashes between pro- and anti-shogunate groups. The latter championed the emperor, led by the samurai of the Satsuma and Choshu domains. Out of the chaos emerged "Three Great Nobles" who engineered regime change, and the greatest of the three was Saigo Takamori (1828–77).

Saigo has a double claim to fame. First he played a key role in establishing national rule unified by allegiance to the emperor. Then nine years later he led a revolt against the very government that he had helped to power. His defeat signaled the end of the age of the samurai. Now Saigo is Kagoshima's most celebrated son, commemorated at Shiroyama Park where he died. The hill offers a panoramic view over the city and houses a large statue of Saigo in military uniform.

Saigo was the model for the hero of the Hollywood movie *The Last Samurai*. Well, that is not really true; Tom Cruise plays the hero. The fictional American who learns to sympathize with samurai values was inspired by real life—the real life, that is, of a French soldier who was sent to modernize Japan's army and got mixed up in the civil war of 1867–68. The film plays on the romantic image of samurai as principled swordsmen who adhere to a code of loyalty. They treasure the spirit of the sword, in contrast to the soulless Howitzer gun used against them. In reality, the samurai were often unruly or arrogant miscreants, but the romantic image has prevailed in the public mind.

The rebels of one age become the rulers of the next, and the city proudly displays statues of the Satsuma revolutionaries in a park near the station. The Museum of the Meiji Restoration spells out how the new rulers emerged from special samurai schools, credit for which is given to the enlightened *daimyo* Shimazu Nariakira. Unusually for Tokugawa times, he promoted a modern way of thinking, and even before the arrival of Perry he initiated a Western-style industrial complex.

It was not long before Saigo became disillusioned with the modernist leanings of the Meiji government, and he retired from politics to set up a school for martial arts. It caught the mood of the moment, and the school attracted some twenty thousand students. In 1877 a faction among them rose in rebellion, and Saigo felt duty bound to join them. After failing to take Kumamoto Castle, the rebels were forced on the defensive and over the next six months lost a series of skirmishes. The final act came on Shiroyama hill, where Saigo was left with just two hundred men in a suicidal fight against government forces.

FOR THOSE SO INCLINED, Japanese mythology is fascinating. The stories are the stuff of fantasy, yet the myths continue to sustain the ruling class by fostering mystique about heavenly origins. Emperor Hirohito may have renounced divinity at the end of World War II, but the coronation of the present emperor nonetheless included a rite symbolizing descent from the sun goddess, Amaterasu. The country's premier shrine, Ise Jingu, continues to honor her as ancestor of the imperial family.

The myth of heavenly descent is known as *tenson korin*. It tells of how the sun goddess instructed her grandson to descend to earth, and how he touched down on a mountain peak called Mt. Takachiho, in southern Kyushu. This has long puzzled me. It is generally assumed that the early rulers of Japan, the Yamato clan, emigrated from the Korean peninsula. If that is the case, then surely they would "descend" onto a mountain in northern Kyushu. Why should Mt. Takachiho be singled out for this momentous event?

Faced with this puzzle, I concocted my own theory. It was sparked by reading about the arrival of the first Europeans to Japan, when three Portuguese traders were caught in a storm while traveling along the coast of China, and their badly damaged ship was swept along by the Kuroshio Current to the Japanese island of Tanegashima. The same current flows towards Kinko Bay, in which Kagoshima is situated, and at the end of the bay Mt. Takachiho is visible.

Because of the current, there are many links between coastal China and southern Kyushu. Japan's earliest rice cultivation, imported from China, is found here, and archaeologists have unearthed skeletons from around this time resembling those of Jiangsu Province. In addition, early myths about Amaterasu and silk weaving are similar to those of the Yangtze River Delta. The ties with China are widespread and substantial.

At this point in the story enter Xu Fu, a Chinese alchemist. According to historical accounts, he was sent by China's first emperor in search of an elixir for immortality. His first attempt ended in failure, following which around 210 BC he was granted sixty large boats, together with soldiers, crew, and three thousand boys and girls equipped with various skills. This time he never returned, and in later years it was assumed that he had reached Japan. How intriguing, I thought. Could the Kuroshio Current have taken Xu Fu's armada to the foot of Mt. Takachiho? Could he be the inspiration for the heavenly descent?

Not far from Mt. Takachiho lies the town of Miyazaki, the port of which gives access to the Inland Sea. It is associated with the route of conquest taken by the Yamato clan, who migrated from Kyushu to the Nara basin. Emperor Jinmu, Japan's legendary first emperor, led the expedition.

Now here is a very odd "coincidence." If you travel to the small town of Shingu on the Kii Peninsula, there are sites associated with the arrivals by sea of both Jimmu and Xu Fu. Just south of the town is a beach where Emperor Jinmu supposedly landed. And in the town itself is a creek where Xu Fu is said to have arrived. (In Japanese Xu Fu is known as Jofuku, and in Jofuku Park is a grave said to be that of the Chinese alchemist.)

The legends of Xu Fu and Jinmu both date from early Yayoi times, when Japan underwent great cultural change. Could it be in fact that the two legendary figures were modeled on the same person? It would mean that Japan's imperial ancestors came from China in search of immortality, landed beneath Mt. Takachiho, made their way across the Inland Sea to Shingu, then proceeded overland to Yamato in the Nara Basin.

The more I thought about my idea, the more likely it seemed, but when I tried it out on specialists there was little support. Alas and alack, there is nothing new under the sun, and I discovered one day that a Japanese professor by the name of Ino Okifu had come up with the very same theory. Wikipedia claims it has since been discredited, though it offers no explanation why. As far as I am concerned, the theory remains a tantalizing possibility. To the world at large Kagoshima may be a volcanic city where the last samurai died, but to me it is a gateway to the mythological past.

On Track ||||||||||||||||||||||||||||||||||||||||||||||||

Kagoshima is the terminus for the Kyushu Shinkansen, meaning that with one change you can get to Tokyo in six hours and twenty minutes.

(In the days of the Satsuma Domain the journey took between forty and sixty days.) Construction of the Shinkansen line began from Kagoshima in 1991, and the extension to Hakata was completed in 2011. The city's main station is known as Kagoshima-Chuo (Central Kagoshima), not to be confused with the relatively minor Kagoshima Station on the other side of the city.

Those wanting a panorama of the city stay in the station complex, for on the sixth floor of the AMU Plaza department store is access to the Ferris wheel. A full rotation takes a leisurely fifteen minutes, and for those who dare, two of the gondolas are completely transparent.

Ibusuki

IBUSUKI—THE MOST SOUTHERN RAILWAY station in Japan. Goal achieved!

Well, not quite. Ibusuki may be the most southern manned station in Japan, but even more southerly is the obscure and unmanned Nishi-Oyama. Like all good railway buffs, I was determined to keep on track to the very end.

With its palm trees and Hawaiian music, Ibusuki has a tropical atmosphere, yet at the same time there is a desolate feel, as if it has seen better days. The town is synonymous with the hot sand baths for which it is famous, but in an age of international travel they no longer have the allure they once did. Trains run frequently from Kagoshima, and so many tours go out of their way to deliver coach loads that it seems half the nation has been buried in sand at one time or another.

From the station, visitors are steered towards a bus to the main facility, and at the reception you are handed a *yukata* and small towel. There are a few instructions but none pertain to the most crucial matter: underpants on or off? This can be confusing in Japan, as when foreigners inadvertently cause shock by wearing trunks in public baths. In a "high-context culture" it is assumed that everyone knows the rules, and of course everyone does— except the foreigner.

Yukata on, underpants too, I rush outside excitedly and feel the fresh sea wind on face and body. "Oi!" shouts someone, and when I turn round a white-haired man is waving slippers at me. People turn around, and I feel I've committed a great *faux pas*. Though I was comfortably barefoot, I thank him, and he says to me in English, "It is very hot," pointing vaguely to the sand. I follow him along wooden flooring down to the beach, where a view opens up over an endless expanse of sea.

We enter a roofed partition, and before me is a startling sight—decapitated heads in an orderly row. They lie motionless, their bodies covered with dark muddy sand, and as in a vision of hell, workers shovel more and more sand on top of them. Ahead of me is a short queue, and as I worry about the correct protocol, suddenly it is my turn. A white towel is wrapped around the back of my neck and I'm motioned to lie down in a shallow grave. My white-haired companion settles into place, we smile, and I lie down next to him. Sand is shoveled against my sides, then over my legs, then on my trunk, then around my head, leaving just eyes, nose, and mouth. I fix my gaze on a patch of blue in the overcast sky.

The sand is heavy, and for one alarming moment I feel trapped by the weight. I think of the tapping technique that helps with panic attacks, then I panic because I cannot tap anything. The French paraplegic comes to mind who wrote a book by blinking once for yes, twice for no. But who would be my amanuensis here? I try wiggling my arms and, reassuringly, find that I can. A soothing warmth permeates my body, and I try to see how my white-haired neighbor is doing, but the compacted sand will not allow. I relax and look again at the little patch of blue.

All the while the sense of heat is growing. It is like a sauna, but with an intensity compounded by the moist sand. The person who entered before me stands up, to my relief. No disgrace now, should I decide to bail out. Ten minutes the guidelines said, and surely ten minutes have passed, but I do not yet have a sense of overheating, so I determine to carry on. Then I realize that my *yukata* is sodden not from the moist sand as I thought, but from sweat from my well-grilled body.

Gingerly I wiggle my legs, breaking the surface of the sand, and there is a welcome flood of fresh air as I sit up. I retrieve my slippers, brush myself down, and head back to the changing rooms for a shower. I feel different, lighter, purged. A cold shower now will cleanse and refresh. The sand bath, I realize, has been a form of burial and resurrection.

LILI JOINED ME AT Ibusuki, where we enjoyed a more conventional hot spring soak and decided on an outing to Chiran, a small town that boasts samurai houses and a kamikaze museum. Samurai and kamikaze—it seemed a fitting prelude to the end of my journey into Japan.

From Ibusuki, the internet instructed, take a half-hour train to Hirakawa and catch a bus for another half-hour. At Hirakawa, however, we found ourselves at an unmanned station. There was no sign of a bus stop and not a single person in sight. This was truly off the beaten track. We walked around for a while and came across a garden in which a man up a ladder was cutting down ripe persimmon. In response to our query, he got down from his ladder and led us to a nearby highway and simple bus stop.

Twenty minutes later we were zigzagging up a mountain side in a bus that swung round curves bordered by sheer drops. One hair-raising bend followed another. Looking down, I wondered anxiously if the pine trees below would hold the weight of the bus if we fell. For her part Lili sat indifferently, enjoying the views and trusting in the safety of the bus. Unlike my propensity to vertigo, she does not fear high places and positively enjoys Ferris wheels. Yet here is an interesting paradox: things that I find easy enough—traveling alone, accosting strangers—are things Lili finds intimidating. One of us is strong on the outside, the other on the inside. Yang and yin, we balance each other.

As the bus climbed ever upwards, we were treated to a view of the sea glittering in the autumn sunshine. Tankers lined up outside a port, waiting to offload, and there beyond them was the unmistakable form of Sakurajima. Yet even here, in the depths of the countryside, the Japanese zeal for Western customs was evident. It was only November 7, but already a Christmas tree had replaced Halloween pumpkins.

Chiran's samurai residences have an English-language pamphlet that says, "A miniature version of Kyoto transplanted into the heart of Satsuma." I showed it to Lili, and together we went, "Ehhhhh?" Nowhere in Kyoto will you find a district of samurai houses. Geisha houses, yes; merchant houses, definitely. Even the occasional imperial villa. But samurai houses? No way. Aristocrats in Kyoto, samurai in Edo is the general rule. Feminine arts in one, martial and masculine ethos in the other.

Generally speaking, samurai as a class comprised five to ten percent of the population, but Satsuma got away with forty percent. This was partly because of its remoteness, and partly because the warriors were dispersed across the domain instead of being concentrated in a single district. Chiran, for example, has a lane of seven residences of high-ranking samurai, concealed behind solid stone walls and fortified entrance.

The area is a center of tea production, and the aesthetics of tea are evident in the clean, austere appearance of the stone-lined lane. Unusually for Japan there are no overhead wires or intrusive modernizations, which is no doubt why the seven-hundred-meter lane was selected by the Construction Ministry as one of Japan's "100 Best Walking Paths." Who could have imagined the Construction Ministry would be promoting preservation?

The residences are still in use, and only the gardens are open to the public. Laid out in the seventeenth century, they are called "Zen gardens" in English, though Japanese has no such expression. The usual way of referring to them is as "dry landscapes." The typical garden consists of raked gravel representing water, with a shoreline of rock and neatly trimmed bushes. In some of the gardens, vegetation is arranged so as to lead the eye upwards from gravel to pine trees, so that the miniaturized landscape seems to transcend the compact confines of the compound.

A short taxi ride away lies the Peace Museum for Kamikaze Pilots. Why is it located in such an out-of-the-way place, one may well wonder? The answer is simple: the site was once a wartime training school for pilots, which also served as a base for kamikaze missions. The museum is generously funded, and the spacious rooms house a collection of planes, with pride of place going to the Mitsubishi Zero fighter favored by the kamikaze.

The exhibits are all in Japanese, save for one major exception: the translation of a touching farewell letter written by a teenage pilot to his mother. Lili's eyes moistened as she read the original, and I could understand why.

Still we differed somewhat in our feelings, for hers were of sympathy and
gratitude for those who had sacrificed their lives. Mine were more ambiva-
lent, for despite its name the Peace Museum came across not so much as a
condemnation of war but more a celebration of self-sacrifice. The museum
held the volunteers up as heroes, but I could not help seeing them as dupes
of a militaristic government. "Never again" was the message at Nagasaki. I
did not get that feeling here.

The ethos of samurai and kamikaze is rooted in the suppression of self,
and Donald Richie wrote of the paradox this presents to foreign residents,
for the very qualities they find praiseworthy derive from darker elements in
a feudalistic past—conformity, repression, obligation. It is an irony of our
times that the hippies who headed for Kyoto in search of liberation took up
Zen and found themselves undergoing a taming of the ego similar to that
implemented by drill sergeants in the US military.

Outside the museum are the inevitable cherry trees, for it is customary
to depict the truncated lives of kamikaze in terms of falling blossom. There
is, too, a reconstructed barracks where the young men spent their final days.
The most poignant element is a sparse wooden dormitory with beds set
close to one another. The neatly folded bedding is set out in a perfectly
aligned row, Zen-like in its precision.

Cherry blossom–kamikaze–samurai–Zen. At journey's end I was
being presented with a stereotype, but it is an image that Japanese themselves have been keen to promote. It is one that sustains the status quo and
makes Japan a deeply conservative country. For all the fervid westernization
of the past hundred and fifty years, the inner core of Japaneseness remains
intact, and the words of Lafcadio Hearn, written over a hundred years ago,
still contain a large measure of truth. "The nation has moved unitedly in
the direction of great ends," he wrote, "submitting the whole volume of its
millions to be moulded by the ideas of its rulers." And the engine driving
this unified force was what Hearn described as "the absence of egotistical
individualism." He credited this to the moral power of Shinto on the one
hand, and on the other to the mastery of self promoted by Buddhism.

THE SLOW TRAIN TO Nishi-Oyama is single-track and bumpy, as if trying
to impress on passengers the remoteness of the station. As befits a loner, I

was on my own; Lili had gone to meet a friend. Nishi-Oyama meant nothing to her, after all, though for me it meant facing up to the reality that my journey was coming to an end. Each day had been an adventure, and I had become addicted to the thrill of the new.

Outside the greenery was greener than ever, due to the moist warmth in these southern parts. Scattered villages were framed by the familiar background of hillside and mountain, while out in the fields old women in large hats were bent over, hard at work. For a while we ran along the side of Kinko Bay, where tankers chugged along the wide channel. In one of the villages the harmony of black-tiled roofs and wooden buildings was shattered by a Western-style house in shocking pink—and it really was shocking. In fact it was so offensive that you wondered what on earth the owners were thinking. Was it a desperate, defiant act of individualism, or simply an urge to add color to a drab existence?

At Miyagahama there was a pleasant grassy area with a lone boat facing forlornly out to sea. A group of high school children boarded the train and stood chatting in such low voices they were inaudible above the clatter of the carriage. To either side was a steep embankment, then came a long tunnel. When we emerged, the magical shape of a mini–Mt. Fuji appeared. Mt. Kaimon, that is, nicknamed the Satsuma Fuji. It took me right back to the start of my journey in Hokkaido and the mesmerizing sight of the Rishiri Fuji.

When the train pulled into Nishi-Oyama, I got off amid a small crowd jostling on the narrow platform. As the train departed, shutters clicked and iPhones were held aloft. In front of us a simple sign simply said, "Most Southerly Station." The train disappeared along tracks that curved gracefully around a bend before heading back northwards up the other side of the Satsuma Peninsula. A friendly fellow next to me explained that the crowd had been jostling for the best photo shot, when train, southerly sign, and Mt. Kaimon are for a brief moment all aligned.

There are six trains a day to Nishi-Oyama, which seems a lot given the few passengers. There is no one at the station to check or issue tickets—in fact there is no station building at all, just a platform. There appears to be no village either, just a few farm sheds and a makeshift shop selling "Kagoshima souvenirs"—dried sardines, pork curry, sweet potato, sea salt, prawn crackers, Chiran tea, and all kinds of pickles. Signatures of *tarento* (television "talent") were pinned on the wall. Japan's most southerly stop was clearly a popular location for the numerous cheap programs in which TV celebrities drop by unexpectedly to surprise the locals.

There was half an hour before the arrival of the next train, and as I finished my bowl of *kitsune soba* (buckwheat noodles with deep-fried tofu) a bus load of elderly women descended on the small shop. I supposed they had arrived for the photo op, so I went to take up position before them. There was only one other man on the platform, a photographer dressed in all the appropriate gear, and I mentioned the coachload of women to him.

"It's not a problem," he said.

"It *is* a problem if they all crowd on here," I replied. "It's not a problem," he repeated. "They are just here for souvenirs."

"How do you know?' I asked.

"Because I come here every week."

"Every week! Why?" I asked.

"I want to do better," he said. "I want to catch the perfect photo."

We chatted a bit more, and he generously let me stand in the very spot he had identified as optimum for the photo. "But I only have an iPhone," I objected, for the spot was rightfully his, but he waved the protest aside. Generosity, courtesy, the search for perfection—he exemplified the finest traits of Japanese culture. It reminded me of a BBC commentator who visited Japan to cover the Rugby World Cup in 2019. Asked for his impression of the country, he said that Japan made him want to be a better person. Here at the end of my journey, I had the same feeling.

Back in Kagoshima I rejoined Lili, and together we boarded the bullet train for Kyoto. The speed was overwhelming, frightening even. First Kyushu, then half of Honshu passed in an anonymous blur. I closed my eyes and mentally retraced my journey from north to south, images coming unbidden to mind as in a slide show. Hokkaido, Tohoku, Hokuriku, Chugoku, Kyushu—from subarctic to subtropical through a wide variety of coastline and countryside. And even as the memories came flooding in, I started pondering my next journey.

On Track ||||||||||||||||||||||||||||||||||||||||||||||||||||||||||

Ibusuki Station offers little for the train enthusiast, save for its boast of being the most southerly manned station. Outside is a footbath, using underground hot water. The station first opened in 1934 and is serviced by the Makurazaki Line, running from Kagoshima-Chuo to the small town of Makurazaki on the Satsuma Peninsula, famous for its dried fish flakes. The route runs round the eastern and southern coasts of the peninsula, offering picturesque views. Only at sleepy Nishi-Oyama do things get interesting, as sightseers descend to see the little train depart from the country's most southerly station. Purists point out there is a monorail further south in Okinawa's Naha, but to invert the slogan of *Animal Farm*, "two rails good." And there let us stop.

A Brief History of Japan's Railways

EFFICIENT, CLEAN, WIDE-RANGING, MODERN, and punctual: Japan's rail network is widely admired as the best in the world. Not only is it well run, but it moves around huge numbers of people. The statistics are startling. Forty-six of the world's top fifty busiest stations are in Japan, and there are over twenty thousand departures a day. On Tokyo's Yamamoto Line trains arrive every two minutes, in conveyor-belt fashion, and if you get off at Shinjuku Station you will be faced with a choice of two hundred exits. Yet far from chaotic, the system works in well-managed manner, such that it copes with a higher percentage of passenger travel than any other advanced country.

Japan came relatively late to trains, as it did to industrialization in general. Not until the modernizers of the Meiji Restoration did it get started, and in setting up the first railway line in 1872, from Tokyo to Yokohama, it drew on British expertise. A key figure was Edmund Morel, who arranged for the import of locomotives and tracks from England. Tragically he died in 1871, the year before the line opened. Such is Japan's gratitude that his grave is designated a "national railway memorial."

The honor of being "the father of Japanese railways," however, goes to Masaru Inoue. In his youth he had escaped illegally from Japan, when foreign travel was still banned. After studying engineering and mining at University College, London, he returned to Japan and was appointed Director of the Railway Board, overseeing the early development. Later he founded Japan's first manufacturing company for trains. He died while on an official visit to London and is buried, appropriately, in a strip of land between two railway lines.

The all-important Tokaido Line, connecting Tokyo and Osaka, was completed in 1889. It meant that travel between the two commercial centers could be done in twenty hours, as compared to a couple of weeks in Edo times. By 1906 the journey was reduced to thirteen hours forty minutes. The same year a nationwide organization, called JNR (Japan National Railway), was created by the Railway Nationalization Act.

Over the next decades a network of tracks was laid out covering the whole country, except Okinawa. It was augmented by private lines run by independent companies (currently numbering over one hundred). As a result, trains reach even the remotest of areas, with over 8,500 stations in all. Steam engines were replaced as electrification was implemented in the 1950s, and in 1958 came the momentous decision to adopt the Shinkansen, meaning "new main line" and known in English as the bullet train. It was a hugely expensive project requiring specially built tracks and stations. (Shinkansen in Japanese refers both to the trains and the tracks, which have a wider gauge than usual: 1.435 meters as compared to the standard 1.067 meters.)

The first Shinkansen was operational by the time of the 1964 Tokyo Olympics, giving the postwar country an enormous boost. Named Hikari, the train took just four hours to Osaka, only stopping at Nagoya and Kyoto. This compared with six and a half hours for the conventional express. There were budgeting and teething problems, but the Shinkansen proved a success, and in 1973 the line was extended to Okayama. Such was the demand that by 1992 the bullet train was transporting twenty-three thousand passengers an hour per direction, making it the busiest high-speed train in the world. To this day there has not been a single fatality.

The success of the Shinkansen led to further extensions, first to Hiroshima and later to Hakata in Kyushu. Other regions looked in envy at the economic benefits, and further lines were added. Now it is possible to travel all the way from Hokkaido to southern Kyushu in just over twelve hours, a distance of 1,452 kilometers. The fastest model is the Nozomi, which runs at speeds of up to three hundred kilometers per hour.

Although bullet trains take the limelight, they have a strong supporting cast. Local trains, often the lifeblood of rural communities, stop at every single station. Some are rackety and crowded, while others have just one or two carriages, which rattle along single tracks. Express trains, as the name suggests, run at higher speeds along main lines. Newer models can be surprisingly plush, with viewing windows for scenic areas. Limited express do the same route but stop at fewer stations, so if speed is your concern those are the trains to get.

The 1970s and 1980s saw JNR suffering malaise from overspending, overstaffing, and over-reliance on the Shinkansen. The accumulated debt was bigger than that of some third-world countries, and so the decision was taken to privatize the network. In 1987 it was broken up into six regional passenger companies and a nationwide freight company. JNR was dead; JR was its successor, standing for Japan Rail. The privatization was done geographically (by contrast in Great Britain it was done by track and train operator). Honshu is divided into three, the largest of the companies being JR East, based in Tokyo. The other two are JR Central, based in Nagoya, and JR West, operating out of Osaka. The remainder speak for themselves: JR Hokkaido, JR Shikoku, and JR Kyushu.

As privatization took effect, nonprofitable lines were closed, land sold, staff reduced, and diversification encouraged (operating shops and hotels around the stations, for example). As a result most of the group operate in the black. The two companies in the red, JR Shikoku and JR Hokkaido, have problems to do with a diminishing rural population. JR Hokkaido in particular is disadvantaged by having to bear the high cost of maintaining rail tracks across vast empty spaces.

As for the future there are exciting plans, though not all may come to fruition. The Hokkaido–Sakhalin tunnel (or bridge), for instance, given present circumstances looks most unlikely. Similarly the ambitious proposal to build a tunnel linking Kyushu with Korea faces problematic issues. On the other hand, there are Shinkansen extensions in the works. Nagasaki was added to the Kyushu network in 2022, the Hokuriku extension to Tsuruga is scheduled for 2024, and in Hokkaido the Hakodate extension to Sapporo-Otaru is due for completion in 2030.

Meanwhile a new type of train threatens to make the traditional Shinkansen look like a laggard. It is known as maglev, short for "magnetically levitated linear motor car." It has already done a test run of just over six hundred kilometers per hour, which means that the route under construction from Shinagawa (in Tokyo) to Nagoya could be covered in a breathtaking forty minutes. The plan is to extend the line to Osaka by 2045, though at the time of writing the whole project is mired in problems to do with the routing.

NOT SURPRISINGLY GIVEN THEIR centrality to life in Japan, railways feature large in popular media, particularly television. Especially common are programs of trips to quirky stations, nostalgic outings with steam engines, or fascination with the nose-length of the latest Shinkansen. Such is the number of train enthusiasts that they have been divided into categories. There are "mourners," who get misty-eyed while attending the last outing of a train; railway foodies, who travel long distances to sample the station *bento* of local delicacies; and "rail thieves," who steal items from prized locations or locomotives to add to their collection. By far the largest group, however, are fanatic photographers known as *toritetsu*, who jostle with each other for the best position, sometimes violently.

Ekiben hitoritabi (Train Lunch Solo Journey) was a manga series published from 2006 to 2011, which featured a railway lover who eats his way around Japan. It was made into a twelve-episode television series in 2012. However, it does not compare with the hit manga, *Tetsuko no tabi* (Travels of a Female Train Fan), which exemplifies the way manga inform even as they entertain. This nonfiction series was inspired by author Hirohiko Yokomi, who wrote a book in 1998 about visiting every one of JR's 4,600 stations. Together with illustrator Naoe Kikuchi, he created a series of train outings in manga form between 2001 and 2006, which show how a young woman is transformed from disinterest into a genuine *tetsuko* (female rail nerd). Each outing is followed by factual information about the trains and railway lines involved. The manga was made into an anime series for television, and at the time of writing episodes are available on YouTube with subtitles.

Rail lore is legion in Japan, but nothing quite compares with the tale of Tama, station master of Kishi Station. The small rural station, which is owned by the privately run Wakayama Electric Railway, won national attention in 2007 when a stray cat called Tama was put in charge. The female calico was provided with a year's worth of food and a stationmaster's hat. Her sole duty was to greet arrivals, but declining numbers meant the future of the line looked bleak. However, as word of her appointment spread, the number of visitors rose dramatically.

In 2008 Tama was honored by the Wakayama prefectural governor for services to tourism. A special Tama Train was created, the station building was given cat features, and Tama won promotion to the board of the railway company, making her their first ever female executive. In keeping with her status, she was awarded two feline assistants and an office, complete with litter box. When she died at the age of sixteen, thousands flocked from around the country to pay their respects, and she was declared Honorary Eternal

Stationmaster and deified as a kami in a small shrine at the station. Thanks to the services of a stray cat, the future of the railway line is in safe paws.

The Tama Train is one of many "character trains" that are to be seen around the country, adding color and cuteness to the railway ride. Unsurprisingly, Thomas the Tank Engine has been eagerly adopted, with books, merchandise, and TV series proving popular, even prompting the opening of a Thomas Land with a Japanese character called Hiro. Many of the character trains reference manga or anime with local associations, such as the Anpanman Train in Shikoku, where the creator of the series was born. *Pokemon, Doraemon*, there is something for everyone. There is even a Hello Kitty Shinkansen running once a day between Osaka and Hakata, with mascot, shop, photo ops, and special decor.

Along with the character trains are luxury trains with special sightseeing opportunities and lavish decor, such as the round-Kyushu train modeled on the Orient Express. There are retro outings too, with steam engines proving particularly popular. All these tourist trains add an extra element to an already impressive rail network, creating what the marketing people like to call a "joyful" train experience. Here is how the folks at JR East put it: "A Joyful Train is not only a means of transportation, but also a package of various pleasures, allowing for the train journey itself to become the purpose of travel."

The wording is seductive, but in my experience you don't need a Joyful Train for the journey to be joyful. Hopefully, *Off the Beaten Tracks in Japan* will have made that clear.